THE GARDEN AS AN ART

THE GARDEN AS AN ART

MARA MILLER

STATE UNIVERSITY OF NEW YORK PRESS

Published by
State University of New York Press, Albany

For information, address State University of New York
Press, State University Plaza, Albany, NY 12246

Production by Diane Ganeles
Marketing by Lynne Lekakis

"The Garden as Significant Form," *Journal of Speculative Philosophy*,
vol. II, no. 4, pp. 267–287. Copyright 1988 by The Pennsylvania State
University. Reproduced by permission of the Pennsylvania State
University Press.

"Gardens as Works of Art: The Problem of Uniqueness," *British Journal
of Aesthetics*, vol. 26, no. 3, Summer 1986. Copyright 1986 by Oxford
University. Reproduced by permission of Oxford University Press.

Library of Congress Cataloging-in-Publication Data

Miller, Mara.
    The Garden as an Art / Mara Miller.
        p.   cm.
    Includes bibliographical references and index.
    ISBN 0-7914-1377-2 (PB). — ISBN 0-7914-1378-0 (CH)
    1. Gardens—Philosophy. 2. Art—Philosophy. 3. Gardens. 4. Art.
    I. Title.
    SB454.3.P45M55 1993
    712′.01—dc20   92-8162
                                                                 CIP

10 9 8 7 6 5 4 3 2 1

To my mother, Mary Hosie Miller

Contents

Illustrations

ix

Acknowledgments

This book first appeared as my doctoral dissertation. I would like first to express my thanks to those who oversaw its transformation from its earlier to its present form: to my editors, Carola Sautter and Diane Ganeles, of the State University of New York Press, and to the anonymous reviewers who recommended its publication. I feel deep gratitude to the members of my doctoral committee, Professors Maurice Natanson, John Smith, and especially Rulon S. Wells, my advisor, without whose patience, originality, humor, and unparalleled breadth of knowledge this project could never have been undertaken, much less completed. A number of other members of the Yale community were generous with time, insights, suggestions, and encouragement, especially Professors Richard Barnhart, Judith Colton, Karsten Harries, George Hogenson, G. Evelyn Hutchinson, Stephen Owen, Jonathan Spence, and King-lui Wu. Professor Kristin Forbath of Connecticut College has repeatedly given invaluable assistance of many kinds. James R. Buckler and Catherine Meehan of the Horticulture Department at the Smithsonian Institution, Professor Richard Quaintance of Rutgers University, and Professor Elisabeth Young-Bruehl of Wesleyan University provided much-needed advice at crucial junctures. Professors Sid Axinn of Temple University, Arnold Berleant of C. W. Post Campus of Long Island University, Robert Ginsberg and Roberta Kevelson of Pennsylvania State University, and Edmund Leites of the City University of New York, heard me through during the critical stage of rethinking the dissertation as a book; their encouragement is more deeply appreciated than they can imagine. Professor Thomas Leddy's paper on gardens read at the Eastern Division of the American Society for Aesthetics provided a much-needed challenge to clarify my argument.

This study could not have taken the shape it did without the contrasting experience of wilderness provided by Larry Dean Olsen, who taught me paleolithic desert survival skills, and Paul Petzoldt and the National Outdoor Leadership School. I am grateful to them. I am grateful also to those who opened their gardens to me, especially Myrtle Bilaitis, Jill Bumford, Richard Coombs; the late Vickie Gruetzner; my aunt, Mary Hosie; Elizabeth Seager, Pat and Debbie Turner, Rosemary Verey; and the Izumi Masayuki family.

Grants from a number of institutions enabled me to expand the context for the philosophical study of gardens. A Summer Grant for Graduate Study from the Smithsonian Institution made it possible to study environmental psychology and landscape preference with Dr. John Falk and Dr. John Balling, then at the Smithsonian Office of Educational Research (since dismantled). The Center for the History of British Political Thought at the Folger Institute provided a fellowship to participate in two seminars on eighteenth-century political thought and culture, which have enabled me to locate English landscape gardens within their historical, political, and theoretical context. I am deeply grateful to the center and the institute, to Dr. Lena Cowen Orlin, Professors Nicholas Phillipson, J. G. A. Pocock, Gordon Schockett, and Lois Schwoerer, and to the other seminar participants for the opportunity to learn from them and to test my ideas on them. The director, Professor Raymond Erickson, and participants in the Aston Magna Academy of 1987 and 1989 not only provided glorious musical experience but also helped me tremendously in thinking through the comparisons with other arts, especially music; I would like to thank the academy, Franklin and Marshall College, and the National Endowment for the Humanities for subsidizing my attendance. The Center for Historical Analysis at Rutgers University provided office space, an informal audience, and other support during the revision stage; I am particularly grateful to Director Rudy Bell and Project Director John Gillis for making this possible and to seminar members Professor Marjorie Beale and Professor Rhys Isaac for helping me work out the final reorganization.

Grants from the Yale Center for British Art, Franklin and Marshall College, and the International Society for Eighteenth-Century Studies allowed me to visit gardens in England, Japan, and France respectively. I would like to thank the members of the 1990 East-West Conference on Eighteenth-Century Aesthetics, sponsored by the International Society, for their valuable responses to the paper I gave there.

I would also like to recognize the valued contributions of the librarians and staff of the Landscape Architecture Library at Dumbarton Oaks, Yale's Sterling Memorial Library, the Yale Center for British Art, the Library of Congress, the Folger Shakespeare Library, Martin Luther King Public Library in Washington, D.C., the New York Public Library, and the Highland Park (New Jersey) Public Library. I am especially grateful to librarians Mary Benson Muller, Judy Malamut, and Annie Day Thacher for their special friendship and support. Dumbarton Oaks, the Yale Center for British Art, and the Honolulu Academy of Arts have graciously given permission to reproduce works in their collections. *The British Journal of Aesthetics* and *The Journal of Speculative Philosophy* have permitted me to reprint work that appeared in an earlier form between their covers. I also thank Larry Grady for his help with editing and proofreading.

My mother, Mary Hosie Miller, has been an unfailing source of support throughout my education. My husband, Scott Robertson, has been enormously helpful and encouraging, and I am deeply thankful to both of them.

PART I

❧

What Is a Garden?

CHAPTER 1

❧

Definitions, Examples, and Paradigms

A. The Questions

This study is motivated by two philosophical preoccupations. First, is it true, as Wittgenstein claimed, that the limits of my language are the limits of my world? The evidence for the constitutive power of language is vast and convincing. Language not only describes the world but also sets up the basic terms for description and perception. To learn a new language (particularly one unrelated to one's native tongue) is to learn a new world, with fundamentally different ways of organizing and recognizing the world, a new way of being in the world, a new self—and not only new Others but sometimes new kinds of Others. To expand within one's native language the ability to speak for oneself, to bear witness to one's experience and give voice to one's own feelings and questions and doubts and objections, is to expand the world—and not only one's own world, but the worlds of those with whom one speaks.

On the other hand, we know that the relation between language and understanding is not simple. It is not the case that translation is impossible, nor that everyone with the same language background understands all other speakers of that language, nor that only people with the same language background understand each other—nor even that language is necessary for understanding or communication. While the conventions of language do much to determine our experience, not all individual experience is linguistically encoded or expressed; some remains recalcitrant to language (perhaps the best documented is the "ineffable" of mystical experience), and individuals are able at times to transcend the conventions of language.

These considerations suggest that there are—*pace* Wittgenstein— limits to the power of language to determine our world.

I would like to suggest that the major challenge to the hegemony of language over experience—and perhaps the only organized or systematic challenge—is art. If this is true, then gardens—if they are art—form an organized and important challenge to the power of language to formulate our world and our perceptions of it.

Organized and systematic, gardens operate at the border between explicit and tacit, between communal or "universal" and individual, between objective and subjective, between the conscious and the unconscious or prereflectively conscious, between deliberate and taken-for-granted. They occupy, or perhaps create, a vast transitional territory between the amorphous, unrepeatable, incommunicable chaos of irreduceably idiosyncratic experience and the readily communicated and comfortable norms of socially generated experience. Language, and especially written language, is peculiarly adept at raising the almost ungraspable, almost unknowable to consciousness, disciplining it with concepts and conventions of argument structure, preparing it to be remembered, expressed, discussed, analyzed, understood, criticized. Especially if it's theory that you want, there's nothing like it. All of the readers of this book belong to cultures which (rightly) value these linguistic processes enormously. Yet this keen appreciation of the power of language has led to an underestimation of other, sometimes competing, claims staked on our understanding and our loyalties by the arts and by physical practices. Within the last several decades scholars, beginning with Carl Jung and Ernst Cassirer and continuing through Rudolf Arnheim, Michel Foucault, Walter Ong, and more recently representation theorists and students of landscape and environmental design as well as of particular artistic forms and practices, have begun exploring the means and consequences of forms of formulating our world. This book works within this new stream of inquiry.

Oddly, while print, and the mass media (film, photography, television) that are viewed as replacing print, are being studied from this point of view, gardens are not. As a consequence, the present study is quite preliminary. In particular, one would want to know how specific gardens, or garden styles, manifest or formulate particular forms of knowledge or belief, how they inculcate or modify non-garden values, and what their relationships are to related linguistically encoded theories. Such questions require detailed individual case studies which are beyond the scope of this book. I would hope, however, that the present work will contribute a framework to address such questions.

Gardens are particularly important for two reasons: because they live, and hence prove their rightness or validity in their very being; and because they utilize, and hence implicate, the whole body of their "audience." (For this reason, I have avoided the impersonal "objective" forms of language which are usual in scholarship in favor of a more vivid personally engaging use of the pronouns "we," "you," "I" that I hope will evoke a more visceral understanding.) Because they live and they incorporate our bodies, gardens are particularly suited to the demonstration of power and authority of various kinds, and they make their claims with an unusually compelling force.

This makes all the more important a second burning preoccupation behind this study, namely, the question whether aesthetic theory as we know it is adequate to art and to its description and to the recognition and analysis of its effects?

The example of the garden strongly suggests that it is not. The hitherto neglected study of gardens, structured and informed by these two questions, will cast considerable light on these fundamental philosophical issues. But before we move to the questions themselves, we need a working hypothesis that answers the question, what is a garden? But before turning to that, a few notes on the limits of the study itself.

B. The Study

While philosophically resonant for any number of reasons, gardens—unlike language and the arts of painting, poetry, music, and architecture, and unlike the concept of nature itself—have received short shrift from philosophers. There are no books and very few articles which undertake the examination of the garden from a philosophical point of view. It is this oversight which I hope the present work will begin to remedy.

In light of the unusual nature of the topic, it is important to recognize from the outset what this study is not. It is not a history— neither of gardens nor the art of gardening, nor of aesthetic theory, nor of thought about the garden. It is not a study of those aesthetic principles in accordance with which gardens have been designed. These principles vary from culture to culture and require individual treatment.[1]

The task here is to uncover the special nature of the garden through an examination of the question whether gardens are works of art. The category "art" in this case is being used descriptively, not normatively; evaluations as to the success or value of a work or a genre must be made independently. "Art" here designates a category of opposition both to language and to all kinds of purely pragmatic organizations, and therefore embraces a continuum of possibilities, including advertising, decoration, and many kinds of ordering or arrangement. This usage is designed specifically for the purposes of philosophers, who might be interested in such things as the ontological status of art, its hermeneutic and communicative functions, etc., rather than for the art world, for whom normative judgments are crucial at all stages. It is not my purpose here to develop a complete theory of art, nor to address basic questions in the field of aesthetics in a systematic way. The only questions which will be raised are those that seem interesting or enlightening in regard to gardens.

The question is pursued through a study of certain aspects of the theory of art, comparisons of gardens with other arts, and the exploration of the cross-culturally valid foundations or preconditions for the creation of gardens. It is hoped that this may shed light not only on the nature of the garden but also on the other arts and on aesthetic theory itself. This study thus differs from most philosophical examinations of art in that it starts with the phenomena—gardens— and tries to generate and elucidate the theory from them, rather than beginning with theoretical presuppositions and deriving observations about art from theory.[2]

C. Definitions

The *Shorter Oxford English Dictionary* offers as definition of "garden" "An enclosed piece of ground devoted to the cultivation of flowers, fruit, or vegetables; often with defining word, as flower-, fruit-, kitchen-, etc. g; b.pl. Ornamental grounds, used as a place of public resort." Yet this is at once too generous and too narrow. Too generous, for contrary to common usage, it would include large agricultural cropland, as long as it was fenced in and used for apples or grapevines rather than for cattle grazing or grains, English having special terms for these sorts of things ("orchard," "vineyard"), and rarely using the term "garden" or its compounds for any sort of commercial plot. ("Truck garden" is an exception.) On the other hand, the definition is too narrow, for many of those things we commonly think of as gardens are not "devoted to the cultivation of flowers, fruit, or vegetables." The plants in the great English landscape gardens built in the eighteenth-century were restricted to grass, trees, and shrubs (plate 1), and

1. Both the architecture of the classical past and the historic personages enshrined there create a sense of all history leading up to this moment, the so-called Whig interpretation of history. The Temple of British Worthies by William Kent at Stowe House, Buckinghamshire, England. Second quarter of the 18th century.

2. Miniature landscape of rocks in the style of Song (Chinese) painting, with a "bridge" over raked-sand "water." It is meant to be viewed from the verandah and is conducive to meditation. Daisen-in, Daitoku-ji, by Kogaku Shuko (1464–1548), perhaps with the assistance of Soami. Kyoto, Japan. Muromachi Period, 1509.

3. This contemporary formal garden utilizes the bi-axial symmetrical geometry and the flat expanses of water of the classic Islamic garden. It also includes a Chinese-inspired "moon-gate" in a minimalist style. Part of the Enid A. Haupt Garden near the "Castle," a collaborative effort by architect Jean-Paul Carlhian of the Boston firm Shepley, Bulfinch, Richardson and Abbott; Sasaki Associates Inc., of Watertown, Mass.; New York landscape architect Lester Collins, and Smithsonian Horticulture Office Director James Buckler. Smithsonian Institution. Washington, D.C. 1987.

had few flowers prior to the importation of exotics like azaleas and
rhododendrons from the plant-hunting expeditions of the nineteenth
century. The rock gardens of Japanese temples (plate 2) have none
of the kinds of plants mentioned; though some may have moss, even
these could hardly be described as "devoted to" its cultivation.
Similarly, neither the Lion Court of the Alhambra, perhaps the most
famous of Spanish gardens (and certainly coming under that rubric
as far as writers of garden books are concerned), nor the Astor Court,
the Chinese-style garden at the Metropolitan Museum of Art, nor the
modern Islamic-influenced section of the Enid A. Haupt Garden at
the Smithsonian Institution (plate 3) could be called "devoted to the
cultivation" of plants, although flowers do make an appearance.[3]

Colloquial British usage, moreover, has "garden" equivalent to the
American "yard," meaning the plot of ground around a house which
belongs to it. Although the lack of cultivation of such an area in homes
of a certain type is often noted in twentieth-century English novels
(especially when the author wishes to imply connections with morality
and class), the fact that it may be nothing but bare dirt does not keep
it from being called "the garden."[4] Zoological gardens, furthermore,
are devoted to the care and/or display of animals, usually with little
regard for plants (the San Diego Zoo being a notable exception).
Although, in spite of their name, we today may not immediately
classify them as gardens, historically they originated with the
menageries that were often parts of Renaissance gardens on the grand
scale, and even when there is no emphasis on plants, they share
fundamental concerns and functions with other types of gardens.

A second difficulty is that a garden need not be a "piece of ground."
The sheer weight of most components of gardens, especially moist soil,
water, rocks, and trees, makes a garden on the ground by far the
easiest and most practical arrangement. But the Hanging Gardens
of Babylon, though not hanging, were raised up on terraces, and "roof
gardens," often extensively planted, are common.

Finally, even enclosure is by no means a constant feature, although
it is shared by gardens of China (plate 4), Japan (plate 3), Persia, and
premodern Europe (plate 5) as well as some contemporary gardens.
Paradise, virtually the paradigmatic garden for the West, the Middle
East, and India, is defined, both literally and figuratively, by its walls;
the word comes from Middle English, adopted from the French
paradis, an adaptation of the Latin *paradisis*, from the Greek, an
adoption of the Old Persian *pairidaeza*, meaning enclosure or park.
The walls of paradise, and the fences and moats that replace them,
keep out the voracious vermin and the trampling herd animals and

Air without Heat.
The Villa of the Emperors Mistress's in Tartary, frequented much by him, for the Walks there.

4. This English copy of an Italian's depiction of the Ch'ing emperor's garden in literati (Han) style is from the earliest illustrations of Chinese gardens to reach England or Europe. (The Italian's engravings were sent to Lord Burlington ca. 1714.) Note especially the naturalistic water and banks and the groupings of several species of deciduous trees. "Air without Heat: The Villa of the Emperors Mistress's in Tartary, frequented much by him, for the Walks there." Imperial Garden. Jehol, China. ca. 1710. From *Illustration from The Emperor of China's Palace at Pekin. . .* (anon.) (London: Robert Sayers, et al., 1753) based upon the copperplate engravings done on site by Matteo Ripa, ca. 1713. Yale Center for British Art.

the thieves and intruders, and even the seeds of weeds and other unwanted plants. But in our age, flower gardens are often fully exposed. This is particularly true of urban and suburban gardens, and most especially of municipal and national gardens, such as those in Washington, D.C. (plate 6), where the purpose is display to the widest possible audience, even including those who are racing past in trains

5. The medieval garden is dependent upon sun, warmth and the plants of spring and summer in order to convey its full effect. At dusk, in winter, it makes little sense. Court with fountain, The Cloisters of the Metropolitan Museum of Art, New York City.

and cars. And what of those cases where the enclosure is a practical physical and/or legal boundary but is obscured from the viewer so that it has no visual or aesthetic effect, such as is found with the *shakkei*, or "borrowed scenery" of Japanese landscape gardens which are enclosed but which rely on the beauty of the surrounding landscape as if it were part of the garden itself, and the ha-ha's or hidden ditches of eighteenth-century English landscape gardens (plate 7) which similarly extend the vision of the viewer beyond the bounds of the garden without interruption? Enclosure is no more essential to gardens than are ground and devotion to the cultivation of plants.

We can only conclude that this definition is far from an adequate guide to the kinds of things that are called gardens. Even if we take only the paradigmatic cases—the grand gardens like Stowe, Chantilly,

6. An anonymous collaborative effort, this contemporary urban garden incorporates
a modern ruin (the former church on that site which burned down in 1970). Like many
modern urban gardens, it does without walls so as to draw in passers-by. This garden
is extremely popular with residents of the neighborhood. St. Thomas's Parish,
Washington, D.C.

7. The ha-ha, or hidden ditch at the boundary between a garden and the pasture land beyond it, prevents the destruction of the garden by grazing animals yet unites the two types of territory into a single picture-space without the intrusion of a fence. Woodland Walk in Alban Wood, by Lancelot "Capability" Brown at Ickworth, Suffolk, England. 1769–1776.

and the imperial garden at Jehol that define the various traditions—
there is tremendous variation among the items that fall within the
category. We need a definition that will encompass both all these
variations and the various colloquial uses of the term. For our purpose
of uncovering the nature of the garden as a cultural and especially
an artistic enterprise, a broad definition will be more useful than a
more restrictive one. Let me propose this, then, as a working definition
with which to begin: A garden is any purposeful arrangement of
natural objects (such as sand, water, plants, rocks, etc.) with exposure
to the sky or open air, in which the form is not fully accounted for
by purely practical considerations such as convenience. (By
"convenience" I mean such considerations as peas in back,
strawberries in front because that's how they can be picked most
easily). Three features of this definition require special note. First,
a garden must include at least some natural objects; an arrangement
that is like a garden but composed of purely artificial objects could
be a garden only in a metaphorical sense. (An example is the sunken
and walled-in space designed by I. M. Pei for the Beinecke Plaza at
Yale University.) Secondly, and perhaps more controversially, a true
garden must have exposure to the open air or sky; enclosed
arrangements of plants become a different category—greenhouses,
orangeries. Gardens which are completely closed in are extremely rare,
but at least one exists; in my opinion this can only be an imitation
of a garden, not the real thing. Third, in a garden, there is in some
sense an "excess" of form, more than can be accounted for by physical
necessity, and this form provides some sort of satisfaction in itself,
and some sort of "meaning" or "significance"—whether aesthetic, or
sensual, or spiritual, or emotional, we shall begin to discover as we
proceed. This "excess" is not meant to entail quantitatively "more"
form—it may mean less, and it would certainly include minimalist
types of form. It is "more" only in the sense that more decisions,
planning, consideration, perhaps measurement or study, went into it.
But it is this "excess of form" that is the invariable marker, or
distinguishing feature, of the work of art; *anything* which exhibits this
excess is a work of art (though it may not be a *successful* work of art).
From the philosophical point of view it is this excess which is
interesting and requires study.

The working definition of gardens used here may seem overly
broad, including as it does potted plants on porches and flower
arrangements. Yet we will learn more about the nature of gardens
in general (as opposed to one particular type or style of garden) by
casting our net broadly, so as to include as many examples as possible

at the beginning, and excluding irrelevancies later, proceeding more systematically as we discover what gardens are and therefore what is irrelevant to them. Because the present project is not to discover or explore an already well-defined category but to uncover the phenomenon of the garden in its fullest implications, we will be willing to include individual gardens that may stretch the definitions, such as that constructed by Pat Turner in Suffolk, which the editors of the famous "*Yellow Guide*" to British gardens have reportedly refused to recognize as a garden. If, on the other hand, we try to determine at the outset a more positive definition of gardens, we risk developing a theory that is culture-specific or restricted to one or a few gardening styles rather than pertinent to gardens as a whole.

D. Examples

Many of the most famous gardens, those which define the notion of garden for us today, became famous precisely because of the challenges they presented to previous models or paradigms prevailing at the time they were made. The eighteenth-century English gardens Blenheim, Stowe (plate 1), and Stourhead; the seventeenth-century French Chantilly (plate 8), Vaux-le-Vicomte, and Versailles; the Japanese imperial garden at Katsura and the Zen rock garden Ryoanji (plate 9); and the American nineteenth-century Longwood Gardens and twentieth-century Dumbarton Oaks (plates 10, 11) and Pepsico Gardens, all vary tremendously in their aims and effects, but they have in common the fact that they broke with garden tradition. (This is one of our first clues that gardens are an artkind, for the role that breaking with precedent plays in gardens is much closer to the role it plays in other arts than in other kinds of social institutions such as sports, the judiciary, agriculture, or advertising. William Kent's substitution of the ha-ha for the garden wall, the fantastic nonrepresentational topiary at Longwood Gardens, and the introduction of fountains and cascades in Italian Renaissance gardens are like Bobby Blanton's development of bass as a lead instrument, Wang Hui's admission of color washes into monochromatic literati painting, and the radical reformulation of color by the Impressionists.) All of these famous gardens have also been considered major works of art, and like other major works of art, they not only operate within the confines of their tradition but also challenge those traditions and traditional assumptions about what art can do and what kinds of effects can be achieved.

LE GRAND PARTERRE D'EAU ET LE CANAL de Chantilli.

8. A "bird's eye view" of a formal garden whose plan is best revealed from a single privileged point of view, the central point upon the highest terrace. As contemporary prints show, the presence of human beings within the garden is as important to gardens like these as to the later "picturesque" gardens, since formal gardens represent the world controlled by the gardenist (invariably an aristocrat or monarch). "Le Grand Parterre d'eau et le canal," at Chantilly, France. First half of the 17th century. From Adam Perelle, *Vues des belles maisons de France*, 1650. Dumbarton Oaks, Trustees for Harvard University.

9. An impassioned attention to detail in the most famous garden in Japan. The timelessness of the rocks and pebbles contrasts sharply with the sense of history with which the planks of the verandah are imbued. Border between the rock garden and the verandah, Ryoan-ji, attrib. Soami (1472–1523). Kyoto, Japan. Muromachi Period, 1499.

10. A modern use of formality. The simplicity is deceptive: pollarding, like topiary, is highly labor-intensive, and therefore expensive. The Ellipse. Dumbarton Oaks, by Beatrix Farrand. Washington, D.C. 20th century.

11. The disappearing path is one of the most universal of garden motifs. The rich textures of the plants, wall and path, especially in contrast to the snow, make this area as delightful in winter as summer. Dumbarton Oaks, by Beatrix Farrand. Washington, D.C. 20th century.

E. Paradigms

1. Grand and Humble Gardens

Many of the most famous gardens earned their initial fame as a result of important breaks they made with their gardening traditions. In the particular gardens mentioned, however, another factor besides their innovative artistic authority comes into play, for their fame is also related to their grandeur—their size, their expense, the magnificence of their aims, and the importance of the families, temples, or other institutions with which they were affiliated. Grandeur is a matter of scale or extent, and hence to some extent of expense, but it is also something more, a matter of pretensions and aspirations. Rarely does a small garden try to integrate itself into the larger landscape. (Rarely does it need to.) A tiny garden is much less likely to take upon itself the task of impressing observers with the wealth and social rank of its owners, and more likely to stress creativity, variety, subtlety, or sheer pleasantness. Just as size alone places constraints on the style (no suburban garden can physically accommodate the grand avenues of trees on the English estates), so size also constrains the themes and issues which a garden can raise: in the gardens of ancient Roman houses, for example, large-scale statuary for the niches and pools of the typical peristyle and nympheum would have been out of place because of the intimate scale; this reduced scale in turn ruled out Olympian subjects.[5]

It will be useful to distinguish between the grand and the humble, if only to prepare ourselves for the eventual recognition of their fundamental similarities. The humble garden is one whose physical limitations are obvious: at the extreme, a single plant in a pot, whether indoors or out. It is not just a matter of size, however, for, as Brecht points out, "A clever gardener can do much with a small patch of ground."[6] The designer of the Gamberaia in Italy would have been just such a clever gardener, for, as Edith Wharton describes it,

> . . . it combines in an astonishingly small space, yet without the least sense of overcrowding, almost every typical excellence of the old Italian garden: free circulation of sunlight and air about the house; abundance of water; easy access to dense shade; sheltered walks with different points of view; variety of effect produced by the skillful use of different levels; and finally, breadth and simplicity of composition.[7]

Even more telling is the fact that of the Japanese gardens, it is precisely those with the greatest artistic ambitions that are the smallest. The Zen gardens of Ryoanji and Daitokuji (plates 9, 2), which are only a few square meters, attempt far more spiritually and artistically than the expansive landscape gardens of Katsura and Heian Shrine in Kyoto and Meiji Shrine in Tokyo. The terms "grand" and "humble" must not be taken to imply a judgment as to how good a garden is, how beautiful, how successful at achieving its purposes.

On the most obvious level, the grand garden is one which is first of all extensive, but also, as a function of extension, expensive to build and to maintain. Even small back yards and the balconies of modern apartments are extremely labor intensive,[8] for gardens are the only art in which changes occur not only gradually over long periods of time, but rapidly; not only by decay or decline of materials but by their increase; not only at the deliberate intervention of an artist-performer, but regardless of whether any human agency is concerned with them at all. (Some of the effects of this ability to change on their own accord will be discussed below.)

As a result of their expense, grand gardens are amenable to purposes of conspicuous consumption, conspicuous waste, and the general display of wealth and social status.

2. Formal and Informal Gardens

A second important division among garden types is between formal and informal gardens. Formal gardens are those which are designed in accordance with nonintuitive, usually mathematical, principles. They may or may not be symmetrical; they are usually geometric, and this geometry is usually readily apparent. Examples are legion among Dutch, French, Italian, Islamic, American, and Renaissance English gardens (plates 3, 5, 8, 11). In addition, they usually have a single privileged point of view from which the overall plan makes most sense. The obvious paragon is Versailles, with its central axis emanating from the king's bedroom in the palace. The appeal to universal principle implicit in the mathematical organization, the attempt to overcome by rigorous discipline the changes wrought by time in the plant life (formal gardens are invariably precisely pruned), and thus to overcome exigency and the experience of time itself, have as a corollary a preference for single determinate views and final recognitions, as opposed to variable experiences while meandering. They are essentially spatial; though existing in time, they deny it.

Informal gardens, on the other hand, are designed intuitively, in accordance with poetic or picturesque principles, or to imitate the natural landscape. "Country gardens," landscape and picturesque

12. Within the "teahouse," a garden would have contributed to the atmosphere of elegance and of participation in quintessential Japanese culture, which was part of what the customer was paying for. Within the print, the garden gives valuable clues to the lovers' mood (p. 42). Domestic-style Japanese Garden, late 18th century. From a print by Suzuki Harunobu. The James A. Michener Collection, The Honolulu Academy of Arts.

gardens, the "jardin anglo-chinois," and Japanese domestic, "stroll" and tea gardens are in this category (plates 1, 2, 4, 7, 12). They are essentially temporal, with spatial adumbration; they revel in the recognition of change and impermanence.

Regardless of style or school, formal gardens embody a denial of time and of the value of the variability of experience. They demonstrate a trust in absolute or universal principles and law completely foreign to the informal garden.

The anomaly is the Japanese Zen-style garden which, true to its rejection of dichotomies, straddles the typical alternatives of garden styles. Although apparently informal, based on sheer intuition and the imitation of natural landscape, its partial yet very real formality is indicated by the precise (though not geometric) control of plant growth (not necessarily shape), and by the fact that it is not designed to be entered but to be viewed from a privileged space along the side (and as with most formal gardens, this privileged viewing location is raised above the ground level, indicative of its somewhat transcendant stance)—that is, its timelessness (or rejection of time and temporality) and its rejection of embodiment. Research reveals the underlying mathematical principles concealed beneath the appearance of natural landscape.[9]

CHAPTER 2

❦

The General Unifying Principles Underlying
the Construction and Appreciation of Gardens

In spite of the significant differences among gardens of different styles and scales, all have a good deal in common. The task of the garden is to mediate those tensions or polarities which are important for a given culture—polarities such as living-dead, animate-inanimate, private-public, wild-domesticated, natural-artificial, inner-outer, personal-impersonal, communal-individual, orderly-chaotic, static-changing. This mediation may take different forms—apparent resolution or clarification, even exacerbation of the tension. The garden is a way of framing the terms within which verbal or theoretical debate can take place. Every garden is an attempt at the reconciliation of the oppositions which constrain our existence; the act of creating a garden, however limited it may be, is not only an assertion of control over our physical surroundings but a symbolic refusal of the terms under which life has been presented to us and an insistence on determining the terms of our existence. As such it is always an act of hope.

A. Signification in Gardens: The Garden as Metaphor

However useful, pleasurable, and beautiful gardens may be, cross-culturally the literary evidence suggests that gardens also play an important symbolic role, serving as a metaphor for the ideal human life and for relations between human beings, the state or community, and divinity or the divine order.[1] Chief among these, of course, have been the garden of Eden and Paradise of the Bible and the Qu'ran, the Song of Songs, the Persian *Gulistan* or Rose Garden of Sa'di, and *The Secret Garden* of the Kabbalah.[2]

The basis for the metaphorical significance of gardens lies in the perceived similarities between human beings and plants. These similarities are both biological and cultural, in the literal sense of providing care for, hence training and disciplining—in specifically human terms, education and government. Plants are not born the way we are, but there the dissimilarity ends. They grow and change and age and die much as we do. Even more strikingly, in doing these things, they exhibit the same dependency on their environment for sustenance and support as we have. They flourish or wither, suffer injury, survive, for similar if not identical reasons. The vocabulary of their existence serves equally well to describe our own; laying down roots, fertilizing, blossoming, budding, coming to fruition, unfolding are concepts which apply to human lives in many different languages.[3] The Chinese writer Huang T'ing Chien explains the analogy in a passage from "Quiet Fragrance Pavilion":

> The orchid has always been highly valued, because its qualities are so characteristic of the perfect person. It thrives in the forest and its perfume is undiminished by the absence of people to appreciate it, and it survives the snow and frost without undergoing any change in its nature.[4]

In neo-Confucianism certain plants—the orchid, bamboo, plum, pine, and chrysanthemum—have come to represent ideal kinds of human life and particular virtues. Lu Yu writes of the plum blossom:

> Exuding a beautiful perfume
> Unobtrusive from sparse boughs
> Undaunted by snow and cruel wind
> Having naught to do with wealth and position.[5]

Lu Kuei-meng elaborates the analogy between human being and pine:

> "A Taoist devotee came from Tientai and showed me a picture called 'Grotesque Pine.' It was indeed a terrifying sight: the roots of the pine coming out from a cave, crawling spirally up along the edge of a crag. Its trunk was exceedingly massive, but stunted, not more than four or five feet in height; its foliage was thick and luxuriant, so that trunk, branches, and leaves huddled together gave one the impression of an injured dragon, a lame tiger, or a tied and caged man of great strength. I was asked if I could explain how a

pine tree could be so warped and twisted. In reply, I said: 'Why should there be any abnormality in the growth of trees and grasses? If they have the right kind of soil and climate, untrammeled by anything external, they always stand upright and flourish. Pines and cedars, being more hardy than most trees, should be better able to withstand adversity. The pine that we are looking at had the misfortune to have issued from a cave, handicapped by all the impediments to growth. How can it be expected to extract itself from its environment? In spite of the setbacks in its early days, it was able to preserve a certain righteous spirit. When it attained maturity, it put up a brave struggle with the rocks. However, the opposing forces were too much for it. Accumulated agonies and frustrations found expression in its gnarled and knotted form, and the world calls it a grotesque tree.

'How is this different at the human level? Heaven endows a person with talents and when they are not appreciated, he feels dejected and withdraws. Then he matures and gathers wisdom, but finds himself jostled and deprived by the powers that be. Then he breaks out in gorgeous and impassioned art, and the world calls him an eccentric person. Alas! when a tree is curbed it becomes deformed, which is the only way for it to express itself. When a person is deprived, he becomes eccentric, which is the only way for him to distinguish himself. Is this not a case of all's well that ends well?' The Taoist devotee declared, 'Well said! Why not write a eulogy for me.' So I wrote this:

> A pine grows in shady crags:
> A grotto its prison, a cave its scourge.
> It suffers from depression
> Which results in deformity.
> It becomes so unsightly
> That even the spirits and ghosts
> Think it quite incredible.
> A Taoist devotee marvels at it
> And forthwith records it
> In weird shapes and words.
> I being a leader among eccentrics
> Have pleasure in writing this eulogy.[6]

For Liu Yen-fu, on the other hand, what is of interest is less the effects of circumstances upon the individual character of plant or human being than the inherent qualities the individual brings to the situation:

> In the eighth moon of autumn, I planted over a hundred bamboos round my studio, carefully keeping intact their roots so that they would not be harmed.

A passer-by in curiosity said to me: "If you plant the Wu Tung tree, you can use its timber to make a lute with; if you plant the pear trees, you can have its fruit; if you love fortitude and loyalty, the pine and the osmanthus are fitting symbols. Why don't you intersperse these amongst your bamboos?" I answered: "The superior man likens the bamboo to virtue. It is hardy because it is not defeated by frost and snow; it is gentle, as manifested by its soft green leaves and downy appearance; it is straight and hollow, having nothing to hide denoting loyalty; it does not grow alone but always has many together—a sign of mutual help; though it may be luxuriant in spring, it does not vie with other plants—an indication of its humility and modesty; it is uniformly the same throughout the four seasons—this shows consistency; it gives special favors to the phoenix (which eats nothing but bamboo shoots)—this shows its love of the man of fine character. Every year, it graduates from shoot to full grown bamboo— an ability to perfect oneself.[7]

The correlation between certain plants and neo-Confucianist ideals grows out of an awareness of the dependence of both plants and human beings on environment and culture. Shakespeare has an equally keen awareness of this dependence, but his focus is different: not the qualities of the individual plant nor the circumstances of its life which control the plant, but human effort. The gardener's speech in *Richard II*, for example, locates, in the interactions of gardeners and plants, a model for the relations of power and dominance to be found within the state:

> Queen [to her two ladies]:
> But stay, here come the gardeners:
> Let's step into the shadow of these trees.
> My wretchedness unto a row of pins,
> They'll talk of state; for every one doth so
> Against a change: woe is forerun with woe.
>   [Enter a Gardener and two servants]
>   Gardener:
> Go, bind thou up yond dangling apricocks,
> Which, like unruly children, make their sire
> Stoop with oppression of their prodigal weight:
> Give some supportance to the bending twigs.—
> Go thou, and like an executioner
> Cut off the heads of too-fast-growing sprays,
> That look too lofty in our commonwealth:
> All must be even in our government.—
> You thus employ'd, I will go root away

The noisome weeds, that without profit suck
The soil's fertility from wholesome flowers.
   1 Servant:
Why should we, in the compass of a pale,
Keep law and form and due proportion,
Showing, as in a model, our firm estate,
When our sea-walled garden, the whole land,
Is full of weeds; her fairest flowers chok'd up,
Her fruit trees all unprun'd, her hedges ruin'd,
Her knots disorder'd, and her wholesome herbs
Swarming with caterpillars?
   Gardener:
Hold thy peace:—
He that hath suffer'd this disorder'd spring
Hath now himself met with the fall of leaf:
The weeds that his broad-spreading leaves did shelter,
That seem'd in eating him to hold him up,
Are pluck'd up root and all by Bolingbroke,—
I mean the Earl of Wiltshire, Bushy, Green.
   1 Servant: What, are they dead?
   Gardener:
They are; and Bolingbroke
Hath seized the wasteful king.—Oh! what pity is it.
That he hath not so trimm'd and dress'd this land
As we this garden! We at time of year
Do wound the bark, the skin of our fruit-trees,
Lest, being over-proud in sap and blood,
With too much richness it confound itself:
Had he done so to great and growing men,
They might have liv'd to bear, and he to taste
Their fruits of duty. Superfluous branches
We lop away, that bearing boughs may live:
Had he done so, himself had borne the crown,
Which waste of idle hours hath quite thrown down.
   [After queen exits]
   Gardener:
Poor queen! so that thy state might be no worse
I would my skill were subject to thy curse.—
Here did she fall a tear; here, in this place,
I'll set a bank of rue, sour herb of grace:
Rue, even for ruth, here shortly shall be seen,
In the remembrance of a weeping queen.[8]

In *Othello* the garden explores the same themes of power and authority, control and dominance, but this time as a function of the relation between the will and the body of the individual:

Roderigo: What should I do? I confess it is my
shame to be so fond, but it is not in my virtue to
amend it.
    Iago: Virtue? a fig! 'Tis in ourselves that we
are thus or thus. Our bodies are our gardens, to which
our wills are gardeners; so that if we will plant
nettles or sow lettuce, set hyssop and weed up thyme,
supply it with one gender of herbs or distract it with
many—either to have it sterile with idleness or
manured with industry—why, the power and corrigible
authority of this lies in our wills. If the balance of
our lives had not one scale of reason to poise another
of sensuality, the blood and baseness of our natures
would conduct us to most preposterous conclusions. But
we have reason to cool our raging motions, our carnal
stings, our unbitted lusts; whereof I take this that
you call love to be a sect or scion.[9]

Do such uses of the garden as a metaphor for aspects of the human
condition reflect anything more than our propensity to homilize on
anything and everything? The tendency to equate plants with the
human condition can be carried too far, as a musical wit of the
Restoration reminds us:

Tobacco, tobacco—Sing sweetly for tobacco.
Tobacco is like love, o love it. For you see I will prove it.
Love maketh leane the Fatte mens tumor—So doth Tobacco.
Love still dries up the wanton humor—So doth Tobacco.
Love makes me sayle From shore to shore—So doth Tobacco.
Tis fond love often makes men poor—So doth Tobacco.
Love makes men scorn all coward Fears—So doth Tobacco.
Love often sets men by the ears—So doth Tobacco.[10]

In the eighteenth-century Chinese novel *The Story of the Stone
(The Dream of the Red Chamber),*[11] in Goethe's nearly contemporary
novel *Elective Affinities,*[12] and in the tenth-century Japanese novel *The
Tale of Genji,* the garden is both a means of expression of individual
personality and feeling, and also (for that very reason) a hermeneutic
tool for our interpretation of the Other who thus expresses and reveals
himself in the garden. A passage from the last book brings this out:

As he crossed the Inner River and left the city he passed a small
house with tasteful plantings. . . .The house being just inside the
gate, he leaned from his carriage to survey the scene. The fragrance

> that came on the breeze from a great laurel tree made him think
> of the Kamo festival. It was a pleasant scene.
> ...Just then a cuckoo called from a nearby tree, as if to urge him
> on....[13]

As a result of the impression the garden has made on him, Genji decides to try to open relations with the lady who lives inside.

Similarly, the garden of the lady Reikeiden is used to reveal to the reader indirectly qualities of the lady herself which it would be too obvious (according to the aesthetics of Heian Japan) to state directly:

> He first went to Reikeiden's apartments and they talked far into
> the night. The tall trees in the garden were a dark wall in the light
> of the quarter moon. The scent of orange blossoms drifted in, to call
> back the past. Though no longer young, Reikeiden was a sensitive,
> accomplished lady. The old emperor had not, it is true, included her
> among his particular favorites, but he had found her gentle and
> sympathetic....[14]

But because of the dependency of the garden on human resources to sustain it, it also reveals a good deal about the owner's social station, financial circumstances, and health (insofar as an ability to pay attention depends upon health):

> Genji had considerable worries. His gloom was deeper as autumn
> came to a close. One beautiful moonlit night he collected himself
> for a visit to a place he had been visiting in secret. A cold, wintry
> shower passed. The address was in Rokujo, near the eastern limits
> of the city...He passed a badly neglected house, the garden dark
> with ancient trees.
>
> "The inspector's house," said Koremitsu, who was always with
> him. "I called there with a message not long ago. The old lady has
> declined so shockingly that they can't think what to do for her."[15]

Such literary references lead to two conclusions. First, while the garden may represent a number of aspects of the human condition— our place in nature, the relation of the individual to the state, human virtue, the importance of order, etc.—it is rarely used to represent anything other than some aspect of the human condition and its correlate the Divine Order. Second, the tendency to generalize from the garden to the human condition is nearly universal, appearing wherever there are gardens.

Such reports suggest that gardens, at least when they exhibit excellent form, may be more than successful fine art—they may be great art, for gardens are universally understood to reveal the individual and the human condition.

B. Multisensuality

Gardens are always multisensual. As early as 1260, Albertus Magnus wrote, in his treatise *On Vegetables and Plants*, of "some places of no great utility or fruitfulness but designed for pleasure...[that] are called pleasure gardens. They are in fact mainly designed for the delight of two senses, viz. sight and smell....Care must be taken that the lawn is of such a size that about it in a square may be planted every sweet-smelling herb such as rue, and sage and basil..."[16] To the delights of color and light, gardens often add the rhythmic motions of clouds, fish, swaying boughs, running water; delicious, pungent fragrances, whetting the appetite, reminding us of warm sunny days to come and evoking memories of events long past; the songs of birds attracted to the seeds or the vinyl bird bath. A pot of cactus enriches the tactile experience of the environment, if only in imagination.[17] These tactile, olfactory, and aural pleasures are indicated even when two-dimensional representation must limit our possibility to enjoy them.

C. The Coexistence of Aesthetics and Functionality in Gardens

The history of garden design makes it clear that aesthetic considerations have informed garden design of all kinds.[18] Recent research has shown, for example, that even medieval gardens, long known to be devoted to practical cultivation, had plants cherished only for their looks and that trees were planted for aesthetic purposes as early as the eleventh century.[19] But if aesthetic value is inherent in gardens of all types, it is also true that gardens have a large number of other functions as well. Gardens both symbolically imply and actually produce a satisfaction of biological necessities—water, shade, shelter, food. The potted chives and basil on the windowsill, the plastic tubs of tomatoes on a fire escape, bring as potent a promise as Chekhov's cherry orchard.[20] At one time or another, gardens have been extensions of medicine and pharmacology, cooking, interior decoration, geography, zoology, farming, religion, and architecture. Gardens may be required to provide food, medicine, intoxicants, dyes, seating for concerts and theatricals and for dinners too large for the dining room, decoration for inside the house, silence, freedom from burdensome rules of behavior, a place to run, animals to feed and watch and play with, fresh air. They have been used to impress one's friends and enemies, secure the health of ill monks, provide peace and quiet for contemplation or meditation, show the route to the City of God, help raise funds for worthy causes, focus the attention on the immediate present as preparation for the rites of the tea ceremony, hide from parents and nannies and unwanted suitors and bullies and escorts, escape the mob of friends in the house, entertain the mob of friends in the house (especially when it's hot and crowded or one's friends tend to spill drinks and cigarette ashes). They have been set to illustrate the nature of the universe or the evolution of plant species or the history of horticulture or the relation of different plants within a biome or the way the peasants live or the relation of the king to his people. They have been designed to embrace a wide range of social activities, from political discussions (discreetly, among friends) through children's games, innocent or illicit canoodling, and practical jokes, to badminton, croquet, bowls, tennis, football, poetry competitions, chess, and *go*. There is, in short, a profusion of functions and purposes.

The space which can accommodate them becomes a sign of human caring. No garden is formally neutral. Plants themselves have sensuous qualities that delight us, the aesthetic pleasures of the "natural object." In even the most pragmatic of gardens, the formal features, while perhaps not "artistic," may yet bring pleasure. In addition, even a purely pragmatic ordering of the garden may articulate to those who are attuned to it a perception of a larger order, a more ascetic enjoyment something like the delight in the "beauty" of mathematics. (This being attuned may be a matter of either paying attention or being in harmony or agreement with the order pre-reflectively, that is, without paying attention.) Bowing to the purely biological order of the garden assigns humanity a role in the natural order, exemplifying a passivity with regard to time, for example, or assigning a moral value to simple physical convenience that articulates a particular view of work and expresses the importance of energy. This type of form is often justified with an explicit rejection of "aesthetic" value: "We have no time for beauty here." The father of one of my students refused for many years to let her mother plant "a few flowers" in the vegetable plot behind their house in Yugoslavia. Yet even this conscious rejection of aesthetics, the strong resistance some people register to "prettifying" a vegetable garden or orchard, must be viewed with caution, if not suspicion. Such cases are not as simple as they may at first seem. They are not necessarily a rejection of aesthetics (even if they are phrased as such) but may be a rejection of a *particular* aesthetic. They may seem to give evidence of the plausibility of the distinction between fine and applied art. But at the same time, this Yugoslavian vegetable garden challenges the doctrine of aesthetic distance under a different logic: the form is meant to set up an antithesis with the outside (anaesthetic or chaotic world), and the work then only gains its aesthetic meaning within the terms of that contrast: the contrast is a precondition for the aesthetic effect. But the work in this case is formally autonomous.

The aesthetic premise of disinterest is consciously eschewed. The order in such a garden is the same as the order of the real world outside. There is no gap; it is transparent, self-evident; hence no art is necessary to make clear the visionary order. The self-sufficiency of a work of art is always relative, however, and beauty can always be overridden by other preoccupations: the blossoms in the orchard may overwhelm a worker seeing them as signs of future drudgery, or may be ignored completely by someone who has just fallen out of a tree.

Every garden is a sign of human caring. Each attempts to create an ethos of a particular kind, a shared environment where beings of many kinds can grow and flourish. Finally, each modifies the environment in such a way as to regulate human interaction and sociability, either encouraging certain kinds of human intimacy and discourse, or staving them off, determining distance and awe.

D. Gardens as Status Symbols

Living rather than inert, exposed to the weather and responding actively to it, gardens change continually, predictably and unpredictably, in ways that matter (relative to a particular style) and in ways that don't. As a result, as mentioned above, gardens take more unremitting effort than almost any other human activity. It is hard to find anything that decays more rapidly, changes form more independently, can be deployed on such a scale or has the potential to cost more money.[21] The advantage of this, from the garden owner's point of view, is that gardens are among the most suitable of all human pursuits for the demonstration of conspicuous consumption and conspicuous waste—and hence of the owner's financial resources and economic temperament. Individual items within a garden may signal

their cost; consider the expensive extremes to which people will go
to collect rare specimens (one thinks of the carp in Japanese garden
ponds, which may cost tens of thousands of dollars each [diamonds
may cost more on initial investment, but diamonds last, and don't
sicken and require special treatment]; of the idiosyncratic rocks
favored by Chinese literati, heavy and brought from great distances;
and of the expeditions to the Himalayas financed by English collectors
of exotic plants in the nineteenth century) or to develop new ones—
the various roses hybridized by the competitive DuPonts, for example.
Methods of planting may also signal expense—municipally sponsored
gardens worldwide seem to favor annuals over perennials; in
Washington, D.C., even the beds of spring bulbs are dug up and
discarded each year. All of these of course are nothing to compare with
the expenses of the old-fashioned Continental formal garden—moving
mountains and forests, digging lakes and rechanneling rivers. It is
virtually impossible to replicate the expense of a garden by other
means. Dinah Shore may have worn her sumptuous gowns only once,
but such meager efforts are put to shame by Louis XIV, who built
and tore down whole pavilions after a single evening's fete.

It is important for the social analyst to realize, however, that
economic class in this direct sense is only one of a number of
dimensions along which gardens are related to social status. Some
of these may (depending upon the social circumstances) depend
indirectly upon economics. Anne Scott-James points out, regarding
the attempted revival of the "traditional" English cottage garden,
that most cottagers wouldn't—or couldn't afford to—take the trouble
to plant a garden unless they could be sure to be in the cottage for
a length of time; undertaking a garden is so arduous and takes such
a long time that it assumes that the gardener can project a sense of
control over her land in the future.[22] This may be a function of economic
status, but control does not necessarily demand ownership. Other
factors such as the expectation of moving might equally prevent one
from projecting control over the land. A sense of stability and of the
predictability of one's tenure—often perquisites of middle- and upper-
class status, but not simple reflections of class in a purely economic
sense—are prerequisites for gardening and imply both a certain kind
of privilege in relation to the passage of time, and the habit of thinking
on a certain temporal scale, which may become part of the definition
of social class. Indeed, one might speculate that the fascination which
playing at gardening had for the nouveaux riches of eighteenth-
century England had (like the play of most mammals) a functional
side as well: it inculcated the habits of planning over the long run
and of considering future generations.

Gardens also reveal the social position of the owner in a nonfinancial sense. Social position includes literal location—whether the garden is part of the community or removed from it, surveying it from a hill or deliberately hidden behind walls or rows of trees or forests, secure enough to permit tantalizing glimpses from the road or requiring real protection from outsiders. But they also include intentional aspects articulating the relation to other or larger social bodies, by means of degrees and types of exposure or invitation. Acceptance, rejection are spelled out by fences, gates, paths, drives, walls, doors. Expectations of certain types of social interaction are signaled by the garden itself, as are the social values of its owner and/or surrounding culture—privacy, exposure, reticence, bragging, conformity, individuality, eccentricity.

Gardens also imply leisure—the leisure to enjoy them, but more importantly, the leisure to have become educated, in whatever senses may be relevant to the particular gardenist's culture. Education, acquired through leisure, may define one's social identity. Gardens then both define and exploit this identity; they may flatter or intimidate or insult the guest by requiring an education similar to the gardenist's—and this emotional response on the part of the guest may be an integral part of the pleasure for guest or host. The contemporary connoisseur of Versailles or Stowe required a knowledge of classical mythology and a reading knowledge of Latin; if the modern visitor finds such gardens less compelling than they were found originally, it is partly because their charms are less obvious to those whose recognition of classical allusion is less immediate. (It is surely also partly because, having no active social relation to Louis XIV and Viscount Cobham and those to whom the latter addressed his garden, we are less vulnerable to the flattery and the put-down, neither inclusion within nor exclusion from the social circle referred to by the garden having much effect on our lives.) Similarly, full appreciation of the rock garden at Ryoanji depends upon familiarity with the ideals and practice of meditation, while the small rock landscape garden at Daitokuji (in the Daisen-in) reveals itself in a special way to those familiar with East Asian traditions of landscape painting. Botanical gardens can be enjoyed by anyone but hold special pleasures for those with a scientific education and a botanist's interest in plants.

Most, if not all, garden traditions are capable of great subtlety and complexity and sophistication regarding the kinds of education the garden requires or reveals. This is education in the broadest sense, not just formal schooling but reading for pleasure, as well as travel, experience of the arts or of the sights of the world, ability to play a musical instrument, and so on. Making a garden is therefore not like fox hunting, which also demonstrates years in the saddle, experience with social rituals, and such cultural values as ability to get along well with animals. Gardens make a potentially infinitely nuanced statement about the gardenist's understanding of what his or her education has been about.

The demonstration of social status, of course, has no direct bearing on whether or not the garden is art. It is merely another of the functions that gardens have been found to serve; other arts, such as painting and architecture, have also proven useful in this way. It is of interest to us here, however, because of the extensive overlap between the decisions made for purposes of demonstrating social status and decisions made for aesthetic effect, and because regardless of which of the two purposes motivates a given decision, it will carry implications for the other.

E. Spatiality

Gardens, like the arts of painting, architecture, sculpture, dance, are inherently spatial. In terms of spatial organization, there are two classes of gardens, those meant to be walked through in a literal sense and those meant to be viewed from the outside without being entered physically.[23] Yet the difference between the two is not as significant as one might suppose, for even those which are meant to be viewed from the outside, including those deliberately modeled along picturesque lines (the eighteenth-century English "picturesque" garden or the Daisen-in rock landscape), first, must be capable of being entered, in order to be maintained, (and the viewer always knows this), and second, are meant to be entered imaginatively, to be recognized and understood as three-dimensional spaces.

There are some real differences between gardens meant to be walked through and those composed solely for imaginative entering, but these differences are primarily practical, affecting the flexibility afforded the gardener and the liberties he or she may take. A garden meant solely for imaginative entering (a very small class) need not concern itself with how something looks from the back; hoses can be hidden behind rocks. More importantly, such a garden may make greater use of spatial illusion, such as the creation of the illusion of vast distances within a small space (for example, by means of making trees farther from the viewer look as if they are at a greater distance than they actually are by planting trees smaller than those nearby, which are supposed to be the same size; this was done at Katsura Imperial Villa in Kyoto).

F. Temporality and the Structuring of Time

Gardens are not, however, a three-dimensional art. Like dance, poetry, and music, they are inherently temporal, hence four-dimensional. Not only do they exist in time (true of whatever exists) but they take time to be appreciated, and they even take upon themselves the ordering or organizing of the experience of time as part of the experience they provide. Most gardens build as well upon the structures of seasonal change, such as Monet's garden at Giverny:

> Monet planned the flower beds to bloom in continuous succession from spring to fall. As restored today the garden unfolds its beauties as it did in Monet's time. Beginning in late March the flowering trees spread a pink and white haze across the blue sky, while narcissus, tulips, forget-me-nots, and crocuses stretch out in a pleasing tapestry below. In May come the azaleas and the rhododendrons, followed by a sea of peonies, poppies, iris, and wisteria and veils of blue, white, and pink clematis supported by tall, rectangular trellises all along the edges of the garden. As these splendors fade, June brings an avalanche of roses in the garden and around the pond—rosebushes as well as climbing roses that cling to the trellises and arch over the central path. In the height of summer the intense colors of geraniums, dahlias, lilies, daisies, saxifrage, zinnias, and French marigolds set fire to the garden, and the pond sparkles beneath water lilies in bloom. In autumn the garden is gilded with sunflowers, black-eyed susans, and cannas harmonizing with the blues, the violets, the mauves of the asters, the bluebells, and the delphiniums; the central path blazes with shades of yellow, orange, and vermilion, and the nasturtiums run wild.[24]

The daily cycles of sun and moon are also exploited by gardens which direct the sunlight, or which, like Katsura Imperial Palace with its Moon-viewing Platform (a pond reflects the moon) and the Mughal gardens with lanterns, are designed to be seen during moonlight.

Finally, many gardens exploit geological time. Geological time is the time of the changes in the earth itself and in the superficial formations with which we are most familiar—the rocks and rivers, hills and mountains, cliffs and shores. In a garden, these features evidencing geological time may be naturally occurring, like the lava formations along the Puna Coast at the Shipman Estate in Hawaii,[25] or artificial, like the serpentine beachfront at Copacabana designed by Roberto Burle Marx and the Elysian Fields at Stowe. They may be presented literally, like Capability Brown's riverscapes at Clivedon and Blenheim, or symbolically, as in the raked sand that represents running water in Japanese Zen gardens. They may be full scale, or reduced in scale, like Alexander Pope's Mount (reminiscent of the mounds in medieval gardens—but also a sacred space like the stupas of south Asia and the Native American burial mounds)—or reduced in scale but deceptively purporting to be full scale, as in Japanese landscape gardens. They may be enclosed within the garden or may themselves comprise what the Japanese call "borrowed scenery," *shakkei*, like the granite cliffs surrounding the garden of Senhora Odette Young Monteiro designed by Burle Marx.[26] They may be the subject, or theme, of the garden, or its topic, the pretense for all subsequent comment, like the cliff sides on which the fifteenth-century Florentine gardens like that at the Villa Gamberaia are based. They may illustrate stasis (as mountains often do) or endless cyclical flux (like flowing rivers) or historical (measurable and directional) change (as a landscape permanently changed by a volcano or violent storm does). And the immeasurable time they present to us may be literally hundreds or thousands or millions of years, or metaphorical eons, the kalpas of human suffering.

But why should we call this a representation of time rather than of space? Many philosophers and architects have agreed that architecture creates space. It is unlikely, given what we know about the diversities of the arts, that two arts should have precisely the same task. It is undeniable that gardens—like painting and sculpture and highways as well as architecture—articulate space. But the several arts do this in different ways, to different purposes.

Gardens articulate space in the interests of articulating time. Let us take the most far-fetched case, the most seemingly static garden, and examine our hypothesis in its light. A moss garden like the Kokiden in Kyoto reveals itself as an exercise in virtuosity, the gardener's garden, attaining the effects of eternal stasis with living materials. (At first sight this might seem to be a variant of the same project as the purely formal garden, the perfectly trimmed topiary for example. Yet the French or Dutch formal garden achieves its ends by means of the assertion of control over the living material, resisting its natural growth; the moss gardener achieves his results not by control over the plant but by control over its environment, not by cutting it back, checking the plant's agenda of growth, but by nourishing it, resisting its death, counteracting the heat and dessication that threaten the struggling plants.) The effect of this garden, however, is neither to eliminate time, nor to distract our attention from it, but precisely the opposite: to call attention to the subtle changes effected before our eyes, by the passage of the sun, the changes in atmosphere, and to our own inner sense of time passing, of our being there over time. By eliminating all the most obvious and usual distractions, it draws attention to the *duree* itself.

Gardens are always experienced first in "real time," that is, time as it is moved through physically and coordinated socially. This "real time" of the garden is identical to and contiguous with that of the outside world; we do not discover a difference in time as we enter the garden, there is no temporal discontinuity as there is in reading a novel, watching a play or film, or (depending on the type of painting) looking at a painting. It takes the same amount of time to drink a cup of tea in the garden as in the house, for a bird to fly in the garden as along a highway.

Gardens thematize time, however, by bringing into the same framework things that "take place" on completely different scales of time. Gardens combine cosmic time (on two levels: the cycle of night and day and the cycle of the seasons), biological time (again often on contrasting scales of trees which live much longer than human beings and birds (plate 4), animals, fish (plate 13), flowers, and insects, which live much shorter), and often geological time (plate 2) (not necessarily scientifically construed, but by means of imported rocks or naturally occurring geological and topographical formations) and historic time (by means of historical allusions, artifacts, and retentions such as ruins). (The garden at St. Thomas's Parish in Washington, D.C., for example, (plate 6) is built around the single wall remaining after the church was burned in 1970.) All of these various kinds of time, with their vastly different scales and their ever-present implied contrast with the time scale of human life, are available to gardening traditions to be juxtaposed and contrasted for effect.

Gardens also affect two aspects of real time, tempo and rhythm. By rhythm I mean the "systematic grouping of sounds [and visual movements] depending on their duration" particularly as they form patterns by contrasting with one another; in the garden these might be made by leaves trembling quickly and delicately in the breeze while at the same time the larger branches of the trees are swaying more slowly, hawks are circling, the sun goes in behind clouds and comes out again, and so on. By tempo I mean the speed(s) at which these

13. Contrasts in texture and pattern are crucial to a Japanese garden, providing both "interest" and "coherence." "Stroll" Garden at Nishi Hongan-ji. Kyoto, Japan. Momoyama Period, 1591.

various things in the garden move. In Harunobu's print of lovers on the verandah of a garden (plate 12), such contrasts of rhythms and tempi are exemplified in the three kinds of plants, the stream, the parallel lines of the planks, and the curves of the lovers themselves. Harunobu exploits the graceful swaying of the flowering shrubs, whose lines echo the lovers' bodies (note particularly the line in the sole of the man's foot and the vertical curves of the woman's kimono) to illustrate the precious evanescence of the lovers' moments together. The flow of time itself is thematized by the sinuous curves of the stream, whose horizontal extensions expand the horizontal curves of the man's knee and right arm, while the lower bank of the stream outlines the bow of the man's sash. (The notion of human life as the surface of a stream has a long history in Japanese thought; indeed the very word for this school or style of art, "ukiyo-e," is "pictures of the floating world.) The contrary possibilities in life, the social structures within which this love takes place, are represented by the solid straight lines of the "man-made" world, the supports and planks of the verandah, the column, and the long neck of the samisen held by the woman. The subjectivity of the experience is manifested externally in the garden.

Tempo and rhythm function differently in gardens than in music. Although gardens have rhythms, these are determined by natural forces, not by the gardenist, and so they cannot be contraposed in succession in order to get different "movements." Tempi, moreover, change to only a limited degree. While not all components of the garden do change their tempi, the gardenist can determine some of them, principally the speed of flowing water and the force of a fountain, and the rate at which—as well as the rhythms by which—a human being in the garden moves.

This last is of particular importance because it affects how the participant views the garden and more importantly the temporality or inner sense of time (not "real time" but psychological time). The tempo set for the participant is never a question of absolute speed, but of speed or tempo relative to the way the person usually walks or walks on a flat and predictable surface. By changing the walkway surfaces (plates 13, 14), the gardenist can slow down the participant's movements and can even draw her attention—by purely tactile and kinesthetic means (not visual)—to the experience of walking. This is a major strategy in Japanese tea gardens, whose purpose is to demand a completely different quality of attention from that which is given in ordinary life, which has been given in fact just a few moments before and a few steps outside the garden. This striking new quality of

14. Walks such as this one force one to pay attention to the act of walking itself, thus concentrating our energy within the present moment. "Stroll" Garden at Nishi Hongan-ji. Kyoto, Japan. Momoyama Period, 1591.

15. A superb beech tree, serving as a veritable axis mundi, uniting heaven and earth in the hemisphere created by the embrace of its branches. It provides shelter, yet at the same time challenges our notion of ourselves as masterful subjects, and thus can be threatening. Dumbarton Oaks, by Beatrix Farrand. Washington, D.C. 20th century.

16. Sand raked like this often represents water. The aged and highly individual trees hardly seem to be tokens of a type, yet they are planted in what amounts almost to an "avenue." Not only in the photo but in the garden itself the shadows are as salient as the trees and sand, leading to a sense of equivalence between "things in themselves" and the world of mere appearance. Daitoku-ji. Kyoto, Japan. Muromachi Period, 1509.

attention is constituted by the exclusion of everything which belongs
to another time, the past or the future, and of all instrumentality per
se. It must be achieved in spite of the spatial and temporal contiguity
of the world inside the tea garden (inside the work of art) with the
"real world." One of the surest ways to effect this transition is by
changing the surface of the path so that the walker must pay attention
to the very mundane act of stepping ahead, so that balance cannot
be taken for granted, so that the tempo with which he or she arrived
at the gate is broken.

Although Japanese tea and stroll gardens have brought the
selection of paths and the determination of the walker's movements—
and consequently of the kind of attention—to the highest degree of
refinement, most gardenists are aware of the differences afforded by
various walking surfaces. And not all pathways require slowing down.
Southover Grange in Lewes, England, (the garden of the school
attended by the seventeenth-century garden connoisseur John Evelyn
when he was a boy) has long, straight, even edges to the flower beds
that are recognized by the neighborhood children as perfect for riding
bicycles, while the edges of terraces are used for playing spy.

The pattern provided by stopping, resting, and continued
movement can also be affected by the gardenist if he or she provides
benches, turning points where decisions are required or quotations
may be deciphered, pavillions or other vantage points with special
views, and so on.

At the same time, the contrast with the movements around one
makes one aware of time in itself, of conflicting scales of time, and
of the directions of time, both unidirectional (time passing) and cyclical
(time returning).

Some gardens thematize human time (what film analysts call
"real time") and set it against other strands of time which the garden
structures simultaneously. Such gardens are meant to be entered
physically but also offer privileged points of view to spectators who
stand above or at a distance. The French formal garden, for example,
offers the privileged viewer a point outside of time from which to
contemplate this human time—balconies or windows or terraces
overlooking the garden. Similarly, the late eighteenth-century
picturesque English landscape gardens often structured views of
laborers and friends through trees or from promontories and
incorporated the human beings who were walking through the garden
as part of the garden itself.[27]

G. The Problem of Two-Dimensional Representation

It is only with the greatest difficulty that writers on gardens avoid losing sight of the full complexity of the experience of the garden: its temporality and the multisensual and the environmental aspects of the garden. The temporal, multisensual, and four-dimensional nature of gardens makes them very difficult to represent in two dimensions. Most studies rely heavily on illustrations—on plans, drawings and photographs—often as a basis for their authors' original impressions and conclusions, as well as for their transmission in print. This is because, since gardens are peculiarly vulnerable to the ravages of time, most of our evidence, especially of earlier gardens, comes not from gardens themselves, but from other arts—paintings, prints, poems. But these representations and reports of gardens are misleading.

The first problem is that any two-dimensional visual representation commits us to one of two approaches, both of which distort. The basic distinction in visual media is that between the bird's-eye view (plates 4, 8) and the immersed or impressionistic view (plate 12). The first, exemplified by plans and aerial drawings or photographs, attempts completeness and is (usually) an idealization. The second, which I will call the located view, is admittedly limited and takes the point of view of a person within the garden, who is always at a specific location. Although it may be informative, it willingly sacrifices completeness for vividness and verisimilitude. While there are works which attempt to combine the two approaches, for example ancient Egyptian paintings of gardens,[28] these are relatively few and do not fully succeed in capturing the reality from the inside.

Both types of visual representation miss the essential temporality of the garden, but they miss it for different reasons. Because the bird's-eye view aims at completeness and a depiction which will be universally valid, it consciously eschews the temporality of the inner experience of the garden. The aim of such an illustration is not the re-creation of an experience but the transmission of information.

In aiming for a complete impression of the garden from the inside, as it were, the immersed view may aim for either a generalized depiction encompassing all moments at once, or a highly individualized depiction re-creating the full impressions of a single moment, as in Monet's paintings of his waterlily garden in various kinds of light or Alan Rokach's series of photographs of the Pepsico Gardens designed by Russell Paige. These are certainly more true to the experience of the garden, but in eschewing temporal succession

they too create a specious present. Like poetry, immersed views can
accommodate temporality to some extent by representing the garden
from a series of stations; this was the avowed intention of Florence
Lee Powell in *In the Chinese Garden*, which attempts to re-create not
only a series of views of the garden but the experience of progressing
through the garden.[29] Japanese and Chinese handscrolls and, to a
lesser extent Japanese painted screens, successfully integrate the
temporal dimension and two-dimensional space by presenting the
viewer with length-to-width proportions such that they can only be
viewed a bit at a time; with scrolls (though not screens) the sequence
is fully controlled by the artist.[30]

This means that if the aim is to understand gardens per se, we
must approach two-dimensional and purely visual illustrations very
cautiously. Using such representations is better than nothing. But,
obviously, one cannot do justice to the full environmental nature of
the garden using photographs or prints, and the photographs should
not be misconstrued as representing the garden as it is experienced.
They are at once too abstract and not abstract enough.

They are too abstract in that, being purely visual, they eliminate
all the sounds and fragrances, as well as the wealth of tactile
impressions that are integral aspects of the experience of any garden.
They reduce an environment which, even in its simplest forms, has
been designed to take advantage of several modes of sensory
experience, to the single mode of vision. Not only that, but the three-
dimensional visual presentation is reduced to two dimensions—a
further abstraction. This may make at times for timeless art—but
unfortunately time is essential to the appreciation of the garden.
Particularly when it comes to depth perception, time is critical. For
half the visual pleasure of the garden comes from the contrasts, the
epistemological and perceptual "play" between appearance and
reality, surface and depth, worked out by means of juxtapositions of
near and distant, of shadows and reflections on the surface of water
and the fish or plants beneath the water (plates 1, 3, 13, 16). The
simple recognition of objects is obscured by the pre-chosen focus of
the observer. One of the peculiar pleasures of the garden is the shift
of focus from one distance to another. In many cases, this is not only
a joy but is essential to the recognition of a species of tree or flower
by distinguishing its outline from the surrounding masses of foliage.
It may be also aesthetic—the lovely shape of a particular pine may
need to be carefully distinguished from other trees behind it. But this
is lost in the photograph unless the color or texture is sharply differ-
entiated. All depth is reduced to two dimensions. Restricted as we are

to the focus chosen by the photographer or artist, without the ability to adjust our focus from the grass at our feet to a distant tree and then to the foliage beyond it, all distant objects become background, all nearer ones subject, as either foreground or middle ground. In the real garden we choose our focus, our subject, with great fluidity.

It is in stymying this process that the photograph shows itself not abstract enough, not selective enough. It is trapped in a single image, where the garden demands an endless rapid fluid succession of selected images. Like any animal moving through its environment, we in the garden constantly shift our perspective. Perhaps no activity is as essential to the aesthetic experience of a garden as this subtle but continuous shifting of focus.

We are encouraged in this method of apprehending the garden by nature itself—for we are instinctively attracted to motion, and it is a rare plant that holds still. Moreover the rhythms visible in the garden are not always simple. Leaves move at their own tempo with every passing breeze; the branches on which they rest may be moving simultaneously at a different pace; the tree as a whole sways in a stronger wind. The leaves of different trees move at different speeds. Running water and fountains keep a constant motion; birds and animals and insects move in ways that are completely unpredictable.

The animal in its environment—and this includes the human being in a garden—is, paradoxically, completely incorporated by the totality, yet also constantly abstracting from parts of that environment, precisely in virtue of his or her attention. Attention is an achievement, based upon the purposes and desires of the organism, and therefore continually reinforcing the self-containment of the organism and its radical discontinuity with its environment. As William James pointed out, attention to one thing is inattention to other things.

Inattention, the gap between ourselves and our environment, and disregard are constant functions of our relation to our environment. Often, they are achieved only at the cost of considerable effort—as I write this, I must continually make an effort to disregard the faucet dripping in the kitchen and the progress of the mail carrier toward our house. It is an attempt not to take seriously phenomena which *seem* important or saliant. At the same time, there are other aspects of my environment, other impressions and sensations, which are available but not demanding of my attention, things like the feel of the chair, the quality of the air, the look of the wall, to which I can direct my attention at any time but which are usually kept in the background. I take them for granted—not only their appearance but also their stability, their continuity, which guarantee in a taken-for-granted way the continuity of the world. Insofar as the garden is part of this world, all this takes place in the same way there. There is a constant interplay between attention and inattention.

The structure of the two-dimensional representation eliminates this dynamic interplay. A central focus is chosen, the rest is eliminated from consideration. What surrounds the focus is never "part of the picture," it cannot be taken for granted. The photograph carries no implications about the world beyond what it says, beyond its own testimonial that such things exist, they are there, they look like this. The relation between the human being and what is looked at has been totally changed.

The garden exists in the midst of such a plethora of opportunities to see, to feel, to hear, to smell. Not all gardens exploit all possibilities to the same extent; some exploit the taken-for-grantedness of the world, others direct attention to certain focal points within that taken-for-granted world. But none of them determine the focus as a photograph does or limit the possibilities of focus in the same way.

H. Organic Form

The ideal of visual art is often described as "organic form." As Suzanne Langer explains it:

> The source of this illusion (for empty space, unenclosed, has actually no visible parts or shape) is the fundamental principle of sculptural volume: the semblance of organism. . . . In the literature of sculpture, more than anywhere else, one meets with reference to "inevitable form," "necessary form," and "inviolable form." But what do these expressions mean? What, in nature, makes forms "inevitable," "necessary," "inviolable?" Nothing but vital function. Living organisms maintain themselves, resist change, strive to restore their structure when it has been forcibly interfered with. All other patterns are kaleidoscopic and casual; but organisms, performing characteristic functions, must have certain general forms, or perish. For them there is a norm of organic structure according to which, inevitably, they build themselves up, deriving matter from their chance environment; and their parts are built to carry on this process as it becomes more complex, so the parts have shapes necessary to their respective functions; yet the most specialized activities are

supported at every moment by the process which they serve, the life of the whole. It is the functional whole that is inviolable. Break this, and all the subordinate activities cease, the constituent parts disintegrate, and "living form" has disappeared.

. . . No other kind of form is actually "necessary," for necessity presupposes a measure in teleological terms, and nothing but life exhibits any telos."[31]

Gardens exhibit organic form par excellence. And they do it on two levels, that of the individual plant and that of the work of art (the garden as a whole). If they did this only on the level of individual plants, of course, there would be no art, no semblance, no Significant Form. Organic form, however, is achieved on the level of the garden as a whole. This fact provides an important key to understanding the peculiar power gardens have to convince. Their illusion is always convincing since it is always based on organic form (organic form being precisely the form exhibited by organisms such as plants). One reason gardens can be successful at revealing the perceived order between macro- and micro-cosm is that they carry evidence of their successful integration of the larger world into the garden in their very existence. In virtue of the fact that, as we have seen, they can only exist physically insofar as they accommodate themselves to the actual climate, weather conditions, geology, etc., their existence is proof of viability and successful accommodation.

I. Death in the Garden: "You plant 'em and they die"[32]

The connection of death with the garden is originary, inevitable, unremitting, and quite complex. It begins with the fact that plants die, that gardens continuously provide us with incontrovertible evidence of death and its generality, while consoling us with evidence that the gardener's art can also keep the plants alive. Gardens originated, moreover, in the attempt to provide our own sustenance. But beyond all this is the fact that the garden is also our symbolic bulwark against chaos, against the randomness death introduces into our world: the mangled bird corpses, the tangled remains of dead flowers, the haphazard lines of dead stalks, the stench of rotting gingko fruits. But we also die, and at certain historical junctures it has been recognized that a certain satisfaction can be gained from establishing the dead within the garden, acknowledging our continued relation with them while admitting a new distance and a lack of reciprocity.

This may be physical or symbolic (or both). At Oatlands, a manor built in 1805 in northern Virginia, the family crypt was set within the garden. Richard Etlin has shown how, increasingly since the late eighteenth century, a garden-like setting has seemed the most fitting environment for our buried dead and the lines between cemeteries and gardens and parks have been blurred.[33]

All gardens, as different as they may be, fall into one of two camps as far as death is concerned. The "natural" or informal garden admits death, even exploits it. The "Edenic" or formal garden, on the other hand, tries to replicate the conditions of the garden of Eden, denying change, death, and the cycle of life. The Garden of Eden, scene of the coming into being of our life, our self-consciousness, and our desires, is also the source of our knowledge of death. Nor is this the fortuitous result of a specific myth, a piece of cultural fantasy. Indeed, if there were no death, gardens would be unnecessary—and they are far too difficult and painful an enterprise to be undertaken if they were not necessary.

Perhaps because of this inherent echo of death, gardens always speak directly, seriously, in their own voice, if you will: they may be gay or lighthearted, but alone among the arts they are never ironic, cruel, desperate, parodic, sarcastic, silly, or even overtly humorous although they are frequently witty.[34]

Only when it is taken up by the other arts, by fiction or painting, can the garden escape its destiny to be serious, to express hope and confidence and order. Such a (fictional) garden can be a thing of terror, the very image of the destruction of all basic human value. The briar forest surrounding the Sleeping Beauty's castle is a perversion of the garden which marks the transition from the outer, public realm to our home: instead of easing the transition, it prevents all further commerce with the outside world. In popular fiction, the hedge maze holds unpredictable lurking death. Hieronymous Bosch's *The Garden of Earthly Delights*[35] has an edge that is missing from a scene of hell: this is not what is yet in store for us but what we already know, a vision of what we live.

CHAPTER 3

🌹

Additional Aspects of Spatiality

Two further aspects of the spatial nature of gardens remain to be considered—territory and environment. Both carry special ramifications for the aesthetics and significance of gardens. The "space" of a garden is not primarily objective space. It is space adapted to biological organisms, organized around and by a kind of mammal. As such, it is always and inherently biological space, richly significant and subjectively experienced. "Territory" and "environment" refer to two of the biological aspects of the garden space.

A. Gardens and Territory

For us as for all reasonably intelligent animals, the ability to survive and flourish depends not only on the external environment but also on the ability to solve problems. The ability to solve problems—to think and to cope with one's environment—is dependent not only on objective factors about the environment and one's individual capabilities but, equally important, also on subjective factors—on self-confidence and perception of control. This means that any satisfactory environment must be empowering. Human beings prefer landscapes which are empowering to those which make them feel helpless.[1]

The Frankfurt School philosophers, who developed the idea of empowerment, understood it to be derived from and founded upon, grounded in, community. Recent work in the psychology of landscape cognition, however, suggests that empowerment is possible even for individuals, on the basis of the individual's relationship to his or her environment. Territory, that is, that part of the environment which represents the control of the individual or his/her group, links the two

53

conceptions of empowerment and may provide a kind of mediation between them. But not all environment-based empowerment is derived from (controlled) territory—because of the interaction between cognition and landscape features, one may be empowered by an environment over which one has no territorial assertion. This needs to be studied further.

As we saw in chapter 2, gardens are especially well suited to the display of social status. The reasons for this are not solely cultural. For culturally specific in their form as garden styles are, as symbolic of ideals, as useful in resolving social and economic and intellectual tensions, gardens' suitability to the display of social status is biological at base—it is first of all a matter of territory.

For predators and the more intelligent animals, the areas where one lives and finds food are not functions simply of climate and the availability of food, water, and protection from the elements. An additional feature, social ordering, structures the environment, making of these areas not mere places one happens to be, but territory, that is, places where one has increased control and perception of control. The act of defining territory expresses control; it also helps to define the self and the in-group. It is also therefore a *social* action, with important social consequences. Definition of territory always requires—and therefore symbolically implies—the compliance or cooperation of others of one's kind.

Territoriality is an important means of reducing competition and aggression, and thus of reducing the amount of tension the animal experiences. The boundaries of one's territory are established dynamically by the animal acting alone and in interaction with others of his species. Because territory is defined among members of a single species rather than interspecifically, it serves to differentiate the individual from his group, and his own group ("in-group") from other similar groups ("out-groups").[2] Gardens relocate the relation to territory which is originally biological within the domain of culture. Although the determination of territory for human beings is far more complex than for other mammals, it is nonetheless first of all a way of solving—or better yet, preventing—problems that originate on the biological level.

The importance of territory for the understanding of gardens cannot be underestimated.[3] Nonetheless, a garden is rarely merely coextensive with territory. There are economic reasons for this: in almost all cases, territory will be larger than the space the gardenist can afford to turn into a garden. But there may also be legal factors which are independent: the obvious case is the garden of a king, whose territory may extend to the whole kingdom, and whose garden, however extensive, is but a small portion.

Humphrey Repton, the late-eighteenth-century English landscape designer, was keenly aware both of the uses of the garden or park to establish territory and of the insufficiency of mere extent to accomplish this social purpose. In "Sketches and Hints on Landscape Gardening," he iterates the point:

> All rational improvement of grounds is, necessarily, founded on a due attention to the character and situation of the place to be improved; while the extent of the premises has less influence than is generally imagined; as, however large or small it may be, one of the fundamental principles of landscape gardening is to disguise the real boundary.[4]

Regarding Tatton, he explains:

> The command of adjoining property, the style and magnitude of the mansion and all its appendages contribute to confer that degree of importance which ought here to be the leading object in every plan of improvement. Vastness of extent will no more constitute greatness of character in a park than a vast pile of differently coloured building will constitute greatness of character in a house. A park, from its vast extent, may perhaps surprise, but it will not impress us with the character of greatness and importance unless we are led to those parts where beauty is shewn to exist, with all its interest, amidst the boundless range of undivided property.[5]

The issues of territoriality and empowerment bring us back to a feature of the initial definition of the garden which we rejected, namely enclosure. Repton rejected enclosure as an aspect of visual aesthetics of the garden. Yet because the garden is a subset of a whole biological environment, its differentiation from that larger environment by means of enclosure can be important. On the biological level, the gardener seeks through enclosure to effect an artificial separation from the larger environment, altering the seamless continuity which permits the intrusion of voracious herbivores or tenacious weeds. Socially and politically, enclosure is an assertion of political and social territory, a warning-off, akin to the signs of occupation made by wolves.

So enclosure works on two levels, as a means of control and as a sign of that control. In a world as insubordinate as the human world is in most societies, enclosure may be necessary if we are to control what is within.[6] The purpose of enclosure is to exclude the unwanted; depending on the type of garden and its surroundings, everything from rabbits, neighbors, and harsh winds to marauding soldiers, stray hamburger wrappers, and wine bottles may need to be kept out.[7] For most of us, the whole world is too big and unmanageable to "improve" (to use the English landscape gardenists' term). The force of enclosure—and of the development of the very notion of the garden—is always to indicate points of tension, terms of contrast, a polarization, indeed an alienation from the world at large. This is true even if at certain points in garden history it becomes desirable to tear down the wall protecting the garden as an indication of the increase in human confidence in the ability to control the world at large.

Even where physical protection is not necessary, therefore, boundary demarcations of some kind or other are often found, with a symbolic rather than a practical value. We need not only to occupy a territory but to define our territory symbolically. A hedge which is far too flimsy to keep out an occupying army or even an out-of-control motorcycle still offers protection from the prying eyes of passers-by. The short stone garden walls of the Cotswolds offer even less protection than the hedge, but they do define the movements of others, formalize the ways by which the house and its occupants may be approached, so that in approaching, the visitor has defined herself as friend or member of the community, one who is willing to abide by a common way of doing things. Refusal or inability to recognize these customs defines one clearly as an outsider, a "violator."

And the territory defined by a garden extends not only in space but in time. The garden demonstrates not only power to control a part of the world but a peculiar sort of confidence because it indicates an expected continuation of that power in the future. (No one gardens only for today).

But the symbolic aspects of enclosure are not solely a function of territoriality; it is not merely the process of defining which is symbolic but also the area defined as a result. A symbolic realm is created in which self-definition and differentiation between in-group and out-group are effected. But because of the means by which gardens are brought about, the garden mediates not only between self and others, and in-group and out-group, but between a number of the poles or oppositions that define human experience, across a whole range of issues and possibilities: Man and Nature, the natural and the artificial, indoor and outdoor, private and social, duty and pleasure, action and contemplation. This is what makes gardens philosophically important, and not just sociologically or psychologically interesting.

B. The Garden and the Environment

Before it is anything else, and in marked contrast to many other human works, especially other works of art, the garden comprises an environment. Yet the environmental character of the garden is in direct conflict with its status as a work of art, for two reasons. First, art depends upon virtuality, the creation and manipulation of illusion, while as we have seen, the essence of an environment is actuality.[8] In spite of the conflict between these two contradictory sets of demands, however, both illusion and actuality are essential, inseparable aspects of gardens. The apparent endlessness of a disappearing path, for example, which is often to be found in Japanese and English landscape gardens and which exemplifies that aspect of preferred landscapes called "mystery," is an illusion; nonetheless it must be an actual path. The illusion of a garden is never pure *trompe-l'oeil*. When we confront a garden, enter it, it supplants, at least in the immediate present, all other environments. It surrounds us. It provides the very ground that supports us and the full range of sensual experience and of information that we are to process.

Second, the environmental nature of the garden violates one of the most cherished preferences of those who cherish the notion of art, the preference for a discrete *object* of aesthetic experience. The remainder of this chapter will elaborate on the environmental character of gardens, while the following chapter will examine the implications of this character for the status of gardens as an art form.

At any given moment, when we are in a garden, it is a full and real world surrounding us: it comprises a total environment. At the same time, a garden is only a part of the environment with which we must daily contend and with which we are familiar. It forms only a part of our world, albeit often a very special part. Its characteristics are chosen and valued for the contrasts as well as the continuities they provide with the outer environment. Yet these contrasts are doubly constrained, by the possibilities afforded by the external environment (I cannot grow bamboo or open up a vista of mountains in my central New Jersey garden) and by the resources which the gardener is able and willing to devote to overcoming those constraints (I can, however, water the grass during a draught). A garden is largely dependent upon its biological environment.

There are, then, three different types of relation between gardens and environment, and they need to be explored independently. First, comprision: the garden comprises a kind of environment. Second, dependency: gardens as living beings and as works of art depend upon their environments to provide certain requirements. Finally, contrast: the meaning of a particular garden is derived largely from the contrast it provides to its surroundings.

1. Comprision

The environmental nature of the garden requires us to bring both to making and to appreciating the garden many of the same faculties, skills, knowledge, and habits we depend upon in other environments. The banks of the garden canal must be able to support us and must be perceptible; we must process information about them. It is just as important that we not drown in a canal in the garden as that we not drown in a canal in the city; this places demands upon both the gardener-as-artist and upon the viewer that are not placed upon a novelist or her readers. The laws of perception and the processes of cognition that we use in the garden are the same as those we use to survive and flourish in the outside world. This means that, whatever may be the relation between survival (in its full complexity—physical and cultural and emotional, of the individual and of the species) and aesthetics in the other arts, in gardens they are intimately intertwined.

2. Dependency

All arts, not only gardens, are dependent upon their environment. The threats posed by modern technology to the monuments of Egypt and the artworks of a number of Italian cities, Leonardo's inadequate preparation of painting surfaces and the slapdash methods of modern painters, the fragility of musical instruments and lacquerware in the face of fluctuations in humidity—all indicate the dependency upon the environment for physical survival. In addition, art must often depend upon a suitable environment for an opportunity to convey its ideas and to display its full aesthetic effects. The French museum which hangs its Monets in a narrow corridor prevents the paintings from being seen as they demand to be seen, as they are. The disc jockey who plays Big Brother and the Holding Company's "Piece of My Heart" following immediately upon another song without a break prevents the work from communicating its precise idea of the quality of a certain pain because the opening notes which make the idea clear can only be understood against a contrast of silence. Outside the work of Arnold Berleant, the dependency of works of art upon their environment has received little attention, although Susan Sontag has written eloquently of the dependency of the photograph:

> Because each photograph is only a fragment, its moral and emotional weight depends on where it is inserted. A photograph changes according to the context in which it is seen: thus Smith's Minamata photographs will seem different on a contact sheet, in a gallery, in a political demonstration, in a police file, in a photographic magazine, in a general news magazine, in a book, on a living-room wall. Each of these situations suggests a different use for the photographs but none can secure their meaning. As Wittgenstein argued for words, that the meaning is the use—so for each photograph. And it is in this way that the presence and proliferation of all photographs contributes to the erosion of the very notion of meaning, to that parceling out of the truth into relative truths which is taken for granted by the modern liberal consciousness.[9]

Precisely because the garden is a total environment rather than a discrete object, it is more robust than the photograph. Yet we can see that the differences between the various arts in these respects are a matter of degree, with the photograph and the garden at opposite poles of a continuum. Like the other arts, the garden is dependent upon its environment for its survival and upon its context for the conditions within which to convey its effects. But the garden, in addition to these kinds of dependency, has the dependency of a living being; in this it is unique among the arts.[10]

Since it is only a part of the environment, limited and therefore to some extent manipulable, yet having many of the features of the outer environment, the garden serves as a model of the real world, either as we believe it is or as we would like it to be. (The term "world" as I am using it is intended to mean the totality of things apprehended, utilized, or suspected by an organism. It is not specific to human beings, but it is always organized, with reference to the survival needs of some living being. "Real" here means "capable of having effects" and would include, for example, phenomena such as fear or an auditory hallucination that arouses fear or that distracts someone's attention. This use of "real" thus includes but is not identical with what Suzanne Langer would call "virtual." [See ch. 7.])

This dependency upon its environment has another important impact on what we understand of a garden. A garden, to be successful, must be successful on two levels: it must satisfy us, and it must survive. If it survives, it seems to prove something—that this is possible, that we (or someone) could control this place, that this kind of life is possible. This fact about the garden makes it an extraordinarily compelling and convincing sort of vision, quite different from what can be achieved in painting or fiction.[11] For insofar as the garden represents an ideal world or an ideal life, it seems by its very existence to prove that world valid. There is a price to pay in terms of artistic freedom—the gardenist is not as free as the novelist or the painter. (There are no science fiction gardens.) But whatever can be said via the garden carries conviction, even when it is not true. The Sun King was not really the center of the cosmos, but Versailles made him seem so.

3. Contrast

All of these relations of gardens with their/our environment affect the aesthetics of garden design and the roles and capabilities of the garden as an art form. "Dependency" on the garden's own physical environment has a major impact on the aesthetics of the various garden styles. As with architecture, a style will usually take advantage of materials available locally, with non-native materials contributing a sense of exoticism and luxury. Again as with architecture, the physical qualities valued by a given style will vary with the locale, often defined by contrast: shade is valued in sunny climates and open sunniness in cool ones. For all the idealization to which it is amenable, the garden can never be a pure flight of fancy. Indeed the idealizations to which it is most susceptible—the tidiness, the order, the elimination of death, the superfluity, the shady coolness, the lushness, the austerity, the extravagance, the colors, the warmth, the light, the quiet, the protection—these values in a given garden are largely determined by the flaws discerned (from the gardenist's point of view) in the surrounding environment.

Take the example of a domestic courtyard garden in New Orleans. Such a garden is built upon the establishment of a contrast with the summer climate, the heat, the humidity, the glare. Its values are defined by this contrast—shade, coolness, running water in fountains. Within this basic paradigm, and relative to the main or overarching idea, the particular flowers in bloom are incidental. As bits of color they can enliven the gloom of the highly desirable shade and offer variety to the repetitious semitropical vegetation—palms and plants with broad emerald green leaves. So the flowers come and go as nature dictates, not in themselves essential to the idea; essential, if at all, only as representatives of a type (although their particularity may be important in formulating other subordinate ideas).

Yet changes in sunlight destroy the idea of this garden completely. Imagine the same garden in November. It is now chilly and gray. The garden lacks all appeal; it has no other values than shade and cool and relief to offer, and these are dependent upon a particular context, the context of seasonal climate. The intrinsic somatic appeal of the garden is the way it makes its idea known; without the right conditions, one cannot understand from the garden itself what it has been made to do. One may reconstruct on the basis of outside knowledge—provided one has heard about the climate in summer, or provided one knows about the values of such austere gardens in Spain and Persia, and one infers that it must be like that. The environmental nature of gardens, and our nature as biological organisms of a particular kind, provide a range of significance, of orderings and values, that precedes and transcends cultural differences and that makes gardens cross-culturally intelligible and meaningful to a large extent.[12] Out of season it is possible to make of it a sort of conceptual art. It is not, however, possible to appreciate it as the work of art it was intended to be, and which it succeeds in being in the heat. Stripped of the heat, and the sun and the humidity, it ceases to be the formulation of a work of art.

C. Environment, Cognition, and Landscape Preference

The processing of environmental information and the interaction of environment and cognition have begun to receive scientific attention recently, along with their emotional, behavioral, and even physiological ramifications. This area of environmental psychology carries important implications for the study of gardens, for we process information in the garden much as we do in other environments.[13] These ways have been developed over hundreds of thousands, even millions of years—some of them are not even specifically human traits. Being relatively weak, slow, and defenseless, human beings like to know far in advance what is coming, and we rely more heavily on sight and sound, as giving information over distance, than on smell, taste, and touch, which provide knowledge only after the threat is so close that we are already vulnerable. At the same time, we are predators, and like other predators we need as individuals to develop sophisticated motor skills and a sense of familiarity or being-at-home outside our own home territory; as a species we exhibit that playfulness and curiosity so useful in facilitating the skills and knowledge in individuals—a playfulness and curiosity that are much in evidence in garden design.

In addition, the history of our species, with its descent from the trees (to which it was well adapted) to the ground (to which it was not) has also played a major role in the shaping of our information processing. Stephen and Rachel Kaplan, pioneers of environmental psychology, have summarized this history and its impact:

> [T]he ground...presented rather grim challenges. First, it was dangerous....This danger was compounded by another awkward circumstance. The ground was well populated by the time our ancestors arrived, and all the convenient niches were taken. To survive, early humans had to range over large territories, but as home-based animals, they had to find their way back.
>
> To meet these dual challenges required two apparently contradictory abilities. It was necessary to know a great deal—about the terrain, about potential predators, about how to get home from many directions. At the same time, it was necessary to be quick, to decide and act with a minimum of delay. In other words, there was a premium on knowledge without contemplation.[14]
>
> There were a number of adaptations to these difficult circumstances. First, humans by and large can only think about things one at a time....The limitation is not on how much one knows, but on how much of what one knows one can contemplate at any given moment. Since humans by and large can only do one thing at a time, thinking only one thing at a time favors prompt action.
>
> In a very general way, two human characteristics seem necessary to the operation of this high knowledge-low contemplation system....First is the human capacity and tendency to build models....[A mental model is] a simplified but coherent conception of some aspect of reality....A simplified but workable conception of the environment is a great help in handling a large amount of information in a hurry....
>
> The second human characteristic necessary for a high knowledge-low contemplation system involves the desire or motivation to know much and to act quickly. To be more precise, the organism must be motivated not merely to know, but to know in a fashion that is simple and cogent, and that facilitates action. The organism must enjoy prompt decisions and be uneasy when decision making is drawn out. This pattern of concerns might be called the desire for clarity.[15]

In other words, certain kinds of information processing favor survival, and certain kinds of environment facilitate these functionally superior kinds of information processing—environments where there are limits on the amount of new information, limits on distractions, limits on unexpected or uncontrollable stimuli, accommodations to visual and auditory perception. Gardens fit this description of environments which facilitate superior information processing and thus survival. This is not coincidental. Gardens satisfy largely in virtue of their sensitivity to human cognitive processes.

But environments are not always under our control. And so survival is also facilitated by a *preference* on the part of the organism for certain kinds of environments. Our emotional responses to environments, in other words, can be shown to be largely functional in terms of our physical capabilities and the types of cognitive processing which we have developed as a species:

> [V]iewed within the larger evolutionary context, preference—even aesthetics for that matter—is closely tied to basic concerns. An organism must prefer those environments in which it is likely to thrive; likewise it must dislike environments in which it is likely to be ineffective or handicapped or harmed in any way. Preference in this context is to no small degree an expression of human needs. In other words, preferred environments will in general be ones in which human abilities are more likely to be effective and needs are more likely to be met.[16]

This view of course flies in the face of much of the theory of aesthetics; since Kant, we are used to thinking of the aesthetic as precisely that which is removed from our purposes and the satisfaction of our needs; Kaplan and Kaplan refer to "the almost frivolous connotation of the term preference, [which] suggests the decorative rather than the essential, the favored as opposed to the necessary."[17] (This view of aesthetics is unfortunately especially prevalent among those who deal with housing and other environments. Real estate agents, for example, often conceptualize aesthetic dimensions as "cosmetic.")

Landscape preference can be evaluated on different levels. In terms of content, fire, water, and caves hold people's attention, and people show preference for landscapes that contain these elements. The latter two of course are features which have been developed, cherished, and accentuated in gardens and parks in any number of cultural traditions.[18]

In terms of cognitive processing, preferred environments are those which favor the selection and management of information, permitting both "involvement" (as William James pointed out, "the best attention is effortless") and "making sense." Involvement and making sense are basic attributes of those landscapes which are easily processed; they have been further analyzed as having four dimensions: complexity or diversity, coherence, mystery, and legibility:

> For an environment to be "involving" it must have some complexity or diversity. Involvement can also come from features that are not actually present but are suggested or implied. The road turning around a bend and disappearing is the classic example of a promise of more information, of what we have called mystery.

> For an environment to "make sense" requires coherence; the parts need to hang together and in some sense "belong" there. Ground textures that provide continuity and the repetition of elements (windows on a building or a row of trees) play a role here. Lynch's concept of legibility, first introduced in the urban domain, is also an important component in making sense. One might view legibility as a promise that the environment will be comprehensible as one continues to make one's way through it. In the natural environment, legibility is enhanced by a sense of depth and by the smoothness of the texture, both of which facilitate seeing where one is headed.

> While the origin of these concepts is in the context of the physical environment, and of landscapes in particular, the concepts themselves are reasonable in terms of human information processing quite apart from a particular setting. Certain properties are common to any cognitive map, no matter what the environment. Likewise, there are certain properties common to any environment that is readily comprehended, i.e., that one readily builds a map of. Coherence is what makes it possible to organize the field, to divide it into units for which one already has appropriate representations. Complexity or diversity provide a sufficient number of representations to fill the mind and to insure that the focus will not be shared with other content. Mystery is an indication that there is the possibility of exploring, of extending one's cognitive map. And legibility is a kind of reassurance, an indication that the informational environment yet to come will be manageable.[19]

The history of the species then seems to have affected not only the way we think and feel about our environment but also the kind of environment we prefer. There is some evidence to suggest that preference for a single type of landscape or biome—the parklike setting with short grass and scattered large trees that approximates the African savanna—is characteristic of our species. In experiments by J. D. Balling and J. H. Falk, American adults showed a preference for savanna at least as strong as their preference for environments with which they were personally familiar (deciduous and coniferous forests), while children demonstrated a significant preference for savanna over all other environments, including their (familiar) home environment. The authors argued that the tendency to produce such landscape elements and arrangements is not accidental but rather at least partially the result of an innate preference for savanna-like settings.[20] (Preferences for environments to which they are adapted, but which they have not directly experienced, have been found in a variety of nonhuman species as well.)[21] Subsequent research by the same scientists evaluated preferences among Nigerian subjects whose home environments were predominantly rain forest (most of whom had never traveled beyond this environment); again, savanna was highly preferred relative to all other biomes; no distinct preferences emerged among the other four types (deciduous forest, coniferous forest, tropical rain forest, and desert).[22] The authors concluded that human evolutionary history has had a major influence not only on such physical features as human posture and dentition but also on some of our behaviors and preferences.

This research suggests that underlying and preceding the preference for the "learned" landscape of our experience is an inherited preference for the type of landscape that favored our emergence as a distinctive species. Such an inherited preference would seem to affect garden design in at least two ways. First, gardens may re-create the essential features of the savanna. As Falk and Balling point out, the English landscape-style garden, typified in the work of Capability Brown and Humphrey Repton, exemplifies the savanna-like landscape.[23] The style became enormously popular not only in Britain but in North America and continental Europe and could be said to have reached the status of an international vernacular not only for gardens but for public parks, golf courses, and (since 1830) cemeteries.[24] Second, it appears that even the most highly stylized treatments of gardens may be understood as attempts to approximate this original landscape. Orians has demonstrated that horticulturists and landscape designers in Japan have tended to modify the phenotype of native tree forms toward those found among trees existing in savanna environments.[25]

PART II

The Garden as a Work of Art

CHAPTER 4

✿

Gardens and Current Theories of Art[1]

In the eighteenth century, European literati considered gardens an important kind of artwork, equal in stature to poetry and painting. In spite of widespread agreement that gardens can and often do display the formal excellence characteristic of works of art, however, this stature has declined to the point where today almost no one thinks of contemporary gardens as works of art. The contrast between these two attitudes is nowhere stronger than in philosophy. For while eighteenth-century philosophers wrote about gardens frequently and saw vital relationships between them and politics and ethics, present-day philosophers ignore them.

How are we to account for this change in status? Stephanie Ross has suggested that the decline is attributable to incidental factors such as the expense of gardening on the grand scale and the difficulty of preserving gardens in their original condition.[2] I believe the problem lies deeper than that, in a fundamental conflict between the nature of gardens on the one hand and certain features of what we choose to call art on the other. The status of the garden as a work of art is extremely problematic, but it repays careful study for it is problematic in ways which are both interesting and philosophically revealing, ways which have to do with both the definition of art and the intrinsic properties of gardens. This chapter will start with a look at the "fit" between gardens and current theories of art and proceed to an examination of the problems gardens pose for aesthetic theory.

A. The "Fit" between Gardens and Current Theories of Art

The demotion of the garden from its former status as an art is odd since according to a number of current theories the garden ought to be the very paradigm of an "artkind." Ironically, the garden has to be rejected as an artkind precisely on the theory designed to be the most generous and inclusive—George Dickie's "institutional" definition of art. According to the "institutional" view, something becomes a work of art if "some person or persons acting on behalf of a certain institution (the artworld)" designates it a "candidate for appreciation."[3] On this view, gardens should be considered works of art since formerly they were and no reason has emerged for their dislodgement.

Such a definition, while useful for certain purposes, offers little insight into why such a designation, enjoyed by gardens at one time, might subsequently be retracted. Given the fact that the "institutional" theory is based on designation per se as the discriminating feature, this inability to account for the rejection of gardens as an artkind is crucial and suggests that the theory is inadequate to the task of differentiating works of art from nonworks of art, that the "institutional" theory in fact does not get at some crucial features which we seem to be employing (whether we admit it or not) in deciding what art is.[4]

A second interesting point is that the garden's "fall from grace" reveals a de facto rupture in our thinking between the aesthetic and art. For many—perhaps most—of us, it is primarily by aesthetic criteria that a garden is judged. In the United States, for example, the expectations people bring to gardens and the pleasures they find there are overwhelmingly aesthetic;[5] nonetheless, gardens are rarely regarded here as an artkind. This deserves our attention, given that most philosophers today do want to claim some sort of integral relation between the aesthetic and art. Monroe Beardsley, for example, states: "What establishes an artkind, on my view, is that a good many of its individual instances are created with the intention (perhaps among others) of making aesthetic experience obtainable."[6] On Beardsley's view, the garden clearly would be an artkind. If it is not accepted as an artkind (as I believe to be the case), then Beardsley's view does not adequately catch our practical de facto definition of art.

Of course, aesthetic satisfaction alone is not enough to make something a work of art—a sunset or an "unimproved" landscape, however beautiful or otherwise aesthetically pleasing, is not a work of art. But what disqualifies the sunset or unimproved landscape from the category of art is the fact it is in no sense artificial; it has not been formed through intentional human activity. But since this obviously is not true of the garden, which probably demands more unremitting effort and attention from its creator than any other art, this cannot be the reason the garden is not considered an artkind.

Beardsley's definition is deliberately broad, for it is designed specifically to "be of the greatest possible utility to inquirers in other fields besides aesthetics—fields to which aesthetics itself should (sometimes) be thought of as a support and underpinning. . . . [such as] art history and anthropology."[7] Beardsley's position offers us an advantage in that it makes possible the inclusion for the purposes of analysis of art some works from cultures which do not employ the category of art. Still the fact that gardens have come to be excluded from the common notion of "art" suggests that there are additional criteria operant which Beardsley's generous definition does not uncover. It seems clear that even the combination of these two criteria, a forming human intention and aesthetic effects, are generally not sufficient to constitute a work of art. There are any number of things meeting both of Beardsley's criteria which we do not regard as works of art—an elegantly set table, the effects of tickertape in the sunlight during a tickertape parade, automobiles, clothing.

But perhaps we *should* regard all these as works of art. The problem here may be that usage and habitual thinking, not only of the general public, of booksellers and magazine editors who make decisions about what to include in the category, but even of philosophers of art, have not kept up with the practices of the art world. For the Metropolitan Museum of Art has a gallery devoted to fashion, and the Museum of Modern Art periodically exhibits objects of industrial design—pens, telephones, coffee grinders—which achieve the aesthetic standards of art. Yet in general we who are not museum professionals seem to prefer the maintainance of our customary biases and preferences to accuracy and consistency. Dickie's theory expands the range of "art" solely on the basis of such innovations in custom. Beardsley's expansion is more theoretically motivated, in that it takes as fundamental the recognition that the "art-hood" of an object is not inherent in the object but is a function of the kind of relation between itself and a human observer which it permits or facilitates. But neither illuminates the situation of the garden.

B. Difficulties Gardens Pose for Theory of Art

Why, then, if current theories of art show no grounds for excluding them, if our general notion of art is expanding at least in practical terms, and if gardens have a history of being regarded as an artkind and can be shown to have form as beautiful, as original, and as self-conscious as other arts, are gardens currently excluded from the category of art?

There are two main reasons. First, gardens enjoy an ambiguous status in a number of different respects—between poles of "art" and/or the "artificial" on the one hand and "Nature" on the other, between art and craft, and between fine and applied art. Second, gardens violate a number of implicit preferences upon which most theory of art is premised—preferences for a single final form of a work of art (for uniqueness and perdurance), for artistic (or authorial) control by a (single) (human) agent, for immateriality, and for what is known as "disinterest" or "distance" or "autonomy." The rest of this chapter will explore the first three of these preferences, which prove so problematic for the status of gardens, with reference to the ambiguities of the "art/craft" and "fine art/applied art" distinctions. Chapter 5 will analyze the issues of "disinterest/distance," while chapter 6 will explore the problem of the garden's nature as Nature.

C. Preferences in the Theory of Art

If we are to understand the puzzling status of gardens, we must look not to the positive aspects of theories but to the often unacknowledged presuppositions of those theories. There are a number of ways in which gardens are very awkward for the rough consensus about art that has developed within philosophy over the past hundred years or so. By "consensus" here I do not of course mean to imply that there has been any consensus of formal definition. Quite the contrary. There has been a great deal of explicit, even heated, disagreement about what art is, as well as considerable experimentation with the boundaries of art by artists. Underlying the debate, however, is a set of assumptions or presuppositions that are still widely shared about what kind of a thing art is and is not, what kind of thing it should and should not be. These assumptions give shape to the discourse itself, often determining the kind of issues that philosophers will find important. They might best be expressed as a set of shared preferences: works that match these preferences help to define the paradigm of art; while works that do not fit these preferences are, to the extent of their divergence from them, problematic and must be accounted for. To be more specific, we seem to prefer works of art which (a) have a single unique form which is stable over time (music which is composed and recorded in notation rather than improvised); (b) are defined and controlled by a single autonomous artist (paintings by "masters" rather than collaborations; auteur theory rather than collaborative theory in film); (c) de-emphasize their materiality and minimize any dependence upon physical conditions for their existence (the so-called fine arts over crafts); and d) set up a relation of psychical distance between the object and the viewer or listener.

For each of these preferences, gardens are intensely problematic.

D. Problem 1: Gardens and the Preference for Uniqueness

Traditionally, philosophers have shown a bias in favor of the one-of-a-kind or "unique" arts, which are the visual arts—painting, drawing, sculpture, architecture. With the exception of architecture, these are what Nelson Goodman calls "autographic" arts—those for which the distinction between original and forgery is significant.[8] These have served as the paradigm, for Western theory and criticism have tended to favor the arts where the single work could be taken for granted. To the extent that an artkind diverges from this paradigm, as the "allographic" arts like music, dance, and poetry do, it has been perceived as presenting problems which it is the task of philosophy of art to unravel. Replication, mass reproduction, the imitation of one artist's work by another, appropriation, and forgery, all become problems for philosophy because we take uniqueness so seriously.[9]

But what exactly is meant by "unique"? Before going any further, it would be as well to explain the reasons for using the term "unique" comparatively and quantitatively. Contrary to popular opinion, "unique" is not a simple term. First, there are at least two different applications of the term, as it can be intended either to include spatiotemporal position of the object or not. When we speak of snowflakes as being unique, we mean in terms of attributes independent of their location in time and space—otherwise the uniqueness of snowflakes is not a matter of amazement at all. On the other hand, each one of an edition of twenty-five prints by Picasso is unique only if numbered—that is, if its location in time and space is taken into consideration; otherwise the differences are indiscernible. Second, "unique" usually applies to the qualities of the object (sensual and sometimes semantic) but whether we mean by that literally *all* qualities or merely all *significant* qualities depends upon circumstance. The distinction is covered up by our use of the single term "unique" for both cases. Generally, regarding art, we are only

interested in significant qualities or changes in qualities—the very
possibilities of art restoration and collection, for example, rest upon
our confidence in that distinction; we don't throw away a Rembrandt
because it has darkened over time. Finally, what is unique is, at least
in the case of art, consistent over time. We are not usually interested
in that kind of uniqueness which changes moment to moment, as the
state of the world might be said to be unique—literally, absolutely—
at a given point in time. "Uniqueness," then, refers ambiguously to
two sets of attributes of the object (one inclusive, the other exclusive
of spatiotemporal location), and it further implies certain
epistemological preferences on our part: the qualities should be
noticeable, significant, and consistent over time.

Now, what is the situation of the garden with respect to the
criterion of uniqueness? I think one can say with confidence that if
anything is unique, gardens are. They are in fact *so* unique that whole
categories of problems are simply nonsensical with regard to them.
Hence gardens remove themselves from the field of problems
cultivated by philosophers in regard to works of art. There are no
forgeries of gardens. There are no full-scale replicas of gardens.
(Although there are very occasionally attempts at full-scale replicas,
such as the Astor Court Garden at the Metropolitan Museum.
Patterned with the greatest fidelity after the Garden of the
Fisherman's Nets in Suchou, inevitably some changes had to be made
to accommodate the change in location, in this case the inclusion of
the court within the museum building necessitating the use of a
skylight; and inevitably the result is a qualitative change that
prevents the "replica" from being mistaken for the "original.") They
cannot be mass-produced. There is no possibility of inauthenticity in
gardens. Why is this?

There are three reasons. First, nearly all gardens include as major
components large numbers of living plants. As living things (and in
spite of the best efforts of modern horticulture), these plants (to date)
are genetic individuals, and they are also very much affected by
environmental factors and by events in their life history. Idiosyncratic
genetic differences among plants in identical plantings—say a row
of junipers or a square plot of lawn—emerge over time in response
to these environmental factors and historical events.

The second reason for the uniqueness of gardens and consequent
elimination of philosophical problems is that both the quality of light
and the particular contributions of the seasons of the year have a
major impact on the appearance at a given viewing and on the way
it will be designed. These are intrinsically ephemeral, and although

there are patterns of recurrence in the daily cycle and the yearly cycle, they do not repeat exactly.

Finally, virtually all of the gardens that we consider works of art—and many that we do not—are designed for a specific site. At best, the design exploits the features of the site aesthetically. As Alexander Pope suggested:

> Consult the Genius of the Place in all;
> That tells the Waters or to rise, or fall,
> Or helps th'ambitious Hill the heav'ns to scale,
> Or scoops in circling theatres the Vale,
> Calls in the Country, catches opening glades,
> Joins willing woods, and varies shades from shades,
> Now breaks, or now directs, th'intending Lines;
> Paints as you plant, and, as you work, designs.[10]

Even where the "lines" of Nature are not followed, however, a garden must suit a particular climate and set of soil conditions—and usually a building as well. Pope is often cited as the first to have articulated the principle of an integral relation between the site and the garden. But this is inaccurate. Pope merely directed attention to a different set of properties of the site, namely the natural topographical features, whereas previous gardenists had ignored the natural topography in favor of architectural and other social features of the site, frequently leveling existent hills, valleys, rivers, and lakes and building new ones in different places. This was especially true of the French and those following their style, including the makers of the English gardens against which Pope was rebelling. (It did not, of course, apply to the Italians or the Dutch, whose formality exploited natural topography.) Yet even in the French case, this was not because garden designers were insensitive to the site but because they were interested in different aspects of the site, primarily its social and architectural features.

The impact of site is so crucial that it is virtually impossible to get the same effect (including specifically aesthetic effects) in two different gardens, even with identical plantings, and even if we assume what is so rarely the case, that identical plantings are viable in two different sites and will grow identically. For the differences between different gardens are exacerbated by a number of factors which affect design but are themselves dependent upon the site: differences in microclimate, in soil composition, in drainage make it difficult to reproduce a given garden somewhere else, even somewhere quite close by the original site; while differences in surrounding buildings or vistas contribute distinctive backgrounds that are integral to our overall impression of the garden. The wall that protects delicate plants on one side leaves the plants on its other side shaded or exposed to cutting winds.

I mentioned earlier that our use of the term "unique" as applied to art implies consistency over time. This consistency serves as a limitation on the degree of uniqueness which we expect of a work of art. Serving as a check on our preference for uniqueness is a second preference for a single basic or privileged form for each work of art (sometimes couched in terms of a "definitive" version). The degree of consistency varies with different arts. In autographic arts, this form is completely realized; in allographic arts, several aspects may remain unspecified by the composer, poet, or choreographer, which remain to be worked out by other artists, usually in the capacity of performers. There may be many interpretations, but changes made to the work by the performer are restricted within certain areas; a core of the work is unchanged. As Goodman points out, this unchanging core, which is crucial to the identity and identification of the work, can be specified in notation.

But there is no such unchanging, *inert* core to the garden. Consistency is extremely difficult to achieve in a garden. There is no point at which a final version is achieved which requires no more of the artist and relatively little by way of maintenance. Because gardens count among their elements living things, change is inevitable; it must be accommodated.

At this point we may conclude that the garden is *too unique* to be a work of art. The season-by-season, day-to-day, and moment-to-moment changes preclude the stability of form that seems to be desirable in a work of art.

Yet we do talk about individual gardens as if they persisted in time. We find enough consistency to attribute to them an identity, however necessary it may be to qualify our statements: "This is a drawing of Stowe as it was in 1731"; "Of course, you're not seeing it at its best; yesterday's storm ruined the blossoms"; "You should see it in June. . ."

What is the underlying unifying principle which allows us to forge a persistent identity for a set of appearances that is constantly changing, to regard a garden which never looks exactly the same as none the less the same garden? The distinctive feature is surely spatial location. The garden at Stowe today is the same garden as the garden at Stowe in 1728 precisely because it is *at Stowe*. As far as determining the identity of a garden goes, spatial location is more reliable than either form or design.

Spatial location, however, is an odd criterion for a work of art. In all other arts, location is an incidental feature. Indeed, the fact that a work of art can be moved from place to place contributes to the value of the work (indeed it is a precondition of the artistic, as opposed, say, to the religious value of the works found in museums) and most especially to the commercial value. Even in architecture, a relatively site-specific art, we identify a building as the same regardless of whether it has been moved or not.

We do not, however, move whole gardens. This is not merely because they are too difficult to move but because, as discussed above, site and location are integral to design and to the successful realization of design. In fact, site and location emerge as the only reliable constant of gardens.

E. Problem 2: The Preference for Artistic Control

All of this uniqueness poses two problems for the garden as far as the theory of art is concerned. For ordinarily we think of the uniqueness of the work of art as the responsibility of the artist. In the case of the garden, however, the gardenist is only partially responsible for the final effects. Modern art has, as we know, challenged this notion that the artist must be fully responsible for every aspect of the final work. But even the weakened version, that the artist must *initiate* the formal features of the work, which accommodates Jackson Pollock, does not describe what happens in the garden. Nor does the further weakened version, accommodating someone like Marcel Duchamp, that is, the artist defines the work as art by selecting or accepting certain pre-existing features of an object. For much of what we see in a garden—the de facto aesthetic effects—is being actively *resisted* by the gardenist, who spends exorbitant amounts of time weeding, pruning, mowing, raking, and otherwise counteracting the changes taking place in his design against his will. In short, no matter how weakly we interpret the control of the artist in the garden, we must acknowledge a radical difference between gardens and other arts as far as the degree of control and the role of responsiveness or receptivity on the part of the artist.

Particularly when we distinguish art or fine art from craft, we tend to recognize the identity of the artist as an integral part of the

identity of the work. *Guernica* determines Picasso for us as much as
Picasso determined *Guernica*; we are as interested—in fact most of
us are *more* interested—in what Holbein's portrait of Henry VIII shows
us of the painter as in what it shows of its subject. But the artistic
character of the artist emerges only through the final form of the
finished works. And a survey of the great gardenists—Le Notre,
London and Wise, Capability Brown, Kent, Bridgeman, Pope, Kobori
Enshu—reveals an immediate difficulty. There is relatively little
reliable evidence of the work of these men surviving which could serve
as the basis for our evaluation. Since there is no final form preserved
intact, we have no sure idea of what the gardenist actually did.[11]

F. Problem 2, continued: Collaboration versus Authority

The inevitable process of natural growth and change leaves the
gardenist in a peculiarly vulnerable position, a position less analogous
to that of other visual artists than to performers in music, dance,
theater. In such "allographic" arts (to return to Goodman's term), the
strict identity of various versions (usually performances) is
ascertainable only provided (1) there exists a tradition of notation that
captures the essential aspects of the work, and (2) comparison of actual
performances with the notation is carried out. Given notation and
comparison of the performed work with its annotated paradigm,
identity in essential respects can be assured, although there is nearly
always a broad tolerance of and even enthusiasm for the variations
encompassed by the notion "personal expression." Without such
notation, however, as Walter Ong has shown in the case of oral
narration, performances vary even on "essentials," and this is the case
even when exact adherence to a single version is valued and is
considered by performers and audience to be maintained.[12] Only
comparison with notation guarantees the literal identity of such works
of art.[13] In the case of gardens, there is no such tradition of notation
and in most cases, given the haphazardness of the records made of
garden plans and appearance, no possibility of re-creating the
"original" effects (assuming them to have been carried out) so as to
determine the appearance and the effects of the garden. George
Clarke, the historian of Stowe, has noted: ". . . Although there are
750,000 items in the Stowe Collection at the Huntington Library and
many of the day-to-day developments are known in minute detail it
remains impossible to say who designed it."[14] This is not simply a
result of the obliterating effects of history. Similarly, at Dumbarton

Oaks, already, after less than half a century, some of the plantings are no longer authentic and no one knows what the original plans and plantings were,[15] in spite of a designer who generally made elaborate and detailed notes and plans, in spite of the creation of a foundation specifically to care for the garden and of a garden-study institute complete with garden library, full-time garden historian, and two full-time garden librarians.

With neither preservation of works in a determinable final form, nor adequate and reliable notations, there is little satisfactory evidence of what individual gardenists achieved. A whole range of critical questions about the relation of the work to its creator(s) which we ask about other kinds of arts becomes unfeasible with regard to gardens.

But is this lack of artistic/authorial control, which after all has been brought into focus as such by our comparison of the garden with arts very unlike itself, rather than by what gardenists themselves have said—can this lack of control be adequate to the phenomenon that is the garden if it is understood only in a negative sense? Is there not some more positive view of the relation of the gardenist to nature? After all, gardens differ widely in the degree of control over nature which is thought desirable. Some, it is true, seek the maximum degree of control, to force nature to appear as static as if the garden were made of nonliving materials. Others minimize either the actual interference of the gardenist in the natural processes and/or the appearance of such intervention, taking advantage of the very impossibility of control for aesthetic effect. Such gardens exploit the fact that the gardenist is only partially responsible for the final effects, that the "finished" product is the result of a collaboration between humankind and nature.

Because the other active participant in the creation of a garden is nature itself, gardens allow for the conflation of what in other arts is usually two distinct issues, collaboration and receptivity to materials.

Western philosophers and critics don't usually think of collaboration as important. Although collaboration is very common in East Asian art, particularly in literati art, where friends may combine their efforts on a single work, some painting, others composing poems or doing the calligraphy,[16] in the West the emphasis on the importance of individual genius has eclipsed the collaborative model. Even where it in fact exists—between architects and painters or designers or gardenists; among performers, composers and conductors; and in film—Westerners view the relation as essentially hierarchical, with one person in artistic command of the total project and the others following directions, able to exercise artistic freedom only within sharply defined areas and always subordinate in what they may do to the master plan. The hierarchies of prestige (as reflected in the allocation of power, money, and recognition and the attribution of genius) reflect the hierarchy of artistic control—and are clearly and explicitly articulated. Architects are superior to interior designers, designers of interiors to the designers of components of those interiors. Composers are superior to performers, and soloists to members of ensembles. We apply to gardens the same hierarchical distinction between artist, who defines a vision, and craftsman, who carries out the vision of another: gardenists (designers and theorists, although they sometimes do some of the labor) are superior to gardeners, who dig the holes.[17]

We tend, when theorizing about art, to ignore more egalitarian collaborations such as string quartets, where decisions are often made collectively. In such a collaboration, no one individual bears the responsibility for the final work. Suggestions regarding interpretation come from different individuals and are freely modified or countered by the others, and the final interpretation may be largely a matter of consensus.[18]

A true collaboration requires that each of the contributors be given the right to speak up and responsibility for the total work as well as for his or her specific contribution. Paradoxically, this also requires a willingness to relinquish final authority and control, and it must coexist with a heightened sensitivity to the contributions and authority of the others. Pat Hickman says of her collaboration with Lillian Elliott on baskets, bas-reliefs, and glasswork, "It is understood who does what on our pieces; we bring to the collaboration our separate skills and strengths and materials. Based on our working together, I've discovered a few ingredients that are crucial to the success of collaboration. The work must be equally shared—from the planning, through producing, and finally to enjoying the full credit for what each has done."[19] But in order for this to succeed, it also requires intimacy, trust in the others' judgment, and capacity to carry out the work. Lillian Elliott points out that ". . .collaboration is not for everyone, and even for those who are successful with it, it is not possible to collaborate with everyone. We feel fortunate to have been able to work together for five years."[20] Collaborators often describe this as a situation of dialogue. David Johnson, a fiber artist who has collaborated with Geary Jones on a series of tapestries, says "Dialogue takes place constantly between us. You might say our woven images are a series of actions and reactions in generation."[21]

The gardenist, in many cases, may be described as in "dialogue with nature," but if so it is a special kind of "dialogue," entailing neither *intention* nor *judgment* on the part of the gardenist's partner. Nor should we forget that not all gardenists see themselves as in a relationship of "dialogue"; in some cases, there may be an overt antagonism. The relationship may nonetheless be described as a real collaboration in that neither partner is solely responsible for the effects and both partners bring about change in virtue of (not necessarily intentional) activity.

G. Problem 3: The Preference for Immateriality: Fine Art versus Craft

Another often unstated preference is for an "ideal," or nonphysical quality, to art. This is not the familiar issue of whether the work of art is to be identified with a physical object, but rather to what degree the materiality of art should be acknowledged. We prefer to ignore, for example, the physical context of architecture. Until relatively recently we preferred oil painting that disguised the physical qualities of the paint itself; painting that revealed itself as paint, as a surface of a particular kind, was inferior. In regard to materiality gardens come perilously close to what we prefer to call "craft," since like craft, they place a heavy emphasis on materials.[22]

What is the importance of the materials to a work of art? Are they to be ignored except as means to the achievement of a particular artistic effect, or are they important in themselves? Insofar as the materials of gardens literally have a life of their own and can rarely be counted on to stay completely within the lines drawn for them, gardens are a very awkward art indeed, constantly challenging the illusion of the artist's control.

1. The Garden as Craft

The relative importance of the materials of a garden suggests that the reason gardens are not considered art might be that the category of craft is more appropriate. There is often a tension in gardens between the craftsman's and the artist's approaches. Of course, the distinction between crafts and art has already broken down, especially for the art world, to a significant extent. Even in the West, artists have often worked in both camps, from Cellini to Anni Albers, and

modern artists like Charles Sheeler, in taking craft for the subject
of art, have revealed its purely aesthetic properties.[23] In discussing
the arts of other cultures, it has never been a useful division; "fine
art" is a peculiarly Western conception with few parallels elsewhere.
Closer contact with other societies has shown that in cultures like
those of the Japanese and the Maori, where the boundary between
art and craft is not rigidly insisted upon, aesthetic standards in the
crafts are very high indeed. Since becoming familiar with these, much
of the Western art world no longer thinks of craft as less distinguished
formally or less excellent than art.

It is not necessarily helpful to think of crafts and arts as distinct
or mutually exclusive categories; the "line" between them is not so
much a line as a broad territory of mutual sharing. Yet two
characteristics distinguish crafts from art and other human activities:
an emphasis on skill and specialized knowledge, and a special
sensitivity to materials. Because of this, crafts may be said to carry
a potential for a different emphasis than fine arts, and the distinction
between art and craft may be worth preserving in order to preserve
this difference in emphasis. While all arts demand some skill and
specialized knowledge and an awareness of the special capabilities
of various materials, and all crafts carry the potential for a high degree
of aesthetic satisfaction, they weigh these values rather differently.[24]

2. The Importance of Materials

What exactly is meant by the craftsman's sensitivity, or
receptivity, to materials? On the one hand, it is an exploitation of all
the qualities of the materials, an awareness of how they may be used
in order to obtain the fullest range of effects, both practical and
aesthetic. Anni Albers's weavings, for example, explored the
possibilities of metallic and synthetic threads, of cellophane and other
plastics, not only for their aesthetic properties—their sheen and
color—but also for their abilities to reflect light and repel water and
dust.[25] On the other hand, craftsmen often understand their materials
in terms of their implications for an understanding of the world at
large, of the nature of physical reality and human capacities. Their
sensitivity to their materials allows them to draw upon the materials
for larger lessons, as Albers explains:

> To restore to the designer the experience of direct experience of a
> medium is, I think, the first task today. Here is, as I see it, a
> justification for crafts today. For it means taking, for instance, the

working material into the hand, learning by working it of its obedience and its resistance, its potency and its weakness, its charm and dullness. The material itself is full of suggestions for its use if we approach it unaggressively, receptively. It is a source of unending stimulation and advises us in [a] most unexpected manner.[26]

Both Albers and the potter and educator Seonaid Mairi Robertson see training in the crafts as a profound education in the nature of the physical universe and in what it means to be human:

> Writing in 1938 [Albers] expanded her concept of material as a culturally guiding force: "Life today is very bewildering. . . .We have developed our receptivity and have neglected our own formative impulse. It is no accident that nervous breakdowns occur more often in our civilization than in those where creative power had a natural outlet in daily activities. And this fact leads to a suggestion: we must come down to earth from the clouds where we live in vagueness, and experience the most real thing there is: material." To Albers, material provides not only stability but also a kind of transcendental quality. Working with material "is a listening for the dictation of the material and a taking in of the laws of harmony. It is for this reason that we can find certitude in the belief that we are taking part in an eternal order."[27]

A fascination with garden materials, with the variety of shapes and colors—and flavors and fragrances—of plants is common among gardenists (plates 4, 11, 12). It emerged early in Europe, became firmly entrenched in the Renaissance and historically received fresh stimulus whenever technological innovation or the discovery of new materials makes possible the cultivation of new species or varieties. But this fascination is not to be equated automatically with either a sensitivity to the plant in its own being or to the intimate relation between the plants' formal qualities and the overall plan of the garden. The cultivation of non-native species requires specialized and detailed knowledge to be successful; it is often the case that the demands of exotic gardening are such that only minimal attention is paid to the overall design and to the aesthetic effects of the whole. (Wisley is the most remarkable exception I've encountered to the generally dismal design scene in exotic gardening.) In twentieth-century gardens like those of Beatrix Farrand, Russell Page, and Roberto Burle Marx, the tension between overall conception and attention to particular plants is overcome by relying heavily on species native to the locale, which will grow predictably.[28]

3. The Importance of Skill

In craft, the technical skill is not fully subordinated to the final aesthetic image but reveals itself in this image as part of what provides aesthetic satisfaction. This is true of some arts, too—especially in playing an instrument or singing, some genres of painting—but it is more usual and more salient in craft. In fact, traditions in which the normal level of technical competence approaches perfection—Middle Eastern rug weaving, Nepali embroidery, Japanese ceramics—often deliberately incorporate symbolic "mistakes." Although these mistakes may be justified on religious grounds—the Muslim weaver is not to be suspected of attempting to approach the perfection of God—the effect of these disparities in pattern is to draw attention to the working of the materials.[29] Where art tries to conceal the hand of the artist and the effort required, craft revels in their revelation.[30]

If we take this lack of interest in the evidence of skill as our guide, then gardens are an art, not a craft. At least by the time of the "great" garden traditions, it had become customary to conceal evidence of toil and skill. So while medieval illustrations of gardens often show the gardeners working, this becomes less and less common from the Renaissance on. In the great garden traditions, it is the result that counts, not the process of getting there.

Yet gardens are not a unitary phenomenon with respect to the differing emphases of art and craft. The different genres and styles place their demands very differently. The enclosed medieval garden seems to have emphasized both pleasure or delight and usefulness; the early postmedieval gardens books delineate a new fascination with skills and knowledge. In the sixteenth century, in both England and Italy, books of garden design, as opposed to guides to the laying out of beds and the care of plants, began to appear. These books reveal a new recognition of the artistic possibilities of the garden that is revolutionary in its implications. Placement of plants was no longer motivated primarily by the biological needs of the plants but was subject to a larger conceptualization of the garden as a whole. (In fact, in Italy the garden soon began to be situated with regard to the outer world and to the outer landscape.) The designs in many of the books begin with simple elaborations of the mandala-like medieval cloister garden pattern and proceed to very fancy, complicated knots. These knot garden designs are at the border between art and craft. They persist in the craft tradition in that they present design largely as a matter of—even a function of—the skill of the gardener in laying out the beds. At the same time, they place a premium on the ingenuity and creativity of their creator, on the ability to envision totally new possibilities. They identify the designer with Daedalus, the supreme craftsman. On the other hand, they show so little of the typical craftsman's respect for materials that they can actually suggest the substitution of colored chalks and gravels for plants!

The disregard for the plant materials evidenced by the substitution of chalks may be seen in other contexts as well—in the geometric shapes forced upon plants in formal gardens and topiary, where the natural shapes of the vegetation are destroyed to suit the designer's preconception, rather than exploited in a dynamic interaction between plan and plant. The issue is not precisely one of skill but rather of repeated, painstaking attention and unwavering devotion, more closely allied to the dusting and vacuuming of an obsessive housekeeper than to the respect a craftsman has for the capabilities of his materials.

H. Problem 4: Fine Art versus Applied Art

1. Statement of the Problem

Another possible reason gardens are not usually classed with the other arts might be that those arts are generally the so-called "fine arts," whereas gardens are more appropriately classed with the "applied arts." The distinction between fine and applied arts has been made on various grounds. First, the applied arts may be viewed as those in which the primary aim is the production of an object which will serve some utilitarian purpose. In this case the aesthetic properties are understood to be separately conceived, and either the aesthetic dimension is found to be "applied" or "decorative," that is, unrelated to the original form, or, on the contrary, it is felt to be too closely bound by the utilitarian demands of the piece. Although it may be appropriate to some objects, this view does not do justice to much of applied art, especially to the so-called "primitive" pieces. From this viewpoint, fine art is supposed to make no concessions to purposes or demands other than itself, while applied art is defined or constrained by a set of demands put upon it in virtue of the practical or social functions it is intended to serve. But in fact this isn't particularly helpful since all arts, even music, the least "concrete" and therefore the least utilitarian of the arts, makes such concessions. To give just two examples, organs in continental Europe during the

Baroque era were often pitched high to save money since omitting even one low pipe would produce considerable savings; this, of course, would alter the sound. Again, one of Beethoven's concerti which was written for three specific performers included a deliberately simple piano part because the pianist the composer had in mind was not terribly good.[31] Fine art is not that which has no such concessions, but that whose concessions we tacitly agree to overlook.

On the other hand, fine art may be understood as that which is not made to fit any pre-existing conception (as distinguished from purpose). Collingwood, for example, has argued that while an artist may have definite ideas about certain features of a work in progress, he does not know in advance exactly what the work will be like. Its final form cannot be predicted and it is this feature which distinguishes a work of art from both craft and applied art, in which the finished product may be fully designed ahead of time. Similarly, following Roman Jakobson, we may understand fine art as that in which creativity, as opposed to appeal to precedent, is brought to bear in the solution of formal problems. In this view, creativity, originality, and individual genius would be highly prized in fine art, whereas applied art values instead the ability of the artist to subsume personality and creativity to inherited tradition. It is worth noting that any of these views would find fine art singularly appropriate to the exploration and elaboration of human individuality, constituting a sensuous hermeneutic, so to speak, for the development of human consciousness. Herbert Read's description applies perfectly to gardens:

> ...the arts have been the means by which man was able step by step to comprehend the nature of things. Art has never been an attempt to grasp reality as a whole—that is beyond our human capacity; it was never even an attempt to represent the totality of appearances; but rather it has been the piecemeal recognition and patient fixation of what is significant in human experience. The artistic activity might therefore be described as a crystallization, from the amorphous realm of feeling, of forms that are significant or symbolic. On the basis of this activity a "symbolic discourse" becomes possible, and religion, philosophy, and science follow as consequent modes of thought."[32]

We will return to this point below.

2. Criticism of the Distinction between Fine and Applied Art

In one sense the distinction between fine and applied art is useful: it acknowledges the radical individuality of the typical work of fine art. This individuality consists not in its objective uniqueness or the originality of its conception or execution (though we may delight in those features) but in the fact that, appreciated aesthetically, an object is considered not as representative or typical or suitable to a purpose but solely in virtue of the qualities it has, regardless of whether those qualities are shared with any other object or not. In contrast, the usefulness of an object is a function of its meeting independently existing standards, and the characteristics by means of which it meets those standards may be shared with any number of other objects, with which, from the standpoint of usefulness, it is interchangeable. This *is* one way of apprehending objects, but it is not the only way, and in fact is opposed to a number of types of relation, not only to aesthetic appreciation, but also to love.

Fine-art theory (that is, any theory of art which posits a basic distinction between the fine and the applied arts) is inevitably unsuitable to many categories of art and to art in general. The distinction between fine and applied arts is not adequate to the phenomena it attempts to describe and in fact introduces more problems than it solves. It ought not to be preserved, for the following reasons. First, it is culture-bound and inappropriate to the description of art of times and places other than the culture in which the theory was originated. It is self-contradictory in that it must exclude objects made for use but whose formal excellence is such that they demand our attention precisely on aesthetic grounds. It disintegrates in the face of modern (formalist) aesthetics. It is overly simplistic. It is misleading in that it attributes the aesthetic character to the object rather than to the subject or a relation between subject and object. It occludes the commonalities among all arts and thus distracts us from important questions. It reduces questions of value, of successful versus unsuccessful or good versus bad art to questions of kind, giving them a pseudo-ontological status. It serves no useful purpose, and thus is inelegant, or uneconomical. Some elaboration of these points may be useful.

Fine-art theory argues for the preeminence of aesthetic values over all other values in regard to the work of art. By this criterion, it must exclude many objects whose form was largely determined by other criteria—belt buckles and locks, drinking vessels and tables, ritual and religious objects. Yet many of these objects, like King Narmer's palette, are now being admired precisely for their formal (aesthetic) qualities.[33] Fine-art theory cannot accommodate such objects, and this inability shows that the theory is self-contradictory since objects like these are being introduced into the canon of art precisely in virtue of their aesthetic qualities. Moreover, the theory is misleading in that it improperly identifies aesthetic qualities as properties of the object rather than as inhering in the viewer's approach to the work, or as constituted by a relation between viewer and object. This makes the theory of fine art useful for establishing the universality of aesthetic perception (as Kant did) and secondarily for the establishing a basis for community. In fact, however, there is no universality of aesthetic perception, and the assertion that there is has the pernicious effects of generating confusion and doubt and diverting attention from a valid line of inquiry into the relation between education (in general, and in relation to art and to specific arts, genres, and styles) and aesthetic perception and sensitivity. On the other hand, this assertion or belief that aesthetics rests on a universal perception can be a very useful ideological tool for instituting and justifying social views. The theory emerged at a time when modern societies were groping for new grounding, new kinds of legitimation with new foundations, and when it was not at all to be taken for granted who was to belong to, and who excluded from, such societies, or on what basis. Most eighteenth-century thinkers who wrote on the subject of aesthetics saw this area as closely related to ethics, politics, and the establishment of community. Removed from the context of this necessity, the theory is revealed as untrue, or more precisely, the distinction between fine and applied arts which lies at the heart of the theory is seen to be misleading and, being derived to meet the needs of the period in which it was generated, as inadequate to examples of art outside that isolated context.

The distinction between fine and applied art serves no useful purpose. It is based upon a prior distinction between the useful or utilitarian, that in which we have an interest, (or that which is determined by the uses to which it will be put), and the aesthetic, in which we have by definition no interest. Again one must be careful to ascribe the features not to the object per se but to the approach taken to it, or the relation established with it. For in fact, interest and disinterest do not inhere in the objects; any object can be made the object of an interest, and anything can be approached without interest, appreciated solely in virtue of its inherent qualities. The distinction between applied and fine art disintegrates in the face of modern (formalist) aesthetics.

One problem is that the view of utility, use, or interest which underlies the fine-applied distinction tends to be simplistic. First, the relation between an object and an experiencing subject are in flux. It is inaccurate to characterize either objects or subjects as permanently fixed within the aesthetic or the utilitarian domain; all such relations fluctuate in time. Our approaches to things, like our approaches to other human beings, commonly vary from the strictly utilitarian to the fully appreciative, the responsive, the loving. Just as someone in even the most loving and receptive I-thou relation will at times regard the Other as just someone-to-hold-the-umbrella-while-I-get-the-key-in-the-lock or someone-to-bring-me-whiskey-tea-in-bed, so, conversely, the most prosaic pea or blueberry may become the object of aesthetic admiration by a person who is washing it. (Ontogenetically, if not phylogenetically, the aesthetic experience may often precede acquaintance with art.)

The distinction is based on an overly simplistic view of utility or interest. All art serves functions, even those most securely within the paradigm of fine art—oil painting, architecture, music. Oil painting may be a means of making evident a political program or its implications, or of taking a stand on political issues. Architecture must not only provide shelter but also organize the possibilities of social encounter and human action. (Here is a case where a major or fine art is considered minor only in those instances where it does *not* fulfill practical purposes—that is, in monuments and triumphal arches.) Handel's music celebrates and justifies the Hanoverian dynasty. The relevant alternatives are not practical versus purely aesthetic values but the subordination of form to use versus finding a form which can satisfy the full range of demands (the practical and the aesthetic) without sacrificing either. Of course this latter is not easy—there is a great deal of bad art—but it is not impossible either. It is a triumph which is even commonplace.

Rather than occupying one of the two positions of a binary opposition, art describes a continuum between the poles of two kinds of purposes: the obvious, well-known and well-defined, often physical purposes on the one hand (knives and forks), and on the other hand, those purposes at the other extreme which are so abstract, so vague, so difficult to get ahold of that they can only be recognized ex post facto. Among these latter would be the awakening of new kinds of moral conscience, the discernment of new bases for relation with others or for the identification of the self, the organization of two- or three-dimensional space in new patterns of coherence, the inculcation of new ways of perceiving light or recognizing human dignity or experiencing historical time. In between the two is a wide variety of semi-articulate purposes: celebrating spring and survival through the winter, legitimating or challenging political authority, winning the beloved, lightening the spirits, asserting dominance or attractiveness, relieving boredom, understanding an emotional experience, and so on. (As Read points out, art drives consciousness, at least as much as consciousness drives art.)

Art is one of our most valuable tools for developing self-consciousness and for extending the boundaries of consciousness. One cannot understand the history of consciousness—by which I do not mean to imply anything like a single, unitary strand of progress in the "evolution" of consciousness—without reference to the history of art. In fact, fine-art theory is well suited to the examination of arts which depend upon and foster a high degree of self-consciousness since it is precisely from an examination of arts which do this that the theory has been derived. Since all fine-art theory starts with the art of the Renaissance (all fine-art theory based on a distinction from applied arts originated in western Europe after the Renaissance), since which time, it is generally acknowledged, self-consciousness was developing its new, modern forms, fine-art theory is well designed to deal with arts which are highly self-conscious. What goes unnoticed is that this is no less true of applied art than of fine art. A number of studies have shown that the processes of individuation, of the articulation of individual identity, especially in relation to the group, and of increasing self-consciousness, are not monopolized by the fine arts but may be served by the applied or decorative arts as well.

I. The Garden as Applied or Fine Art

Gardens may occupy either position or more commonly an ambiguous position between the two. It is true that there are some gardens whose form is determined almost solely by practical considerations. This is especially likely to be true of vegetable gardens and commercial gardens. In other gardens, such as the suburban American front lawn with shrubbery at the base of the house, the form is determined in defiance of convenience and productivity, by an allegiance to traditional forms. This allegiance may be entirely unself-conscious and taken for granted, or it may be an act of self-definition and protest, as when it is insisted upon in the Las Vegas desert. One can only tell by looking at the situation of the individual case, including the local geography and climate.

Yet some gardens are unquestionably fine art—created by persons recognized as artists (William Kent, Sen no Rikyu),[34] highly creative and self-conscious and deliberate in design and execution, slave to no purpose, masterfully exploiting the artistic materials to full aesthetic effect.

If even these gardens—Stowe, Ryoan-ji, Stourhead—are ignored in discussions of fine arts, there is something wrong with the way we are understanding—or at least defining—art.

CHAPTER 5

𝄢

The Preference for Distance and Disinterest

Since Kant, the focus of the distinction between art and everything else has been the notion of aesthetic disinterest. Yet the notion is not generally valid and should not be used as grounds for the dismissal of gardens from the category of art. This is not the place for a full-scale analysis or critique of disinterest, and I will limit my remarks to those aspects which directly pertain to the problem of gardens as art.

A. Varieties of Disinterest

Disinterest has been characterized by different philosophers in widely varying ways; each of these versions presents a different way of approaching what is largely agreed upon in Western philosophy to be a fundamental difference between the work of art and all the rest of reality. In spite of the variation in the characterizations, however, there is at base a common insight, namely into a fundamental schism between art (and nature approached aesthetically) and the rest of life, a self-containment on the part of art.

Although the distinctive "otherness" of art from the rest of reality was noticed by Plato, it was Kant who gave it its decisive modern form.[1] For Kant, the basis of the distinction is whether we have an interest in the *existence* of the object as opposed to observation or intuition or reflection of it; our interest in its existence depends upon whether we need to use it to achieve some pragmatic purpose. Kant's "disinterest" defines the work of art in virtue of its relation (or more precisely its lack of certain kinds of relation) to the external world. Kant's version avoids the mistake of viewing the aesthetic as a division inherent in the world; he makes it clear that although objects of certain kinds facilitate our apprehension of their separate status, it is the shift in attitude adopted toward the object that is crucial. The same attitude may be adopted toward other objects as well; and of course it is perfectly possible to obliterate the distinction and approach a work of art in a purely instrumental way.

In an article entitled " 'Psychical Distance' as a Factor in Art and an Aesthetic Principle," Edward Bullough approached the same problem from a different perspective, viewing the autonomy of the work of art as a function of a psychical distance set up between it and the viewer. Bullough refined Kant's formulation to accommodate some objections that had arisen to earlier versions, especially the tendency to focus attention on physical existence and physical properties. For Bullough, the physical properties of the work of art are not important in themselves, but only as means to an end, namely the "psychical distance" between the viewer and the work. Bullough's "psychical distance" specifies the relation of the work of art to us and the formal means of achieving that relation.

Psychical distance, which he distinguishes from actual spatial distance between the work and the spectator, from represented spatial distance, and from temporal distance, is that which "appears to lie between our own self and its affections" as we experience a work of art, "obtained by separating the object and its appeal from one's own self, by putting it out of gear with practical needs and ends."[2] Although this distance can be achieved outside of the experience of art, it is inherently at odds with our "normal" outlook:

> As a rule, experiences constantly turn the same side towards us, namely, that which has the strongest practical force of appeal. We are not ordinarily aware of those aspects of things which do not touch us immediately and practically, nor are we generally conscious of impressions apart from our own self which is impressed. The sudden view of things from their reverse, usually unnoticed side, comes upon us as a revelation and such revelations are precisely those of Art. In this most general sense, Distance is a factor in all Art.[3]

Relinquishing the reference to one's own needs and ends does not, however, mean that the experience is impersonal:

> Distance does not imply an impersonal, purely intellectually interested relation of. . .[the] kind [to be found in science]. On the contrary, it describes a personal relation, often highly emotionally colored, but of a peculiar character. Its peculiarity lies in that the personal character of the relation has been, so to speak, filtered. It

> has been cleared of the practical, concrete nature of its appeal, without, however, thereby losing its original constitution. One of the best-known examples is to be found in our attitude toward the events and characters of the drama: they appeal to us like persons and incidents of normal experience, except that that side of their appeal, which would usually affect us in a directly personal manner, is held in abeyance. This difference, so well known as to be almost trivial, is generally explained by reference to the knowledge that the characters and situations are "unreal," imaginary. . . . But, as a matter of fact, the "assumption" upon which the imaginative emotional reaction is based is not necessarily the condition, but often the consequence of Distance; that is to say, the converse of the reason usually stated would then be true: namely, that Distance, by changing our relation to the characters, renders them seemingly fictitious, not that the fictitiousness of the characters alters our feelings toward them.[4]

Another way of viewing Bullough's "psychical distance" is as a condition for the presentation of art—distance is that which guarantees that the performance will be allowed to proceed uninterrupted by the kind of interventions that would be required were the actions to be taken as part of real life. Autonomy in this sense is necessary to nearly all art, though not only to art, and operates on even the most primitive level. (Performances are always carried out until they come to an end.)

Stefan Morawski's version analyzes disinterest/distance, which he presents as "relative autonomy of structure," as one of four attributes for the work of art. The first three of these can be taken to apply to the garden clearly and unproblematically: 1) a structure of sensuously given qualities; 2) the artifact of skill or virtuosity; 3) individual expression. The fourth, "relative autonomy of structure," is more troublesome for gardens, though ultimately more revealing. As Morawski describes it, autonomy is defined by internal relations. This "relative autonomy" distinguishes the work of art from other kinds of closed structures of sensuously given qualities and therefore is necessary if we are to be able to distinguish art from structures such as "the surgeon's table with doctors and nurses standing round about it, a crowd of people suddenly running down the street together, a report or account of something that has just occurred." This relative autonomy is what permits the work of art to be a microcosm—although Morawski is at pains to point out that functioning as a microcosm by no means entails the independence of the work of art from the macrocosm. The work of art remains a part of the rest of the world and is subject to the forces pertaining in that world—in Morawski's words, the microcosm "is not just genetically dependent upon the macrocosm. . .but it can reflect, or, in more cautious phrase, express it as well."[5] The work of art as a microcosm is defined by its internal coherence; its relative autonomy refers to

> systems of qualities [which] whether immediately sensuous [as, presumably, in gardens] or indirect and semantic [as in literature] subsist in themselves. . . .[T]he moment of relative autonomy coheres with qualities that are so structured as immediately to seize our attention. Calling attention to structure plainly means. . .focusing upon its internal field, upon the autotelic qualities which function independently of the external world.

B. Critique of Distance

There are good reasons for preserving this separation between art and the rest of life.[6] At the same time, the separation must be approached cautiously. There are serious problems with the theory of disinterest. The aesthetic attitude ought not to be taken as the primary or only proper response to art. Distance in Kant's sense is a historical innovation, introduced at a particular time and not inherent to all art or all aesthetic experience.[7] Aesthetics and the concept of art are by no means utilized in all cases where we find works of art, but are highly culture-specific, emerging only about 250 years ago and restricted geographically to Europe and those cultures immediately influenced by Europe.[8] Yet art and a wide range of complex responses to art are virtually universal phenomena.

As a distinguishing feature of art, disinterest or aesthetic distance is misleading because art is only one category (though a most important one) of things which may be approached aesthetically.[9] Most importantly, the attitude of distance is not restricted to aesthetic objects. Rather, the aesthetic attitude is one specific type within a much larger range of psychical distance, which remain largely unexplored by the philosophers of art. The training of torturers, for example, also makes use of psychical distance, instigated formally. One would, however, prefer a theory that gave adequate grounds for the differentiation of art from torture.

The view that art should be disinterested has encouraged a disregard of, even a blindness toward, the plethora of uses to which art is regularly put, so that we are liable seriously to misunderstand art, its functions, and its efficacies—and ultimately its role in our lives.

Distance has erroneously been used as the defining feature of art, by which to judge an activity or product "art" or not, and as a result, a number of activities and works—gardens among them—have been miscategorized.

Bullough would say · that anything which is experienced aesthetically is so experienced because of psychic distance. He does not consider psychic distance in any contexts other than the work of art, but we can easily summon up any number of other situations in which distance may occur, sometimes with aesthetic effect. The flight crews of bombers often describe the beauty of the bomb as it falls. The mere perception of beauty in such circumstances may be troubling since we often want to believe that beauty and goodness are correlated. In such cases, the distance is created less by formal features than by the individual's need to create or enhance the distance between himself and what he sees or does. In the case of personal acts, the need to create distance stems from feelings of moral guilt; in cases of catastrophe, such as are described by the victims of bombing raids, distance also occurs, presumably less from guilt than from a need to stave off despair. Such victims also sometimes describe small scenes of acute beauty, their capacity to notice such "details" incomprehensible to them.

So distance alone may precipitate aesthetic awareness without any formal instigation. It can be seen as in some sense the antithesis of identification. At the same time, distance cannot define art as a separate category from the rest of life; distance theory is a misunderstanding of how we in fact understand art. Literature, for example, requires that we identify with certain characters. The activity of identification is just that which we use in everyday life a) in order to act as ourselves when action is not based on instinct or whim, but we must identify with a particular role (lawyer) in order to act; and/or b) in order to act morally when we are not following some rule but trying to understand a situation and a person. The "aesthetic" distance that prevents members of an audience from interfering with the attempted killing of the heroine on stage is based upon a) understanding of the situation as "not real" and b) taking upon ourselves the role of spectators, which in much formal theater requires nonparticipation. But either is sufficient in itself to prevent people from taking action in real life as well as in art. It is not uncommon for us to find, for example, young children threatening each other with the most violent ends; in such cases, we try to discern whether they mean what they are saying or are playing, whether they are serious or pretending. If we find they are playing or pretending, that does not mean it is art. Again, we often accept a role in everyday life that prevents our interfering with certain actions with which we would interfere if we were following our inclinations, as spectators or participants in sports or court proceedings, we accept sharply defined roles that carefully restrict the ways in which we may act. Similarly we may define ourselves as spectators within real-life situations where action is called for, not because we are misapplying the concept "art" but because we find it incongruent with our role. Cases where observers do nothing to stop child abuse are quite common; the reasons for non-interference often have less to do with fear or lack of concern than with the roles they have undertaken for themselves—the "good neighbor," or the guidance counselor who is legally required to report the abuse but to refrain from direct intervention. The relation(s) between art and distance are variable.

C. Distance and Disinterest in the Garden

We saw in chapter 3 that the elements in the garden and their arrangements take on from the very beginning a primary significance based on their significance in the larger world, a significance, or more accurately, range of significance, which is derived from hundreds of thousands of years of evolutionary development. As one might suspect, this common psychobiological heritage is more effective and more salient in gardens than in many other arts and institutions. It is so deep-rooted that it challenges the very concept of the aesthetic; if the aesthetic is that which is pleasing or satisfying but with regard to which we preserve an attitude of disinterest, the garden is not a matter of aesthetics. Its very primordiality provides a substratum of shared values, orderings, and preferences which underlie all subsequent cultural variation and are nearly universal in its appeal.

There are, then, three perspectives from which the garden is at odds with the theory of distance, corresponding with the three different views on the nature of distance. From the point of view of disinterest, it is too enmeshed in our purposes and needs. From the point of view of distance the garden is too close to us. From the point of view of autonomy of structure, it lacks self-sufficiency. I will examine each of these in turn.

1. Disinterest (Kant)

Gardens are not only environments. They are also sites. By "site" I mean a place designed and designated for a specific activity or purpose, as we speak of choosing a campsite or a site for a house or a new business.

We saw in chapter 2 that while aesthetic considerations have informed garden design from earliest times, functionality has also been crucial at all stages. As a site for activities, the garden is not only, or even primarily autotelic, but is a seamless part of our endless daily purposes. Its effects on us are by no means limited to the aesthetic but affect us physically and psychologically as well, as is attested by the medieval custom of joining infirmaries with cloister gardens. The impact of gardens may be particularly significant in urban environments where other opportunities to experience vegetation and water may be rare. R. S. Ulrich has shown that views of vegetation have a beneficial effect upon hospital patients: ". . . surgical patients assigned to rooms with windows looking out on a natural scene had shorter postoperative hospital stays, received fewer negative evaluative comments in nurses' notes, and took fewer potent analgesics than . . . matched patients in similar rooms with windows facing a brick building wall."[10] Ulrich cautions that

> Although the findings suggest that the natural scene had comparatively therapeutic influences, it should be recognized that the "built" view in this study was a comparatively monotonous one, a largely featureless brick wall. The conclusions cannot be extended to all built views, nor to other patient groups, such as long-term patients, who may be suffering from low arousal or boredom rather than from the anxiety problems typically associated with surgeries. Perhaps to a chronically understimulated patient, a built view such as a lively city street might be more stimulating and hence more therapeutic than many natural views. . . . Investigations of aesthetic and affective responses to outdoor visual environments have shown a strong tendency for American and European groups to prefer natural scenes more than urban views that lack natural elements. Views of vegetation, and especially water, appear to sustain interest and attention more effectively than urban views of equivalent information rate. Because most natural views apparently elicit positive feelings, reduce fear in stressed subjects, hold interest, and may block or reduce stressful thoughts, they might also foster restoration from anxiety or stress.

Such an example points up two problems with Kant's notion of disinterest. First, Kant utilizes a very literal, almost physical definition of needs, uses, and purposes (the sort that would be described as "lower order" needs in Abraham Maslow's "hierarchy of needs"), ignoring a whole range of emotional, psychological, political, religious, intellectual purposes and needs which arts of all kinds constantly address.

Second, Kant disregards the positive role of uses and purposes in challenging and stimulating artists; as Jacques Maritain pointed out, completely unrestricted freedom renders art meaningless or superfluous, not free.[11] Artists have long recognized the value of purposes and constraints, which may function in a positive way, just as the constraints of materials do for craftsworkers. In a radio interview in which he was asked to explain how the revolutionary musical style of the group Cream was invented, lead guitarist, singer, and songwriter Eric Clapton explained that they had undertaken a concert tour early in the group's career, before they had many songs to play. They had a number of alternatives: to shorten the length of time they would be on stage (this they judged would have been unpopular), to play songs written by other people (acceptable, since this is what most musicians do, but boring), and so on. Their highly creative response was to play each song longer. This required a new kind of development of the music, entailing expressive improvization, and ultimately led to the popularization of a new musical style. The example is interesting since it shows the vulnerability of an art form not only to situation and the talents and temperament of the artists but also to the audience: Clapton also noted that their choice was influenced by the type of audience they were getting in those days. Similar forces are at work in the development of garden design. Speaking of the designer of the classic Italian style gardens, Edith Wharton writes:

> He had now three problems to deal with: his garden must be adapted to the architectural lines of the house it adjoined; it must be adapted to the requirements of the inmates of the house, in the sense of providing shady walks, sunny bowling-greens, parterres and orchards, all conveniently accessible; and lastly it must be adapted to the landscape around it. At no time and in no country has this triple problem been so successfully dealt with as in the treatment of the Italian country house from the beginning of the sixteenth century to the end of the eighteenth century; and in the blending of different elements, the subtle transition from the fixed and formal lines of art to the shifting and irregular lines of nature, and lastly in the essential convenience and livableness of the garden, lies the fundamental secret of the old garden-magic.[12]

Historically gardens came to be considered important works of art only when most of the practical purposes of the garden—growing of foodstuffs, etc.—had already been eliminated from the "pleasure" garden and relegated to a separate kitchen garden. The garden as

a means to the production of food and medicine was overturned by
the Renaissance. But this is not to say that other less tangible
purposes were not being served by the garden. As a recent article
points out, the eighteenth-century "tea gardens" like London's
Vauxhall, met a complex of social, cultural, and physical needs:

> Several reasons explain why tea gardens developed and why they
> became important centers for recreation and socializing. The English
> upper classes have always leaned toward outdoor activities. But by
> the late seventeenth century the rise of capitalism had begun to bring
> many of the gentry to the cities for much of the time. The outdoor
> facilities for amusement were limited in the English cities: Streets
> were not yet fit for strolling, private gardens were disappearing under
> brick and mortar, and riding in carriages or on horseback was
> impeded by the crowds of working people in the few parks. Moreover,
> the growing ranks of investors and businessmen valued the manners
> and dress that marked their upper middle class status, and wanted
> venues in which to see and be seen.
>
> Tea gardens met the criteria of being country places in an urban
> setting and public places of high fashion. Tea carried with it the high
> status of an expensive commodity. Coffee houses, also then in
> operation, catered to men; but the new tea gardens attracted both
> sexes.
>
> The gardens became places in which ladies and gentlemen could
> enjoy each other's company in nice surroundings out of doors.
> Admission was a few pence and the practice was to stroll with tea
> in hand in public view. On Sundays, all of London society flocked
> to the tea gardens—music, tea and promenades were the central
> attractions. People took their pleasure in the walks and bowers. They
> sat in arbors of honeysuckle and admired the plashing pools. They
> ate bread and butter and drank tea and alcoholic drinks.[13]

Far from being detrimental to the aesthetic status of the work of
art (as Kant saw it), our "interest" in it and the practical constraints
derived from its intended function(s) may well serve as a formal
stimulus to creativity, much like the rigors of musical and poetic
forms. Thus the plan of the garden at Rockefeller Center, for example,
was subject to a number of nonaesthetic considerations. It had to help
to direct pedestrian traffic off Fifth Avenue and in toward the fountain
and those shops whose windows face the inner court and so cannot
attract passers-by, and it had to occupy the center of the walkway
leading to the court so as to channel the pedestrians along the doors
and windows of the shops lining the walkway.[14] The plan that was

drawn up to meet these requirements is highly successful as an urban garden and suffers no more from the requirements than a sonnet suffers for its length. Obviously certain effects cannot even be attempted within such limitations, but the fact that the constraints are not inherent to gardens per se or that they are commercially motivated does not affect the aesthetic effect.

Most art throughout history has been heavily constrained by nonaesthetic purposes. And in fact it is often very difficult to determine whether some apparently purely aesthetic aspect might not have had some more mundane function. Even the most superficially "decorative" objects may serve important functions—purely through their decoration. Thus it has been suggested that the gold- and silver-foil folding screens of the Rimpa school in Momoyama and Edo Japan and the displays of silver and pewter utensils in the open-shelved cupboards of colonial America were used to brighten up dark interiors; given modern research into the relationship between lack of light and psychological depression,[15] this puts such "decorative" objects at the center of a viable environment. Similarly, both anthropologists and semioticians of art have found that the decorative designs on clothing and utensils may be important markers of identity and of personal identification with the group or a totem. It would be indefensible to maintain that no one whose art was religious or brightened an interior experienced art properly.

The garden taken as a work of art cannot be adequately described by a theory which views the work of art as autonomous or aesthetic values as primary. This suggests, however, that the Kantian-based theories are inadequate to the task of understanding art as a whole.

2. Distance (Bullough) and the Garden

What does it mean for a work of art to be also a site? What are the implications of this for the garden as a work of art?

For one thing, we enter it. It is spatially and temporally continuous with the rest of the world in which we live. There is no change of scale. Psychic distance is severely challenged, as physical distance is literally destroyed. We do not merely look at the garden, we are surrounded by it, bringing the same psychological habits of perception to the garden that we bring to any other environment. In addition, the tempo of our experience of the garden is the same as that of ordinary life. To the extent that special tempi may be called for, we ourselves initiate the change, as we do in our normal environment, rather than respond to changes initiated externally, as we do in listening to music or watching a film or drama.

Bullough's version of distance is always triggered formally, by physically identifiable features. It is the formal features, such as the proscenium arch and the frame, which prevent us from taking the work as a seamless part of literal reality. It might seem, prima facie, that the walls of gardens would function identically to mark off the work of art from the "real world," but phenomenological examination shows this not to be true. In the case of both the proscenium arch and frame, the device itself remains during our whole experience of it. Although of course attention is shifted away, it continues to provide the very condition of the viewing experience. Cases of unframed paintings, like East Asian handscrolls, show how crucial the frame is to the fabrication of distance: without them, the viewer enters the painting (imaginatively) rather than maintaining an independent position outside the frame in the real world. To be sure, awareness of the wall persists in some gardens, too, such as the small walled gardens of medieval cloisters, New Orleans courtyards, and walled Zen gardens like Ryoanji. But in other cases no such formal marker exists, and such physical barriers as may be necessary for the protection of the garden are hidden, and thus *formally* nonexistent (see the ha-ha in plate 7). In most large gardens even if there is a wall, one leaves it behind and it cannot therefore function as an immediate frame or condition of all moments of our experience.

Even more problematic for the theory, however, are those cases where the formal boundary marker—the wall or verandah—partakes of both worlds in such a way as deliberately to blur the distinction between the work of art and reality. One thinks first of a Zen garden like Ryoanji, where the wall partitioning off the outside world, and quite successfully excluding it from thought if not literally from view, acquired over the years a patina, a mellowness, the result of weathering, that made it an inseparable part of the garden aesthetically. When it became necessary to replaster it and the stark new surface was revealed, many people were quite disturbed at the new effect and described it as destroying Ryoanji and as giving quite a different aesthetic experience. In a case like this, the garden wall is not a facilitator of distance, a marker of the metaphysical difference between two realms. Its primary function is to indicate where the intentions of the artist/gardenist cease to take effect. The fate of the wall at Ryoanji underscores the futility of human intention as a definitive criterion for gardens.

The arts Bullough discusses, painting and the theater, are susceptible to this analysis, as would be literature. But arts differ considerably in this respect. Some arts, such as architecture and gardens, not only take their places within the continuous fabric of daily life, they destroy all possibility of distance between the "observer" and the work, as the "observer" must enter them, be physically engulfed. Music is an even odder case: we are surrounded, as by a cathedral, yet physically it enters us. It is no easier to turn our attention from the music that we do not wish to hear than to avoid the taste of food in our mouths. (That is, it *can* be done, but this is the exception, not the rule.) Similarly, it is often said that what prevents culinary art from being a fine art is that it is too close, we cannot maintain aesthetic distance; but if this is the reason cooking is not art, it is also true of music and would mean that music is not art either.

3. *Autonomy of Structure (Morawski) and the Garden*

There is of course a rather wide range of styles in garden design, and distance, disinterest, and structural autonomy differ slightly with each of them. It is safe to say, nonetheless, that in virtually all gardens which are meant to be something more than a place to grow vegetables, the relative autonomy of the structure is marked. We have discussed what Morawski means by this notion above; it remains to be seen however how it is to apply in the case of the garden, probably the most problematic of the arts for Morawski's theory. One interpretation can be dismissed outright: the *Pragnanz* or "precise compactness" of the Gestalt theorists, who "hold coherent systems to be those in which no element is superfluous and none can be replaced by another."[16] There do indeed exist gardens which satisfy this description, including some formal gardens (plate 10) and Japanese rock gardens in Zen temples such as Ryoanji, parts of Daitoku-ji, the dry garden, and the forecourt of the teahouse Shonan-tei 2 at Saiho-ji. But they are extremely rare and contain few plants other than mosses, for in most climates if other plants are used, the shape and texture—and the sheer number of elements—change continuously as the plants undergo seasonal budding, flowering, withering, and dropping of leaves. On a strict interpretation of Pragnanz, however, the crimson of autumn maples, the very presence of any leaves at all, would have to be deemed superfluous since they are not necessary to the same garden in winter. Gardening is a constant process of accommodation to the changes imposed upon us as designers by the different elements of our media.

A somewhat looser definition of the autonomous structure than the Gestalt theorists concede is then necessary in the case of the garden.

CHAPTER 6

❦

Environmental Aesthetics and the Effects of Art[1]

A. Environmental Aesthetics

Alternatives to the Kantian-derived theories are being developed by a number of thinkers who are interested in overturning the subject-object dichotomy at the core of the notions of "disinterest" and "distance" and who are exploring, under the rubrics "environmental aesthetics" or "participatory aesthetics," the possibilities of a more interactive model of art. Arnold Berleant, for example, proposes a radical reinterpretation of art in terms of an "occasion for" experience instead of an "object of" experience.[2] Berleant has suggested that even the arts which have traditionally been thought of as best appreciated from the "aesthetic" or distanced point of view, like (Western) portraits and landscape paintings, are better encountered as partners, equals, in a relation than as objects of an experience. The distinction he makes, of critical importance on several levels, is particularly valuable in regard to gardens.

Berleant's theory posits a revision of the two fundamental relations which constitute the work of art. First, the relation between the work and its "meaning," as described by Berleant, is fundamentally different from the relation as described by any theory based upon a notion of an object of aesthetic experience.[3] Interdependent with this is a second reformulation, a re-vision of the relation between art and the human subject who encounters it. I would suggest that Berleant's reformulation of these two relations implies the revision of a third relation, so far not developed by Berleant himself, namely, the relation we have as viewers of art to all of subsequent reality. Implicit within Berleant's thesis is a challenge both to our traditional concept of art and to the assumption that reality is apprehended independent of artistic mediation.

Berleant alludes to the relation of art and meaning as one of "embodiment." More accurately, as he points out, this is not a relation at all, but an original unity, for there is meaning to either of the terms in isolation from the other. As he says, there is no question here of making physical, for that would imply the prior existence of one of the terms—the content or referent or meaning, and it is just this relation between meaning and form that has proven so resistent, so intractable a problem in the philosophy of art.[4] Whether this content be conceived in terms of subject matter, in which case the task of art is representation, or in terms of the feelings which the treatment of the subject provokes or portrays, in which case the task is conceived as expression, makes little difference to Berleant's thesis. The fundamental distinction between the meaning or content and the work itself, the resolution of which is invoked by Wollheim under the rubric "fit" or "appropriateness," is itself the mistake which gives rise to our problems.

But a second and perhaps ultimately more far-reaching difference is that the relation between us and our art is refashioned. This means that both terms of the relation must be reinterpreted. On the one hand, the work of art cannot exist as art without human consciousness, intention, appreciation. What is true of Duchamp's "Fountain" is true of every work of art—it "is nothing without the human contribution."[5] But if, as Berleant claims, what art must provoke are "occurrences of the unity of perceiver and art object in an original act of experience,"[6] then the human subject must also be reinterpreted. For the embodiment of which Berleant speaks is our embodiment—"embodiment in the sense of being united into a body that is the condition of the wholeness of human being, that condition before those divisive acts of thought that alienate consciousness from body, thought from feeling, people from their world."[7]

If wholeness in this sense of an interactive unity with our environment is a human possibility (and environmental psychology as well as some philosophical theory suggests that it is not only a possibility but the general condition of our experience in the world), then it is the "divisive acts of thought," the alienation of consciousness from body, of thought from feeling—and of feeling from behavior—that are learned or striven for. Wholeness is our everyday condition, alienation (in this restricted sense) is the achievement, socially constructed.

This suggests an interesting possibility. The introduction of this special aesthetic distance is not without its practical side. Modern life requires distance from our own emotions, mastery over instincts and inclinations, ability to put feelings aside. This is particularly true of modern medicine and modern warfare, but even lower-level everyday skills such as working at the same task for eight-hour days and commuting through traffic jams require a degree and kind of self-discipline quite different from that in non-industrialized societies. Art itself (not all art but art as it has been taught since the eighteenth century) teaches these skills—intellectual-emotive skills—of distancing. Therefore distance or disinterest is not itself disinterested, but highly motivated.

I think that no one questions that one can, if one has a mind to, cultivate the disinterested approach to art, as aestheticians—but not artists—have been recommending over the past two hundred years, just as doctors cultivate disinterest with respect to pain and blood. Berleant's point is that this is an inappropriate and ultimately unsuccessful way to approach art. If by aesthetic distance we mean a restraint from purely practical utilizations of the object (here the term is fully appropriate), then we are describing a real condition for art; but if we mean anything more, we are simply mistaking the nature of aesthetic experience, which is better conceived as engagement than distance. I would like to propose that if this is the case, as I think it is, then the greater part of the history of aesthetic theory since the eighteenth century has been a collective exercise in the promulgation of alienation. The appreciation of art in this now-classic modern sense (that is, post-eighteenth-century) becomes the practice of divisive acts of thought, and the practice of art the inculcation of devisive thinking.

Disturbing as this view may be to our various traditional ontologies of art, it is perhaps more threatening yet to our notion of ourselves. If the qualities of the work of art cannot be described purely in themselves, independently of the mind which perceives and orders and appreciates them, neither, in this view, does the human subject stand apart from her experiences. This part of Berleant's theory, of course, is not new—it is a familiar tenet of phenomenology, existentialism, and empirical psychology, and a premise of religious art and of Chinese and Japanese art.[8] But oddly enough, it is rarely taken seriously within the field of Western aesthetics. Yet where art exists, it must change the human being who has entered into relation with it. There is no such thing as moving on untouched. To see, in this sense, is to be altered. However imperceptibly, a new self, new possibilities, are created in each encounter. I suppose that this is what the Japanese novelist Yasunari Kawabata meant when he said that "Looking at old works of art is a matter of life and death." It nourishes and sustains us. It makes our life—as we know it—possible.

There are a couple of ways this can happen. Surely any of us can recall some experience with a painting, a play, a building, after which we felt we would never be precisely the same again, we could never experience things exactly the same way. A novel by Thomas Hardy breaks our framework of assumptions about the nature of causality or human efficacy; a Rembrandt portrait makes us search the streets for faces with similar inner qualities which we had never until then suspected existed; a movie shows us a new way of imagining our own sexuality. Again, this phenomenon is familiar, not new. My point is that these should not be taken as anomalies; they are the *paradigms* of artistic encounter.

But there is a second way in which art changes us, less dramatically because more routine. Styles, whether of schools or of individual artists, both embody and encourage ways of seeing, which may then become routine—for us as individuals or for a whole society. They are routine not just as ways of seeing art, but as ways of seeing and understanding the world itself. In an important early study of the picturesque garden, Christopher Hussey pointed out just such a transformation on the part of the "picturesque," which he describes not as a style, or a school of art, but as a way of seeing[9] It is a way of seeing which originated with works of art, was subsequently fostered by theoretical essays, and finally came to be a completely transparent way of approaching not just works of art but the world itself—the surrounding landscape, one's own house, and the friends and family who appear within that landscape.

Implicit within Berleant's project is the rejection of what amounts to a naive realism in regard to the subject matter of the work of art persisting in the philosophy of art—a realism that discounts the role of art in constituting the world which is to be "represented" or "expressed" within the work.

B. Works of Art and Personal Identity

Both the work of art, obviously, and the human self, less obviously, are human constructions—partly inherited, defined within constraints established and often insisted upon by society, and partly personal, the result of our intention and efforts at self-formation.

What is the relation between the work of art and the human subject who encounters it? The question can usefully be approached from two perspectives, either as an analogy or metaphorical relation or as an analysis of an encounter.

1. The Relation of Art and Self as an Analogy

The insistence of modern (eighteenth-century and since) aesthetic theory on a single and persistent final form of the work of art parallels in certain interesting ways the obsession with personal identity dating from about the same time. The comparison between the work and human life is encapsulated in the often-invoked phrase *arts longa, vita brevis*. The phrase, which became popular in the eighteenth century, cast no fresh light on the human condition: one had already been aware that life was disappointingly short, but the more usual comparison, familiar from the First Epistle of Peter, was with plants, whose coming and going we could easily witness and indeed were in the habit of engineering: "For all flesh is as grass, and all the glory of man as the flower of grass. The grass withereth, and the flower thereof falleth away: But the word of the Lord endureth forever."[10] The words of Peter illuminate the desperation with which we call on the work of art to endure: he reminds us that it is not just our years which are short and unreliable but our glory as well. This last deficiency, however, is one which art can remedy: where life and fame and glory betray us, the physical object can sustain us, show who we were (if we were the subject of the portrait, for example) and of what we were capable, if we were the artist. (Since the Renaissance, the artist has been called upon to express his individuality in his art, and the public has become interested in the artist as a personality; portraiture, which originated with utilitarian purposes, such as the arrangement of a marriage when the two parties live too far away to meet in person, has been gaining interest and popularity.) Art becomes, then, the triumph and vindication of man over the conditions of his existence in an increasingly secular world, that is, where one looks less and less to the afterlife for salvation.

This helps make sense of the odd fact that, while the greater part of the world's art has been religious—and a good deal of what the eighteenth-century gentleman would have seen in Italy on the Grand Tour would have been religious—the aestheticians of this period were adamant that proper appreciation of an aesthetic object excluded all religious feeling. Art was being called upon to create a category not independent of religion, but supplanting religion.

The work of art is able to meet the challenge of representing, recasting, man as a being who perdures only because it is artificial, made by him. The special appeal of the garden (as a work of art and not merely a sort of place with an inherited traditional design) in the early modern period is derived from the fact that it allowed man to

remake the world itself, and to remake nature. From the fifteenth-
century Italian gardens on, one improved nature—the wilderness
inherited through Adam and Eve's sin—by revealing its inner,
obscured rationality,[11] or by imposing rational form upon it. From the
beginning of the "natural" movement in the eighteenth century, one
remade Nature herself, not putting the mark of man on God's world,
but putting oneself in God's place and remaking Nature.

The next step was the garden as autobiography or self-portraiture,
invented by Alexander Pope.[12]

2. The Impact of Art on the Self

The work of art reveals itself to me, but in doing so, it also reveals
what Suzanne Langer calls the illusion—the structure of some
particular human feeling or range of human feelings. In the case of
gardens, this "feeling" or illusion is some particular perception of the
order of the world.

This structure repeats itself to me in repeated viewings.

In encountering such a structure, which remains substantially
identical with itself over time, I encounter myself. I come face to face
with memories of myself as I was, and as I felt, in previous encounters.
The sameness of the structure prompts recognition of the difference
in the viewer. This is inevitably part of the experience of a work of
art. I remember that I loved it desperately the first time I encountered
it, or found it trivial, or that I could not understand it at first and
only found it arresting after I had myself matured or had become
familiar with other works of its type or had had certain kinds of
experiences, or had gained knowledge about what the artist or his
culture were up to. Perhaps after several encounters, its first brilliance
came to seem tedious or repetitious or superficial. For all the variation
possible in my several responses to it over time, it has in virtue of
its staying the same given me a still point from which to measure
my own changes. Through it I learn to recognize myself. It is true that
I might do this through other means as well. But self-knowledge is
always difficult (epistemologically at least and often emotionally as
well) and is not to be taken for granted. Any means to it is to be given
its due. Art has an important role to play in the development of self-
consciousness, as it is specially suited to showing us our own changes.

On the other hand, it is not simply a question of knowledge of
oneself. Having a self, being a self, is not simply a matter of knowing
facts about oneself, although it often operates on that level: I am the
one who can be counted on in this family; I am the one who is so good

with dogs; I am the one who cooks well or is mechanically inclined or likes butter pecan ice cream and hates olives. These things are part of our sense of who we are. As explicit tags, they become increasingly salient in modern societies, where individuals are often called upon for action independent of their groups, where such action may be abstract, unmotivated, and long-range rather than concrete and immediate, and where individuality is so highly prized, and where being accorded respect often depends upon the ability to project to others an image of a coherent identifiable self.

Particularly in an age of alienation, the maintenance of any internal sense of who we are based on either traditional identifications with our group or community on the one hand or on our feelings and immediate perceptions on the other becomes increasingly tenuous. Increasingly we are expected to act in violation of our feelings—not merely to curtail the impulse we may feel to strike out and kill someone who has humiliated us (a self-restraint that has been urged upon us, more often than not, throughout history) but to continue to stay at a very boring task for eight hours day-in day-out for forty years. From an economic necessity, the hiding of one's feelings and the consistent and habitual adoption of patterns of behavior in violation of our feelings becomes first custom and then a cultural ideal. In most cultures, it was incumbent first upon the aristocracy, but now it is expected of most everyone. In such a situation, one does not hide one's feelings solely from others, one learns to hide them from oneself. They become unrecognizable, alien. If one is to have passions at all, one must first learn how. (I believe that this is in fact the case—that we learn how and what to feel and how to interpret feelings largely from art. If so, this would give a new and probably unintended force to Langer's theory. But this is not the place to show this in detail.)

It is not just economic and cultural alienation that push us toward this, not just the adoption of an ideal of unfeelingness that seems the only attainable ideal. A huge proportion of us in the twentieth century are being raised in situations where to recognize our feelings would be absolutely unbearable. Our very survival depends upon an inability to recognize the extremity of what we must endure. (This is true not just in war but the conditions of normal modern life: life in dysfunctional families and with alcoholic or drug-abusing parents; systematic dislocation; forced migration—more people have been forced to leave their homes since World War II than during any comparable period in human history.) When the consistency of character and personality (a moral value in the West for two to four hundred years) of those we grow up closest to is being eroded by drugs and alcohol and there is no extended community to whom we can appeal for constancy and predictability if not relief, and our very house and neighborhood are changed every few years, how can we recognize ourselves? We rely increasingly on the kind of external "tags" described above. But our world changes so quickly, and its standards change so quickly, that we may never learn to recognize who we are from how we feel. Nothing is the same long enough for us to revisit it.

In such a situation, art acquires a new urgency: it does not simply give our feelings a sensual form, make them external and communicable, as Langer maintains. Rather it reveals them to us for the first time. It becomes "the still point of the turning world."

Self-identity, more than knowledge about ourselves, requires experience of ourselves, an inner feeling, or recognition, of who we are. This is partially dependent upon, at least it is reinforced by, a special kind of memory, not of the facts of who we are, but of *experience*—how we felt and what we saw. We have such memories, often triggered by a fresh experience of something that was only a tiny, though a very vivid, part of an earlier experience, as Proust showed and as Neisser discusses in *Memory Observed*.

The return to the work of art is not precisely the same thing, for it is not merely a memory of an experience, but a fresh experience which may be superimposed upon a memory more or less clear. On the other hand, if the art is worth its salt, the return to a work is more, rather than less, meaningful. Such an experience has three layers simultaneously: the same experience over again (one is aware of having "always" felt like this when hearing this music: this has always meant this much, meant it in this way), the memory of previous experience, and a new experience.

To the extent that our experience of a work changes over repeated encounters, we gain knowledge of ourselves (and of course of the work as well); to the extent that it feels the same, we inhabit ourselves, are confirmed in ourselves, recognize ourselves.

There is a tension here between the need to be the same person returning to the work of art—indeed, the work of art creating one as the same person through the return and re-encounter with it—and the changes that the work itself effects in the self through subsequent encounters. For as Husserl showed in *The Phenomenology of Internal Time Consciousness*, we never return precisely the same to subsequent encounters with the same phenomenon.[13] Even where the phenomenon is unchanged (*pace* Leibniz, who showed that no phenomenon or thing in the world, but only an idea, could remain the same over time. . .), even where, less plausibly, we ourselves have not been changed by

events and experiences in the interim, subsequent experiences of a
phenomenon include within them our knowledge and experience of
the previous encounter. And so they are different. Our notion of art
must accommodate this dynamic tension if it is to do justice to the
phenomena of art.

Gardens are adept at revealing to us aspects of the temporal
structure of our daily lives. They recall to us our memories of previous
times in the garden. To a large extent, they utilize these stratified
or embedded memories in creating their effects. That is, I visit a
garden and know it immediately to be a place where I have been
before. But my memory of it will include not this simple bare fact,
but the ways in which those previous enterings were themselves
steeped in memories of previous occasions. Thus this garden is not
merely one which I have visited, which I therefore recognize, which
bears the stamp of a particular kind of familiarity. This garden of
which I write now is one to which I used to go; my present memory
of the garden evokes memories of the garden as a place which was
intimately familiar. Perhaps another never became so familiar to
me—it always bore the stamp of strangeness, of occupants and
inhabitants who surprised me by their presence, or of awkwardness,
reminding me subtly that I did not quite belong here, I was here on
sufferance. It is impossible to consider a garden without bringing to
bear an awareness of whether one actually lived with that garden,
or visited occasionally; over a long time, or a short. I remember the
exact occasion when I first heard Brahms's German Requiem or Janis
Joplin's version of "Piece of My Heart"; these were sufficiently
significant occasions in my life that they became what Neisser calls
"flash-bulb memories." Because I remember the exact occasion, with
all its details—where I was lying or standing, the time of day, the
room—I know about how long these works have been part of my life.
But with music, unlike gardens, the quality of this wealth of previous
experience does not impinge upon my awareness during a subsequent
experience. The quality of previous experiences is not integral to
present experience in music, as it is in gardens. Gardens seem to have
as their "subject" time and temporality per se.

Nor does my present experience of a play or piece of music refer
me automatically to my next. Yet this is exactly what happens in a
garden. The first crocus implies the hyacinths and forsythia, the first
rosebud its own blossoming, the first rose in full bloom the bed ablaze,
the bed ablaze their dying and the end of summer. Something similar
occasionally happens in other arts, but it is the exception and not the
rule. Seeing a ballet, we wonder what Nureyev makes of this role, rush

out to get tickets for another performance of the same ballet, the same company, with him dancing the lead. Anyone who loves the music of a living composer through others' performances wants to hear the composer's own interpretation. Yet this desire, this reference to another version, is a sometime thing in other arts. It is essential and inevitable in gardens.

Moreover in gardens it is distinctly temporal: the "other interpretation" is provided by the garden itself in another time. The better we know a garden, the more fully this tension between the present and the future versions asserts itself, to the point where the gardener himself is likely to lose all satisfaction with present beauties in his awareness of the possibilities to unfold in the future—or of the work he must do to assure them.

In addition, my experience of the garden takes place at a certain time of day, and this time of day is integral to the experience as it is only incidental (usually) to my experience of music or poetry or ballet. The matinee is not an essentially different experience of the work of art than the evening performance; it will be very hard to recall when a given performance took place on internal evidence. This is not so in the garden. Morning coffee in the garden makes one want the poignantly different experience of tea in the afternoon; or a view at sunset. There is simply no separating the time of day, the quality of light—and the weather, the atmospheric conditions—from the experience.

Garden design frequently takes these factors into account and exploits them. Some garden styles deliberately structure our memories of previous visits and incorporate objectifications of those previous experiences into subsequent visits. So the ritual of naming parts of the Chinese garden, which has originally taken place as an interaction among friends, is carried out by a subsequent stage: the placing of signposts and plaques with inscriptions alluding to the name previously chosen. Or a sapling is given to a child on a special occasion, planted, and becomes a part of the garden. Or a string of Chinese lanterns is strung up for a party, and left up because we can't bear to renounce the lingering delight of that evening.

In addition, nearly all gardens exploit as best they can the peculiar delights of the different seasons. In virtually all climates with deciduous trees, gardens are not all evergreens, but invariably include trees whose foliage turns colors in the autumn, and flowering trees for the spring.

Many gardening traditions also structure the garden to take advantage of certain times of day. This is relatively rare in the West, but prevalent in Asia. The Mughal garden Shalimar, for example, had niches in the walls for candles so the garden would be lovely at night. Since barbeques and outdoor grills have become so popular in the United States, all manner of candles in colored glass containers, pseudo-Japanese lanterns, indirect lighting, plastic Chinese lanterns, and other kinds of light have been made available so people can eat dinner at a leisurely pace with time for the coals to get hot and for drinks without worrying about having to eat in the dark. Regardless of the ultimate success of the lighting arrangements in artistic terms, such an occasion is bound to be exciting and special.

Katsura, the eighteenth-century Imperial Palace outside Kyoto, deliberately structures both time of day and the time of the year. The Moon-viewing Platform overlooks a small pond which openly declares its suitability as a reflecting surface for the moon. It thus calls out to be seen at night—but since it is particularly the harvest moon that one traditionally takes the trouble to organize parties to view, it also suggests a particular time of year, the end of summer.

This dynamic relation between the work and its human participant forces a dynamic relation between that same human subject and the world—not just by analogy, because the world takes the same role as the work of art in relation to the subject, but because it is the function of the work of art to change all subsequent viewings of our interactions with the world.

The implications of this are as follows:

1) Art often has as its aim the transformation of our understanding (of self and of the world) and of behavior, of society and imagination.

2) Regardless of whether it intentionally assumes these aims or not is irrelevant; it has such transformation as one of its effects (although not necessarily in a uniform and consistent way).

3) The competing claims presented by the various works of art are often best decided by some process other than art: in courts of law, in legislative bodies, in therapy sessions, or whatever. Art offers visions and sometimes makes their implementation possible. It does not have the final word on whether its programs should be adopted.

3. The Evil Lover of Good Art

I am claiming that art has ethical, political, social effects, the combination of which I will call "moral" (bringing to bear the original meaning of "customary" as in mores, and remembering, as somebody said, that it is often matters of deportment or manners which require the greatest courage to break); it manifests these effects in five ways.

First, arts create the visions of ourselves, of others, and of our world, which make certain kinds of actions and beliefs possible or impossible, likely or unlikely, plausible or implausible. Second, they teach us about the world and ourselves (as Robertson and Albers, cited above, described). Third, they present us with a form which engages us and by which we learn to recognize ourselves. Fourth, as Langer suggested, they reveal the structure of our feelings. Finally, as Langer has shown, some arts, like architecture, actually create the ethos within which ordinary life takes place. The "illusion" thus created is not something we are free to ignore. Partly (but only partly) because of the nature and permanence of its physical presence, the "illusion" created by architecture, for example, establishes very strong constraints on behavior, constraints that are harder to ignore than the constraints of, say, poetry on belief.

But the view that art has such moral efficacy leads to two hard questions. First, how do we justify artistic freedom? Second, how do we explain cases where a very bad person, even a very "bad" society, appreciates what is generally accepted as great art?

One answer to the first question is that art is a form of play, of escape from reality, and that this escape is necessary. This view sees such play as effecting changes within the individual (reduction of tensions) but often ignores the ways play—at least in its artistic forms—may change our understanding of the situation which makes the situation intolerable.

I would suggest that art may offer a whole society new ways of understanding itself and portions of itself and its situation, thus paving the way for political and other changes in the society—and eliminating the need for further play to reduce those specific tensions. Art which succeeds at this task makes itself obsolete, if not incomprehensible. If this is so, then we must allow the artist a free reign because part of what must be changed is the standard by which his art is judged reprehensible. This is the realization of conservatives who oppose the very real challenge that art may pose to the status quo.

A second challenge to our theory is this: if art is morally efficacious, how can we explain the fact that many apparently evil people love great art? If Goering was a lover of Mozart, how can we consider Mozart's music a moral force? There are five possible answers, four of which must be dismissed as seriously unsatisfactory:

1) We could say that art is not effective in the way I have claimed. This is the most common position held, and the position of all branches of formalism. Art has no such powers, and when it attempts to rectify or compensate for the problems of the world, as for example did

Harriet Beecher Stowe's novel *Uncle Tom's Cabin,* it is either to that extent no longer art, or it is simply making a category mistake. This view has a certain plausibility, given the fact that so much evil persists in the world in spite of the omnipresence of art, and its criticism is telling: Any defense of my theory must be able to account for the persistence of evil in the face of art.

2) We could say that art loved by a bad person must be bad—in this case, Mozart's music must be bad. Most of us would not stand for that, but additionally this response is ridiculous because art loved by bad men may also be loved by good men, and usually is. ("Loved" here in reference to art is being used to indicate not merely an affective relation but also a presumption of extended or repeated and voluntary exposure; I use the word since it carries the necessary connotations of interaction and openness.)

3) We could say that such a person only seems to appreciate this music, but that really he does not, or appreciates it for all the wrong reasons—perhaps because it gives him a more glamorous or respectable image. If this is the reason, then art is not as robust as I want to claim. And although it is true that in many cases art must be understood—or even subjected to interpretation—before it can be efficacious, it is also true that in other cases it is efficacious without such deliberate interpretation, or that at least on some levels, interpretation may be automatic, subliminal, pre-reflective, almost a psychophysical reaction. And if we want to claim that art changes our understanding of the world or itself, it cannot be the case that we must already understand it before this takes place.

4) We could say that it is impossible to judge the effects of Mozart on Goering and that without this music he would have been worse. This is not satisfying, although it is true: we cannot know such things with assurance, and since no one is entirely without redeeming features, it is undoubtedly true that Goering could have been worse. (In fact art may even have done the rest of us a disservice in helping to camouflage his true nature from those who, seeing his love for art and thinking him therefore a sensitive and respectable man with an appreciation of some of the finest things our civilization has to offer, were blinded to his true nature.)

5) The real reason for the coexistence of art and evil lies in the interaction of three factors:

a) Art competes with any number of other forces for its power over the human soul and imagination. Many of these forces—economic, psychological, and so on—are stronger and even undeniable; art is always deniable, that is the point. So art is always at a disadvantage relative to these other forces.

b) Art is not a single monolithic presence but a congeries of disparate and competing visions, varying widely and often at odds.

c) Many works of art, perhaps most of those we consider greatest, do not aim at internal consistency within that resolution of the tensions with which they concern themselves. Far from it: they actively and purposefully incorporate ambiguity and ambivalence and juxtapose contradiction and endless adumbration."[14]

C. The Concept of Art Resolved as a Matter of Degree

If there is a problem with Berleant's theory from the point of view of a traditional philosophy of art, it is just that it seems to capsize the very concept of art, without doing justice to the special status of the work of art as a special category of being. The rules which describe our perception of and interaction with works of art are the same as those describing our perception and interaction in other cases. The distinctions between fine art, on the one hand, and craft, folk art, mass art, popular art, and nature on the other, all collapse. The philosophical problem of the definition of the work of art is not to be resolved but rather dismissed as a red herring.

But should the relative differences in the emphasis upon and the satisfaction derived from either originality or conformity of expression be taken as indicators of fundamentally different categories of objects, activities, and experiences? Should they not rather be taken as differences in degree? As Alison Lurie makes the point in *The Language of Clothes*, "In dress as in language there is a possible range of expression from the most eccentric statement to the most conventional."[15]

Recognition of the continuum between art and non-art, or everything else, resolves this problem. It brings another advantage, too, in that the fact that there are borderline cases, gardens which we are not sure whether to call art or not, need not disturb us. There are borderline cases in writing and painting, too. Between the Rembrandt portrait and the whitewashed wall are not only paintings aspiring to be art of varying degrees of artistic success but also murals combining decorative purposes with larger artistic aspirations and skills.

CHAPTER 7

☙

The Signifying Garden: Gardens as Art[1]

I have argued that gardens might well be considered an artkind in spite of the problems they pose for aesthetic theory because they do, nonetheless, fit such current definitions of works of art as those of Monroe Beardsley and George Dickie. In this chapter I would like to set up a framework that will facilitate recognition and analysis of gardens as an art. This framework is derived largely from Suzanne Langer's work, especially *Feeling and Form*. While Langer herself does not discuss gardens, an extrapolation of her theory to include them is justifiable on the basis of the theory itself, particularly in the light of her discussion of the principles of generalization. Her work is especially illuminating because she is one of the few philosophers who starts with careful examination of individual arts and builds up the theory from there and because she does not depend upon the distinction between fine and applied art.[2]

A. Art as Semblance or Illusion

Semblance, also called "illusion" or "virtuality," and Significant Form, the two central concepts of Langer's aesthetics, are useful points of departure because they take meaning or significance as essential to the work of art and focus attention on the form. Semblance may be understood as the concept by which Langer approaches that disjuncture effected by art from the rest of reality, her approach to what philosophers more commonly refer to as distance, disinterest, or autonomy.

Langer begins her discussion with the observation that "every real work of art has a tendency to appear. . .dissociated from its mundane environment," yet she dismisses the "aesthetic attitude" as

unnecessary for the apprehension of art, noting that it is deemed
unnecessary especially by those "who spend their lives in closest
contact with the arts—artists, to whom the appreciation of beauty is
certainly a continual and 'immediate' experience," (rightly) pointing
out that "it is not the percipient who discounts the surroundings, but
the work of art which, if it is successful, detaches itself from the rest
of the world."[3] This impression created by the work of art, one of
"otherness," is the impression of an "illusion."

Illusion is a term to be used with caution. In Langer's thought
"illusion" is contrasted with reality, "reality" having a severely
restricted meaning: it is that which can be measured, weighed, and
dealt with scientifically. But illusion is not to be confused with
delusion. Delusion is subjective, private, individual, and verifiably
false. Illusion is intersubjective, widely shared (what Kant, somewhat
misleadingly, called "universal"), and produced communally as well
as privately. Although illusion is not subject to scientific measurement
and verification, and hence is not part of what Langer calls reality,
it does have effects in the world that people experience, the
"*Lebensweld.*" To a large extent, illusion—and therefore art, which
creates the illusion—structures the Lebensweld. Illusions are human
constructions and impose an artificial (though often natural *seeming*)
order on the world.[4] Because of their consistency and range, their
"givenness" or appearance of "naturalness," and their near
omnipresence, they are powerful, yet there are important limitations
on the power of these illusions. First, they are only possible within
the constraints of biology and psychology. Second, the actual effects
and achievements of these illusions may far outreach those which were
intended by their makers; effects transcend intention. Third, insofar
as it is socially constructed, the illusion partakes of the "givenness"
or impersonal and taken-for-granted quality of the non-man-made
world; the illusion may simulate reality for its observers.

The creation of illusion is what is most essential to and definitive
of art; hence the illusion can be a guide for the process of
differentiation of the specifically artistic aspects of a work of art from
those aspects which do not pertain to its artistic nature (such as
weight). Thus, for example, in discussing the contribution of "practical
arrangements" such as steam heat to the architectural significance
of a building, Langer states very directly that they "have no
architectural significance, though they be 'built into' the
house. . .They affect the utility of the building, but not its semblance—
not even its functional semblance. They are material factors, but not
architectural elements."[5] That is, they are reality, but not illusion.

B. Elements of Semblance

The "semblance" of a work of art is created by means of its "elements," which must be sharply distinguished from its "materials." Materials are actual components of the piece not as a work of art per se, but solely as a physical object or system. Elements are "factors in the semblance, and as such they are virtual themselves." It is fairly easy to see how the distinction applies to painting, for example:

> Paints are materials, and so are the colors they have in the tube or on the palette; but the colors in a picture are elements, determined by their environment. They are warm or cold, they advance or recede, enhance or soften or dominate other colors; they create tensions and distribute weight in a picture. Colors in a paint box don't do such things. They are materials, and lie side by side in their actual, undialectical materialism.[6]

Extrapolating, we find the materials of sculpture to be wood, marble, bronze, ivory, and so on, while the elements would be their colors, their texture and finish (whether rough or smooth, shiny or matte, etc.); the materials of music are vibrations, but their elements are tones, rhythmic patterns, and so on. Elements are always phenomenal, that is, perceived.

The materials of the garden are the stones, rock, cement brick, water, earth, air, and vegetation of various kinds. The elements of the garden are colors, textures, shades of light and dark, fragrances, motion and stillness, various tempi and rhythms of plants or water, relative warmth and coolness (not to be called temperature, because as an element it enters the picture only when it is felt, not measured).

These categories are not mutually exclusive. The same tree, water, or earth may be considered as either material or element; which we choose depends upon our purposes. Insofar as the earth becomes part of the appearance, it is an element, not a material; insofar as it holds up the rest of the garden, it is a material. Water is an element only insofar as it is to be seen or heard; insofar as it is necessary for the growth of the plants, it is not an element, but a material precondition for the creation of the work of art.

This two-way distinction between materials and elements is inadequate to the analysis of gardens, however, for the elements of the semblance are more complex in gardens than in the other arts. "Elements" in Langer's sense have no meaning and no representation in and of themselves, while the elements of the garden do. Elements

are sheer appearance out of which meaning is constructed. But the
semblance that the garden creates consists not merely of such
sensuous qualities (Langer's artistic elements) but of sensuous
qualities that are inescapably meaningful because of our lived
existence. Such meaningful elements I shall call "components." The
welcome impression of cool shade that we feel as we enter an arbor
on a hot sunny day is integrally related to our physical existence at
that moment. Similarly, water in the form of ponds, rivers, streams,
waterfalls, fountains; paths, walls and fences; beds of flowers or raked
stones are neither mere materials nor mere elements but meaningful
elements, or "components," which are inevitably understood as parts
of our environment. Ryoan-ji (plate 9) comes as close as a garden can
to pure abstraction. Even here, however, representational and
propositional meaning is all but inescapable; in spite of its abstraction
and the fact that it is a Zen garden and Zen discourages exegesis,
people proliferate theories about the alleged representational and
metaphorical content of the rock groupings on the sand. The
environmental nature of gardens, coupled with our nature as
biological organisms of a particular kind, provides a range of
significance, orderings, and values that precedes and transcends
cultural differences and makes gardens to a large extent (though not
completely) universally intelligible and meaningful. This level of
meaning is neither representational nor symbolic, and neither culture-
dependent nor culture-specific.

C. Significant Form

Significant Form is the characteristic feature of art, the means
by which the semblance is created. More precisely, it is that sort of
form which articulates an idea of human feeling—not a concept of or
label for feeling but a form which makes evident the inner structure
of the feeling. It conveys information about the feeling. Langer
suggests that artistic ideas apply to feelings, to that range of
experience that is so recalcitrant to clarification by (nonartistic)
language. Each art is appropriate to a different range or type of feeling.

What is a feeling in this context? As used by Langer, "feeling"
is another somewhat misleading term. The feelings articulated by art
are not feelings in the ordinary language sense of emotions or
sentiments. They may include such sentiments or emotions, but they
are not identical with them. Since the feelings articulated and the
semblances created by the various arts differ in accordance with their

forms, it is difficult to give a single definition adequate to all the
various arts, and Langer does not try to do so, preferring instead to
specify the various kinds of illusion possible in the different arts. So
the semblance of all visual art is one kind or another of virtual space;
that of music is virtual time.[7] Extrapolating from Langer's theory, we
find that gardens create both virtual space and virtual time; their
primary illusion or "feeling" would be a perception of a spatiotemporal
order or harmonious relation between the macrocosm and the
microcosm that I call "virtual world." The exact forms vary with the
individual garden, depending upon the tensions and conflicts which
the culture and the artist are attempting to reconcile.

D. Virtual Space

   Langer finds the particular kind of Significant Form created by
visual art to be virtual space; correspondingly, she sees the creation
of virtual space as the primary task of visual art:

> The purpose of all plastic art is to articulate visual form, and to
> present that form—so immediately expressive of human feeling that
> it seems to be charged with feeling—as the sole, or at least
> paramount, object of perception. This means that for the beholder
> the work of art must be not only a shape in space but a shaping *of*
> space.[8]

The "architectonic process" effected by a work of art is "the
construction and ordering of forms in space in such a way that they
define and organize the space"[9] which, "being entirely independent
and not a local area in actual space, is a self-contained, total system."[10]
The mark of virtual space is that the evidence of it given by our senses
is inconsistent.[11]
   Gardens are largely (though of course not only) visual. Therefore,
if she is right, gardens must create virtual space. This they do, in
numerous ways. The pictorial space created by "picturesque gardens"
out of three-dimensional space, the illusion of deep distance created
in Japanese stroll gardens and the shallow rock landscape gardens
situated off verandahs (plate 2) are virtual space in even the strictest,
most literal sense.
   But this is problematic in that virtual space is virtual just in the
fact that it is not actual:

> This virtual space is the primary illusion of all plastic art.... Being
> only visual, this space has no continuity with the space in which
> we live; it is limited by the frame, or by surrounding blanks, or
> incongruous other things that cut it off. Yet its limits cannot even
> be said to divide it from practical space; for a boundary that divides
> things always connects them as well, and between the picture space
> and any other space there is no connection. The created virtual space
> is entirely self-contained and independent.[12]

But the garden is always actual space, with actual three-dimensional
objects in it, and frequently with us human beings in it. Therefore
it would seem that it cannot be virtual (i.e., non-actual) space—at least
not at the same time in the same respect, that is, as a work of art
like painting and architecture. It becomes important to know,
therefore, what exactly the virtual space of the garden would be like.

For not all virtual space is alike. Different arts create different
kinds of virtual space—or create it in different ways. And other visual
arts are able to incorporate living human beings within their space.

All visual arts take their place within actual space, have actual
dimensions. As physical objects, they are themselves actual. Actual
and virtual are not contradictory; they indicate two different potential
viewpoints from which the work can be apprehended. In a given case,
these two approaches may compete or complement each other. Which
approach we assume will depend largely on our purposes in looking
at the work at that moment. Are we trying to find a place to put the
thing to get it out of the way, or to appreciate it as a work of art? The
theatrical set designer must treat the space as actual even while she
creates of it virtual space.

The discrepancy between the virtual space and actual space is
factual, but it is not always apparent. Like the virtual space presented
by mirror, it may confuse us, seduce us into believing we can enter.
Occasionally this is exploited by a work of art, as in *trompe l'oeuil*.

The virtual space of painting has an analog in those actual
gardens which we are not allowed to enter. (This "not allowed" is
established by the conventions of appreciation, since of course
gardeners do enter such gardens for purposes other than appreciation,
namely maintenance.) These are gardens like the Japanese rock
gardens and moss gardens and others where the viewing place is
predetermined and off to one side and/or raised: many of the new
corporate and institutional gardens within buildings—and
occasionally in courtyards—which are to be looked at only through
glass, such as the indoor garden in the Madison Building of the

Library of Congress. In addition, individual beds within various kinds of gardens are rarely to be entered. The Persian pleasure gardens were meant to be enjoyed from the shade of the porticoes. This is not inherent to gardens, nonetheless, since in far more cases walking around the garden is crucial to its appreciation—even of those which do provide a single privileged point of view on the garden.

In the other visual arts, however, most cases do not encourage the confusion or conflation of the virtual space of the work of art with actual space. Except for gardens, the question is not likely even to come up in purely geometric or abstract arts; it is only pertinent to representational art. But here the differences are usually underscored by a number of signals. As in language, redundancy is the rule rather than the exception. Frames are common example of such a signal. Even in East Asia, where frames were historically unknown, hanging scrolls were in fact traditionally "framed" by a series of enclosing rectangles of brocade. In gardens, walls mark off the boundaries in much the same way—which is why it truly is revolutionary, as Walpole observed, to "leap the fence" as William Kent did and eliminate the wall. The Japanese verandah may similarly be regarded as the equivalent of a frame for a garden.

Changes in scale, nonrealistic coloring, bold outlines, etc., are also signals, clues to the fact that we are looking at an illusion rather than reality. But we cannot conclude that their primary function is to indicate the distinction between art and reality. If the consensus about the drawings of the cave dwellers at Lascaux and similar sites is correct, even the acute stylization—the reduction in scale, the monochromism, the heavy outlines—of those paintings did not prevent people from understanding the paintings as the animals. Although this seems a little strange to us now, it is not terribly different from the way modern people react to the movies and popular music—they often take it for reality. Interviews with actors from the television series are full of stories of viewers mistaking them on the street for the fictional characters they portray, even asking them about their fictional families and what it's like to live in their "houses." Confusion of artistic illusion and reality should be recognized by philosophers as one of the normal responses, quite possibly essential to art, rather than merely aberrant and ignorant.

E. Gardens as Semblance: The Virtual World

Gardens create and utilize illusions of many kinds—illusions of permanence and perdurance, of distance, of plenty, of peace and harmony; illusions that one is in a wild forest (the cages of the singing birds in Marie de' Medici's aviary near the amphitheater in the garden of the Tuileries would be covered with branches to create this effect;[13] similarly, Elizabeth and Edwin Clarkson's North Carolina garden, Wing Haven, which relies upon thousands of wild birds, creates the illusion of a world in which different species live in complete harmony[14]) or that inanimate things live, that the past is present, that there is no decay, no death, that it is always spring, that one's property extends without limit, that the mundane order of physical reality reflects a cosmic order or a divine sanction.

As a subspecies of visual art, the garden takes on the creation of some sort of virtual space. What kind of virtual space? One that is three-dimensional; environmental in the sense of enveloping, encompassing us; continuous with the rest of our world—not discontinuous like mirrors and paintings.

But gardens are not merely spatial—as we have seen, they also exploit time in various ways, purposely directing our attention, incorporating the rhythms and tempi of natural phenomena or deliberately disregarding them.

Moreover, gardens utilize components from the everyday world. Roads, lakes, and streams; the scenery from the surrounding countryside; buildings; real animals and plants; the sun; the sky; the clouds; even people may (depending on the type of garden) be incorporated into the garden.

What we have, then, is a virtual world.

What is a virtual world? Virtual is Langer's term, adopted from physics, for the kind of reality that illusory phenomena have. They are illusory in that they cannot be measured or established scientifically. This comes out in her discussion of illusory powers ("The Magic Circle") but is applicable to other illusions as well: "All forces that cannot be scientifically established and measured must be regarded, from the philosophical standpoint, as illusory; if, therefore, such forces appear to be part of our direct experience, they are 'virtual,' i.e. non-actual semblances."[15] They nonetheless are not chaotic or without organization; they have their own inner consistency, objectivity, and patterns of coherence. They are objective in Kant's sense of eliciting highly similar reactions from different subjects; it is not that each subject reacts uniquely. They can therefore be studied. They can be said to have effects. But their effects in virtue of their illusions (or virtual semblance or powers) are not effects on the actual world directly, but on the structure of our perception.

The garden organizes components of the actual world in such a way that our attention is directed toward certain features while others are ignored. Some features are brought within the grounds, others are eliminated or kept away. (Note that of all kinds of art, the garden is the only one where it makes sense to draw the distinction between "eliminating" and "keeping away" because it is the only one with components that move of their own accord.) It may therefore be not only virtual but "ideal," a perfect form of the world. But it is never ideal in the sense of drawing primarily upon ideas for its efficacy. It is able to put itself across only by means of physical sensations and appearances. Therefore it always has already solved in some sense any tension between physicality and spiritual or mental life. This is why there are no perverted gardens, as imagination would seem to require: The garden has no way to trap man in his body to his discomfort and humiliation, because the terms are set up and resolved on the physical level. "Perverted gardens," gardens which are set up to be horrid, to exemplify the opposite of everything we want and expect in a garden, might seem to be a good idea—but in fact malice is attributed only to fictional woods, not to gardens.[16]

The garden embodies an order or harmony; this is true cross-culturally. Although the elements which are put in order differ, they nearly always include human beings as one of the terms. The identity of the other terms depends on what is most in need of being ordered.

The creation of a virtual world, a variety of "ethnic domain," means that gardens have three important roles to play in relation to social reality. Most obviously, and as we have seen, they serve as the site for human activity, which, regardless of whether it is performed socially, in the sense of in groups or interactively, or by individuals in isolation, is socially conditioned. The garden as a site is continuous and contiguous with everyday time and space: no transformation is necessary to bring the lawn chairs from Sears to their spot next to the azaleas. Nor do we undergo any essential transformation in ourselves or in our social roles, as is the case on the sites of some religious rites and on the stage. In fact, however, the garden has a more foundational role in the creation of everyday social reality than we are likely to recognize. At the very least, it may be said to confirm the basic terms on which a given society is founded, most notably class relations, in-group/out-group definitions, and temporality, the internalized sense of time, especially as that is channeled and utilized by society. In addition, within everyday life it has two rather more specialized roles to play. 1) More than just confirming the status quo, the garden, which as art is relatively freer than many other social institutions, may respond during times of social conflict or transition and contribute to the establishment of new patterns of social relations and of temporality. 2) In relation to architecture, the garden assumes the special functions of transitional space, that is, of space specially designated to effect transitions from one category of social reality to another.

At the same time, no garden operates only on this mundane level. Every garden moves with an almost unnerving equability back and forth between the "is" of everyday reality and the "ought to be" of the ideal.[17] Every garden is the embodiment of someone's vision of how life should be, the creation of a realm at once idealized—and often to a large extent imaginary—and liveable. It creates an ethos in which the terms of life as we feel it ought to be lived may all be included.

Finally, gardens may actually be constitutive, in the phenomenological sense, of certain crucial features or categories of social reality, particularly as they are susceptible to the formative forces of a given culture. Two such categories are personal identity and selfhood, and the We-relationship.

The "We-relationship" is a notion developed by Alfred Schutz, who describes it as a relationship among consociates in which "the Other's course of action, its motives (insofar as they become manifest) and his person (insofar as it is involved in the manifest action) can be shared in immediacy and the constructed types. . .will show a very low degree of anonymity and a high degree of fullness."[18] How is it possible that gardens should play such a role, even on occasion (for I am not arguing that they are a necessary condition for the constitution of the We-relationship)? There are three capabilities inherent in the garden that are conducive to this process. First, the garden physically isolates "us" from "the others," the crowd, automatically constructing us as an "in-group." Usually this carries implications of a basis for the felt cohesion that is far more permanent and far-reaching than our happening to be in the same place would seem to imply. (This is the dynamic underlying the image of the garden in the film *The Garden of the Finzi-Continis.*) Second, as we saw in chapter 2, structures of temporality are coordinated by the garden and thus our internal sense of what is happening and how it is liable to be coordinated. Third, and most importantly, we are given the same surroundings and the same foci to command our attention. This in itself is not enough to instigate an instantiation of the We-relationship, of course, but it does help. (Movies and radio programs command and focus the simultaneous attention of all their viewers, but without necessitating any of the sense of shared reality).

None of these guarantees the constitution of the We-relation; any of them may be overridden by compelling factors in our own personal responses. But the garden creates a presumption of community, as against a presumption of individuality or isolation or anonymity which is pervasive in many other environments. It is this presumption of community, not merely the privacy and romantic associations afforded by gardens, that makes their traditional association with love and politics so appropriate.

PART III

The Garden as Great Art

CHAPTER 8

❧

Great Art: Significant Human Content: Theoretical Issues

A. Introduction

The recognition of the garden as an art form leads to a second, perhaps more provocative question: Can the garden be great art? Granted there are great gardens—Blenheim, Stowe, Stourhead, Versailles, Katsura, Ryoanji—and great gardeners—Capability Brown, William Kent, Le Notre, Kobori Enshu. Are any of these admittedly great gardens great also specifically as works of art? Can we expect of them not only sensuous pleasure and formal excellence but the kind of illumination of the human spirit and of the human condition that we find in other arts? The persistent (and cross-cultural) habit documented in chapter 2 of interpreting gardens in religious, political, social, and psychological terms rather than as purely aesthetic or physical entities, suggests that if gardens should turn out to be art at all, they will be capable of being "great" art.

For by "greatness" in art philosophers generally mean art which is not merely superb formally but which has, in addition to formal excellence, "significant human content." A number of philosophers have argued that works of art fall into two categories, "great" works and "small."[1] Greatness, on this view, is a complex matter, requiring not only aesthetic or formal excellence but also a second independent source of value. The question for gardens, then, would be, can they embody (or represent or express) this sort of content? Great art is that which goes beyond excellence; to be great, art must meet two conditions: it must be formally excellent (in my view all the gardens illustrated in this book have formal excellence) and it must have important content.[2]

Before we consider gardens as great art, however, we must devote some attention to the concept of artistic greatness per se. My own position is 1) that art can have meaning on four levels, the obvious level of subject matter, reference, or representation (dismissed by Clive Bell as irrelevant); the level of the formal qualities and organization; the level of the medium itself (that is, as Marshall McLuhan pointed out, "the medium is the message"); and the environmental level, which includes such matters as arrangement and placement of the work, its interactions with other works and with non-art, etc.; 2) that meaning on the first level is optional, while meaning on the latter three levels is inevitable, and 3) particularly in the case of good or important works, the presence or nonexistence of meaning in the first sense is often integral to the work. Yet most discussions of great art and/or the "meaning" of art are referring to the first level only.[3]

In this chapter I would like to clarify what is meant by great art. Subsequent chapters will examine the notion that ideas may be expressed in art and develop the contrasts between ideas in art and in language and in gardens (chapters 9 and 10), and finally, examine some of the ways in which ideas may be expressed in gardens (chapters 10 and 11), thereby demonstrating how some gardens may achieve the status of great art.

B. The Theory of Great Art

The concept of artistic greatness per se reveals itself upon examination to be problematic in two ways. First of all, as Bertram Jessup points out, significance itself turns out to be complex. In fact we are not satisfied with mere significance but require it to be of a certain kind—enduring or permanent significance. Endurance is problematic even in the case of formal excellence—preservation of formal qualities in paintings or buildings presents challenges, on the one hand, while, on the other, those very changes may become aesthetically essential later on, as in the case of certain types of Japanese ceramics whose glaze is expected to crack with age or modern buildings which are expected to achieve their color by rusting. Such changes may be anticipated or not, planned or not by the artist; in addition, tastes change, and as Pope's criticism of symmetrical gardens, cited above, shows, even formal qualities may cease to appeal. Yet compared to content, form endures in a way we might almost call robust. Enduringness of content is far more problematic. As Jessup explains it,

In respect to many if not most great works of art of the past a factual
perplexity arises for the 'serious content' view. It is that the 'serious
content' which they contain, at least in the plain sense, has
undergone radical changes; so that, for example, what was at the
time of creation [of the artwork] a burning truth, or at least a live
option for belief, has become a palpable falsehood or a primitive
superstition. And what was once a noble ethical vision becomes a
questionable or even an abhorrent dogma.[4]

The two criteria seem to be irreconcilable. If we insist upon
significant content, enduringness seems impossible to attain; once
we insist upon enduringness, we must jettison the concept of
significant content.

Jessup presents and rejects two responses to the incompatibility
between the "serious content" and the "enduringness" criteria:

The first and radical possiblitity is that the 'serious content' view
may be rejected in favour of a completely different theory of great
art, one which stands for 'significant form', 'plastic value', 'decorative
quality' or something else which makes content either innocently
irrelevant or harmfully distractive. The absolute alternative to
'serious content' is some kind of formalism, as in the theories of Clive
Bell, Roger Fry and Ortega y Gasset. This is, of course, the second
major tradition, stemming. . .from a rejection of Plato's major premise
about art and enjoying strong favour in the pure art, dehumanization,
and non-objectivist doctrines and practices of our time.[5]

Although some might maintain a pure formalism with respect to
gardens, I believe it cannot be said to do them justice, given either
the sorts of things we have seen people say about them or what we
have learned about the implications of their environmental nature.
But Jessup, rightly, I think, rejects this formalist alternative on behalf
of all arts because "it seems. . .to entail the rejection of art as well
as the theory." He proposes a second way,

a way of amendment rather than of rejection of the 'serious content'
view. Serious content is preserved in appreciation of great art in
which it is found, but it is taken aesthetically rather than in a real
life way. With this amendment, serious content will be taken as
necessary to great art, but necessary only because it affords a richer
material for aesthetic uses than merely neutral material or trivial
content.[6]

Jessup's "taken aesthetically rather than in a real life way" is
no solution to the dilemma, however, since it merely expands the range

of works which can be found to be great (i.e., from those whose resolutions and formulations with which we may personally agree and which we find valid and significant, to the much larger group of all those which anyone at any time found significant) without any attempt to explain greatness or account for the irreconcilability of greatness with enduringness. It is a muddled move, moreover, for how we know them to be significant to others without finding them so ourselves is an epistemological puzzle; significance is always significance to someone, and if the someone is not ourselves, we need presumably to look for evidence regarding someone else's mind. Furthermore, it does not allow us to distinguish between those works in which content is identifiable but not significant, a purely decorative treatment of the human form, for example, and those in which the content is integral. Jessup's solution is itself too easy; it is less a resolution of the conflict than a postponement to another level of discussion. If we aestheticize our response to significance, we have abandoned the "great art" position and returned to purely formal concerns. And engagement with the work of art is once again reduced to a purely aesthetic response. In the end, Jessup has no resolution to the problem he has analyzed.

Jessup's difficulties have a triple source: 1) his laxity in conflating two disparate definitions of serious content; 2) an implicit positivism or essentialism, evident in the fact that he locates serious content primarily on the level of solutions or formulations rather than questions or issues to be probed; and 3) a positivist, even naive, confidence that we can identify what is right and true with enough certainty that our identification can be used as a guide in the (conceptually dependent) task of identifying great art.

The resolution of the apparent antagonism between the criteria of significant human content and of enduringness[7] depends not upon an aestheticization of our response to the work but upon our defining serious content in a way that is appropriate to art. The difficulty arises, I believe, with a confusion within the definition of serious human content, and it can be resolved by the separation of the two distinct meanings, for only one of them goes out of date in this problematic way. Jessup conflates two competing definitions of "serious content" with profoundly different implications; he is too easygoing when he "attempts to bring together some of the characteristics which are currently asserted or implied to belong to 'great art,'" for the different characterizations conflict.

The first of the two definitions given by Jessup is "factual truth, religious belief, and moral, social and political rightness;" this is the view of what art should do as derived by Jessup from Plato and the art-for-life's-sake school.

The second definition is never given explicit formulation; it is suggested by a passage which Jessup quotes from Pepper, who writes, "So far as the work appeals to our common instincts and our deeper emotions, it can move men of whatever age or culture." Similarly, Walter Pater, at the end of his *Essay on Style* focuses on the types of issues rather than truth and rightness. He speaks of

> the distinction between great art and good art depending. . . not on its form but on the matter. . . . Given . . . good art;—then, if it be devoted further to the increase of men's happiness, to the redemption of the oppressed, or the enlargement of our sympathies. . . , or to such presentment of . . . truth . . . as may ennoble and fortify us. . . it will also be great art."

Resolution of this problem is possible only if we locate significance on the level of questions or issues rather than answers; provided we understand significant human content in Pater's and Pepper's sense, there is no conflict with the criterion of enduringness. Only this second version of significant content can resolve the dilemma which Jessup has uncovered since (as we have discovered empirically) the specific formulations of significance offered by art (as by philosophy and science) may not last. Only a concern with general issues rather than with specific solutions can be of enduring interest. Serious content cannot imply either truth or rightness since we are so rarely sure of either, and when we are surest, we are most likely to be wrong. Our knowledge of truth and our visions of rightness change.

Use of the first definition complicates the notion of serious content without contributing explanatory power. It adds a further condition to the concept of significance (which by now, for Jessup, means "meaningful + enduring + true"). In fact, the addition of the requirement of truth would mean that we could not have great art that focused on matters the truth or falsity of which could not be determined—no art that dwelt on the meaning of life or the importance of love. It gives art no credit for asking the right questions. It demands of the work truth and rightness, our ideas of which are constantly changing, and of the author/artist, a privileged access to truth which we in fact no longer expect even from philosophers, scientists, and priests. It is a burden which no work of art can bear. We do not want to be obliged to disqualify the *Divine Comedy* because hell isn't quite like that. Surely a work of art, like a work of philosophy, might be both serious and valuable although morally or socially wrong, or even in parts false.

The danger of Jessup's position is not merely that epistemological and hermeneutic problems would multiply unbearably. More important is that the role of truth and of moral, social, and political rightness is different in art than in other spheres of human activity. A work of art cannot be expected to give the ultimate solution to questions of fundamental philosophical import. The most it can reasonably be expected to do is to give a good formulation of one or more issues and to raise new or important questions. The formulation need not be right or true to be worth our while. It may be useful if it does nothing more than illustrate aspects of the issues in such a way as to increase our understanding. This may be done by, for example, illustrating character, or the effects of society upon human beings, in a new way. But art is not devoted solely to the solution or elimination of the problem but also to our understanding of it. Therefore it does not focus only on the issues but also on how we understand them and how we understand ourselves in our approach to them. Anything which clarifies these processes of understanding, if only by illustrating them, is a significant contribution. This Dante has done (among other things), and this is what makes the work great (rather than merely fine) art.

Works of art become passé not when their solutions to the eternal questions are proven wrong or distasteful but when their formulations of these questions have become too simplistic or are seen to be based on assumptions which we no longer maintain.

C. A Fourth Criterion: A Form Adequate to the Content

But is this revised formula (aesthetic or formal excellence, plus significant human content, plus enduringness) sufficient for the description of great art? It is not, because art is not a matter of adding qualities together arithmetically. With the addition of serious content, the requirements for form are changed; form must now be adequate to the content. By "adequate" I mean both appropriate and commensurate. It is in fact the inadequacy of the form to the content which accounts for the low evaluation we usually give to popular arts. Take for example murder mysteries and detective stories. As a genre, they tend to be formulaic. Nonetheless a number of exceptional examples exist in which the form is extremely pleasing, character is well developed, the language beautifully, creatively, originally used. The themes likewise deserve our most scrupulous attention—the meaning of the death of an individual, the effects of vengeance, the meaning and possibility and conditions of justice, the inadequacy of our understanding of the motives of another—or ourselves. Nor do these themes fade into insignificance with the passage of time. The problem, then, is the way in which the forms of such novels and movies remain oddly impervious to their own content. Too often the treatment trivializes its themes. In cases like these, in spite of the fact that all three of Jessup's criteria are met, the work cannot be called great. (Note that the case of literary propaganda is somewhat different, in that the writing itself tends to be uninspired and monotonous; since both excellent form and significant human content are separately required, this is not great art in spite of taking on the noblest themes.)

On the other hand, the inclusion of this fourth criterion reveals the inadequacy of the original form-content conceptualization of the work of art. For if the form is not adequate to the content, we may not perceive the content at all—either may not perceive that there is serious content, or may not be able to distinguish the actual theme "intended" by the artist from some much more general concept under which it may be subsumed. To give an example, suppose a painter has in mind a depiction of light itself as we perceive it (as opposed to light taken as a symbol of holiness or as a sign that a door is open or a lamp lit). If the form is not adequate to this attempt to call into question the very nature of seeing, then we will look at the painting for its representational content—perhaps a chair and a table—or its colors. Neither of these is particularly significant human content; the work is not great art.

By "great art," then, we mean art which meets four criteria: excellent form, significant human content, enduringness, and adequacy of form to content. If gardens are to be great art, they must meet all four.

I will not here undertake to demonstrate that this is possible. Although I believe it has been done in many cases, to show just how this has been achieved would require detailed and in-depth studies of individual gardens that would take us beyond the limits of this book.[8] We will, however, take a closer look at significant human content and one garden's mediation of death and memory.

D. Significant Human Content: Levels of Meaning

I stated above that most discussions of art focus on only the first (namely propositional or representational content) of the four levels

on which art can bear meaning. This is problematic for gardens, for
the other three levels, formal qualities and organization, medium, and
interrelation with the environment, are at least equally important
yet tend to be neglected under the prevailing disciplinary paradigms
of both art history and philosophy.

1. Level One: Propositional and Representational Content

Of course many gardens do include at least some propositional
and/or representational content. The rock landscape of the Daisen-in
in plate 2, for example, is obviously representational, as is the Temple
of British Worthies at Stowe in plate 1, while gardens in virtually
all the European and Asian styles include carved quotations or visual
or verbal allusions as well. Art historical studies of gardens have done
fine work on iconographic and literary programs of gardens, while
philosophers have made some real strides in understanding
propositional and representational meaning in general.

2. Level Two: Formal Qualities and Organization

Formal qualities and organization are practically equivalent to
"style" and in some cases "genre." Yet where "style" and "genre" are
invoked by art historians they are often understood to be free of
content or meaning. (There are important exceptions to this generality,
such as the understanding of Cubism as an artistic counterpart to
relativity theory, or the view of Impressionism as the instantiation
of subjective perception.) But the organization of form is precisely what
structures the relation of the "viewer" or participant to the garden;
it thus plays a crucial role in determining how we are to interpret
that garden. In Roy Strong's and Michel Baridon's views, the formal
gardens of European monarchies are visual and kinesthetic correlates
of monarchical power and the political theories that are used to justify
it.[9] Horace Walpole also recognized the essential connection between
this type of garden and monarchy, although he overlooked this
particular line of evidence, stressing instead the aesthetics of control
over the shape and positioning of plant material and the historical
fact that the use of huge old trees (in English gardens) depends upon
the landowner's independence of royal power. (In France large trees
could be confiscated by the king for lumber.) The use by monarchical
gardens of a single privileged point of view, centered and raised

above the garden as a whole (plate 8) gives credence to the notions of both absolute power and absolute reason to justify the power. The "picturesque" garden depends upon a viewer who is also outside the garden, but in this case there are any number of equally valid views (though all may be structured by the gardenist). The full significance of this type of organization remains to be explicated, though important work has been done by Christopher Hussey, John Dixon Hunt, and David Marshall.[11] The use of repetition in Renaissance knot gardens, to give another example, is like the use of repetition in so-called "pure" music (that is, music without words). One senses it is meaningful, yet the meaning is clearly not on the levels of either representation or propositional content. As I see it, knot gardens served the purpose of weaning human consciousness of space from its "natural" or pre-scientific sense of space as always and inherently subjective, that is, organized around and from the perspective of a human subject and carrying inevitably the values of that subject. Knot gardens, along with some other artistic media,[12] made it possible to think of space as purely objective, and to experience our own space as objective.[13]

3. Level Three: The Meaning of the Medium

As we have seen, the medium of the garden is itself meaningful, for the various components are inherently meaningful, within a given context. Beyond this the medium of living plants makes possible the conviction gardens bring to their messages, for in view of their success in virtue of being alive, they compel acquiescence in a way analogous to the logic of theoretical argument. It also cues us to the tacit comparison to our own lives. Other media within gardens, such as rocks or topographical features, function not only as items within the representation but also are essential to the interpretation of the temporality of a given garden and to the recognition of its tempi.

4. Level Four: Environmental Meaning

The environment similarly may carry meaning on the level of representational content, as when a property is visually extended to include surrounding landscape not in fact owned by the gardenist. It also is crucial to the sense of appreciation we bring to the garden, however, since the outer environment is what provides the terms of contrast. It therefore sets up the terms for many of the values which are expressed in a given garden. In a harsh winter climate, a medieval cloister garden makes little sense.

E. Gardens as Great Art: An Example

The garden pictured on the cover, a small sunken garden located between the formal gardens and the Capability Brown riverscape at Clivedon in England, illustrates the power of a garden to address the great issues of life, in this case the meaning of war and the relationship of the living to the dead. This garden was built originally to commemorate the local men who had died serving in the First World War. The reduction of their lives to identical flat stone markers with no individuality other than their names is in counterpoint to the living forms of plants among whose rich three-dimensional variety of textures, colors, and shapes the human visitor makes her way. It is not that the markers lie underfoot, exactly, for the visitor has been graciously provided with a way to circumvent them, but if they are not trod upon it is because the visitor chooses not to do so. Their stillness and lack of individuality are formally analogous to the paving stones of the walkways and a total contrast to the vigor of the plants and the other kind of stone in this garden, the classical columns which thematize historical connection per se and establish the dignity of the setting. The garden marks its connection with the march of history in another way, too, for the symmetrical perimeter walk with intersecting central axes is a medieval garden form, though in this case it has been distorted from circle to oval. The sense of war (not death itself but death in war) as a trap which embraces both the dead and the living is admirably caught by the steep vertical surrounding walls. (Interestingly this use of a steep vertical wall confronting the viewer was used to similar effect in the Vietnam Memorial by Maya Lin in Washington, D. C., although there the wall has a linear direction which echoes the historical development of the war which gave the sense of an encounter in which we sank ever deeper.[14]) The beauty of this garden is outstanding, and the sense of tranquility almost overwhelming, but its force comes not simply from "formal excellence" (beauty) and the emotions it expresses, but from its significance as a subtle and complex juxtaposition of historical past and present life, of intensely personal subjectivity and anonymous objectivity, of life and death, of natural death and the inexorable yet unnecessary death of war, of the choices to serve in war or to escape it, to wage war or to avoid it, to pay homage to the dead or to walk on them, and what is not ours to choose, the lucky fate of not having to choose. Drawing upon these pairs of oppositions, it recreates the notion of honor, intensifies our awareness of honor and of its value, while the equivalence of the paths, the futility of choosing one path over another, underscores the complimentary awareness of fate.

CHAPTER 9

꙳

Ideas in Art and Language

The notion of significant human content in art is strikingly close to the notion of an idea. The medium most commonly associated with the expression of ideas is language. (In this work I will refer to ideas expressed in language as "concepts.") But the linguistic and artistic formulations of ideas differ significantly; this is clearly indicated by certain features of art itself and by certain of our responses to it. In this chapter I would like to identify two distinct nexus of essential differences in the ways art and language signify or convey ideas and information. The chapter following this will provide a more detailed examination of the differences between what is possible via language and via gardens. The conclusion will indicate some of the implications of these differences for the theory of art.

A. Artistic Ideas as Significant Form

Suzanne Langer explored the issue of artistic ideas in *Feeling and Form*. She finds the expression of ideas in artistic form, which she calls "Significant Form," essential to all the arts and identifies it as the basis for the unity of the arts, whose differences in media would otherwise call into question the very possibilty of meaningful similarity among them.[1] Langer asserts that "the oft-asserted fundamental unity of the arts lies not so much in parallels between their respective elements or analogies among their techniques, as in the singleness of their characteristic import, the meaning of 'significance' with respect to any and each of them. 'Significant Form'. . . is the essence of every art; it is what we mean by calling anything 'artistic.'[2]

Langer differs from Clive Bell, who also puts Significant Form at the crux of artistic identity, in her insistence that such form is not purely self-referential but rather signifies *something*. So although Significant Form is not referential in the linguistic sense, it does relate to things other than itself. Langer defines Significant Form as a kind of articulate form symbolic of human feeling, and art as the creation of such forms.[3] "Articulate" in this case means not that it is expressive but that (1) it is complex, composed of more than one element, and (2) its internal structure is given to our perception.[4]

B. Differences between Art and Language

There are two basic differences between ideas as they are formulated in art ("artistic ideas") and ideas as they are formulated in language ("concepts"). First, concepts direct us to similarities, while artistic ideas retain an utter particularity even when they also are generalizable. Second, concepts are independent of their form, while artistic ideas are inseparable from form.

1. Artistic ideas are not concepts, which indicate similarities among members of the category they construct. A concept is a way of devising a category, based on explicit, or at least on explicable, criteria. A concept is used to help us recognize and identify similarities among things which do not necessarily appear similar except with reference to the concept, and to disregard those differences among members which are deemed irrelevant and which would otherwise be distracting.

The "Halleluia Chorus" and Gauguin's *Brittany Landscape with Swineherd* are not ideas in this sense. They do not help us to discern similarities among things in the same way that "liberty" or "Wissenschaft" or "savoir faire" do. The artistic idea is always particular, always primarily itself, not the representative of a class but an individual object.

This brings us to an important question. Ideas always apply to objects or events (or, of course, to alleged, imaginary, or pseudo-objects or events; no ontological claim is implied). To what does the artistic idea apply? It is not that the artistic idea is not capable of generalization; it is. But the problem of judgment, in Aristotle's sense, by which we determine how ideas apply to individual objects and events, is different with artistic ideas than with concepts or other kinds of ideas.

Take as an example a portrait of a king. To what or whom does it apply? In one sense, this picture may be a picture of a particular man; yet this is not a *necessary* meaning behind all pictures of kings but rather a late development in painting. An earlier meaning is kinghood itself—a composite of power, authority, perhaps divinity, nobility, various kinds of social, mythic, and character traits. It is not always easy to decide regarding a given picture whether what is being portrayed is the qualities (physical or spiritual or psychological) of an individual, or kinghood in general, or the effect of a certain rather unusual degree of power and autonomy (and if the latter, whether it's the effect on an individual or a type). Any and all of these may enter a single portrait.[5]

Another example is the pessimism (as it is often seen) of Thomas Hardy's novels. Why should it be considered pessimism at all? It is so only provided we view the events not as isolated occurrances in the lives of individuals but as typical in some way. But typical of what? Of rural life in late nineteenth-century England? Of rural life everywhere? Of all human life? The determination of the appropriate range of generalization of a work—and the conditions for that determination—are cruces of interpretation.[6]

2. A second major difference between artistic ideas and concepts is that the former are inseparable from their form. (Categories have no ostensible form.) A number of phenomena bear this out:

a. This is the basis for the conviction, prevalent in contemporary philosophy, that multiple copies of a work such as the copies of a print or sculpture, or variations in versions of works such as performances, are problematic—not only financially, but more importantly, theoretically.

b. Copyright law makes a distinction between an idea (which cannot be copyrighted) and the expression of an idea (which can).

c. Although philosophers of art insist that the history or provenance of a work should be incidental and unimportant (pace Leibniz), in fact collectors, dealers, and even many lovers of art do not feel that way or act on that basis. There is a tension—more precisely a schism—here between philosophical theory and people's attitudes toward art, which philosophers sometimes dismiss by implying that the collectors and dealers and amateurs have impure and improper attitudes toward art. But this respect for the history of the work, for what is in its most theoretically respectable terms called authenticity, is another facet of the basic fact that works of art are essentially sensuous forms, inseparable from their instantiation. (The importance of the instantiation and its history is acknowledged by East Asian connoisseurship and at least traditional theory of art. In both Japanese tea ceremony and Chinese painting, the recognition of the relationship between the work of art and previous users or viewers becomes an important part of the process of appreciation.)

There is a good deal of confusion and debate about these two points, which (if we follow Langer on philosophical confusion[7]) shows that the problem of art is fundamentally misconceived. It is the reluctance to come to terms with the irreducibly individual nature of the work of art that gives rise to so many of these problems. (And individuality, whether of a person or an object, is always interactive and historical, as Leibniz recognized.) The philosophical problem here in respect to the work of art parallels the problem with respect to love and interactions of others (commonly called the "object") with self.

d. We don't finish with a work of art—at least not in a simple way. We keep going back. The idea, apart from its sensuous instantiation, does not suffice. The main exception to this generalization is for the artist. This, incidentally, is a good reason to follow Weiss's advice and distinguish between the artist and the audience of a work, because they approach it so differently.[8] The artist struggles to realize an idea; his involvement with the work, his need for that particular work, ceases when he successfully realizes the idea in the form or recognizes that he has taken that particular work as far toward the realization as he can and gives up. After that he rarely returns to it.

For the audience, on the other hand, the closest parallel to a work of art is a person whom one loves. (The temporary boredom or satiation we feel when we have been with a work of art too long finds its analog here since of course few people like to be with each other every minute, no matter how strong the love.) We continue to require stimulation from other human beings in addition to the loved one, without this having any bearing on the love. But there is a recognition that those others do not supplant the loved one, or substitute for him. The continual (though not continuous) presence of the loved one is vital. Continued interaction with the other is vital. Memory, the idea of the person, is not enough. All of this coexists with various utilitarian satisfactions one may receive from the loved one. These things are apart from utilitarian considerations—the myriad ways in which we benefit by the existence and/or acts of the other.

Here again the difficulties philosophy has with art parallel the difficulties it has with love and with the intricacies of the relations of the self to others. The tradition that minimizes interactive aspects of art and the individuality of the work as embodied in physical form and history, and that idealizes aesthetic distance, is the same tradition that idealizes the isolated and self-sufficient self and understands personal identity without essential reference to others. Taking sight as the paradigm for knowledge, and knowledge as the paradigm for relation, this tradition isolates the knowing (seeing) subject from interrelation, establishing, in Buber's terms, an I-it relation rather than an I-thou. The self is constituted as a subject in contrast to— and often by means of its domination over—an object, rendered powerless to affect the subject by its very objectification. The process, many of its effects, and the means to those effects are quite similar in both cases, whether the "object" be a human being or a work of art. (The stakes are higher, of course, when the "object" is a human being than when it is a work of art.) The process is not inevitable; alternatives are beginning to be worked out theoretically, although their study does not yet occupy as large or secure a place in philosophy, psychology, and the study of art as does the work on subject-object relations.

e. We relatively rarely translate a work of art from one medium to another, however. More common is the translation of a work from one style to another, as in, for example, Monet's "Olympia," or Trutat's "Reclining Bacchante," both "versions" in a sense of Titian's "The Venus of Urbino."[9] But in neither case is this ever for the same reason as linguistic translation, that is, to render the (completely) incomprehensible comprehensible (or to take a more pessimistic note, to give the illusion of comprehension). Further, when art historians discuss the differences among such versions, it is precisely the *differences* in meaning that they explore.

f. In addition, in discursive (as opposed to artistic, ritual, poetic, and some performative) usage of language, once an idea is conveyed, it is unnecessary to retain that exact form any longer. But art is more like love than argument (pace Edward Albee and those with views of love *as* argument). We rejoice in and continue to require the persisting presence of the object. We are not done with it because we've seen it once. This is partly because discursive language moves to conclusions, which once they have been accepted, suffice in the absence of the argument itself. The conclusions are meant to supplant the argument. In fact, in a certain sense, that is the point of argumentation. Having reached a conclusion, we want to be done with it or move the conclusion from its place as a conclusion to a premise in a further argument. (I am speaking here only of disciplined discursive language, as takes place in modern science, in philosophy, occasionally in political debate; rejection of proven conclusions is common enough in undisciplined verbal squabbling.)

g. Discursive language values logical consistency far more than art does; in fact, many schools of art make a positive value of inconsistency or contradiction.

h. We often have an intuitive sense that to change the formal features of a work of art is to make it a different work. There are limits to this, of course: orchestral works may be rewritten for the piano; a Milton Avery painting may be taken as the design for a needlework. But overwhelmingly, Western philosophers prefer to have a single form be definitive. (As noted, both philosophers of art and collectors prefer if in addition to there being only one version, there be only one copy of this privileged version: a preference that we do not insist on in the case of philosophical texts, for instance.) And only if form and meaning or content are inseparable, does it make sense to find, as philosophers often do find, that multiple copies of works of art, such as prints or sculptures, and variations in versions of works such as theatrical and musical performances, are problematic.

In contrast, concepts—ideas that are formulated in language— are understood to be in an important sense independent of their form, of the words used to enclose them. This is what is called the arbitrariness or conventionality of language. That it is valid is born out by the practice of translation from one language to another. This practice is often problematic and perhaps only rarely fully satisfactory, but the frequency with which we resort to it testifies to its general usefulness.

CHAPTER 10

❧

The Signifying Garden: Gardens and Language

These important differences between concepts and artistic ideas—the unspecified range of generalizability of the work of art, its radical individuality, the inseparability of form from content in art, the possibility of translation in language but not in art, and the desire for continued contact with a work of art even after one has come to understand it—all bespeak the most radical divergence between art and language as means of thinking and communicating. Yet given the current propensity to interpret all signifying systems as "language," the comparison seems to warrant close scrutiny.

A. The Analogy of Gardens and Language

Two common features prompt the analogy between gardens and language. First, both gardens and language are regularly used to communicate and are interpreted as meaningful. Second, there are a number of similarities between the two in terms of the ways they encode meaning. Both gardens and language consist of well-established yet extremely flexible arrangements of elements. In both, meaning is constituted on three levels, that is, on the syntactic, the semantic, and the pragmatic level. But these commonalities scarcely justify the correlation of the arrangement of gardens with linguistic syntax, or the assignment of meaning to the elements with linguistic semantics. For the key to the differentiation of gardens from language is this fact: except when they are very closely related, languages are mutually unintelligible; gardens are not. The unintelligibility of languages is due to the fact that the assignment of linguistic meanings is essentially conventional, or as Saussure put it, the relation between signifier and signified is arbitrary. As we will see, this is not the case in gardens.

Language is commonly regarded, especially by nonlinguists, as a highly articulated structure for conveying information. On this view, any such signifying system—including costume[1] and genetic codes[2]—comprises a language, and the important differences between systems are limited to their modes of production—sounds in language and colors, shapes, textures and patterns in clothing. Secondary differences involve the different kinds of information which different systems convey. Costume or tatoos inform the observer of the personality and/or the social identity—rank and origins—of the wearer; barks, tail waggings, and position of ears indicate an animal's feelings or disposition.

I would take issue with this view for the following reasons. Focus on different modes of production makes it easy to overlook the truly radical differences that exist among different systems regarding what can and what cannot be conveyed about the content. It encourages a tendency to imagine that the messages presented in nonverbal systems can all be translated to language as well and that nothing is lost in so doing, and therefore that language gives messages which are essentially the same as the messages in nonverbal systems (except for being perhaps more convenient or otherwise more suitable— matters that are not essential to the nature or content of the message but rather concern the transmission of the message). But the chief differences between language and other semiotic systems concern neither mode of production nor the social ramifications of the transmission but the nature of the message itself. There are several such differences.

B. Differentiation of Language and Gardens:

1. Semantics: The Relation between Signified and Signifier

a. Language: The Arbitrary Nature of the Sign

Since Saussure, the arbitrary nature of the linguistic sign has been recognized as the "first principle" of linguistics and semiotics. "The bond between the signifier and the signified is arbitrary. . . .The idea of "sister" is not linked by any inner relationship to the succession of sounds s-o-r which serves as its signifier in French; that it could be represented equally by just any other sequence is proved by differences among languages and by the very existence of different languages: the signified "ox" has as its signifier b-o-f on one side of

the border and o-k-s (Ochs) on the other."[3] (Although there is some
evidence that certain languages associate certain sounds or sequences
of sounds with a particular range of meaning—In English, for example,
the pattern CC+/er/ ending a verb seems to indicate a trivial action
composed of repeated smaller actions: jabber, chatter, fritter, clutter,
stagger—this kind of association between meaning and sound has been
taken to be the exception rather than the rule; in fact, the very fact
that these associations vary from language to language points up the
essential arbitrariness of the sound-meaning relation.) "Arbitrary"
in this connection means "unmotivated, i.e., arbitrary in that it
actually has no natural connection with the signified." But it does
"not imply that the choice of the signifier is left entirely to the
speaker. . .[for] the individual does not have the power to change a
sign in any way once it has become established in the linguistic
community."[4] In sum, the signifier "though to all appearances freely
chosen with respect to the idea that it represents, is fixed, not free,
with respect to the linguistic community that uses it."[5]

b. Meaning in Art

Langer points out that the situation is completely different in
music and the other arts, where two types of nonarbitrary relations
may be found coexisting. First, the sensuous qualities of the signifier
are appreciated for their own sake and not just in virtue of what they
"mean." (This distinguishes poetic or artistic language usage from
nonartistic usage.) Second, these qualities are arranged and
juxtaposed so as to enable them to enter into dynamic interaction with
the other sensuous qualities within the work. (In general, qualities
outside the work such as colors or musical tones are not expected to
enter into consideration; this is implied by the self-sufficiency of the
work of art.) Significance in art is very different from the kind of
significance (usually called "meaning") found in language. For Langer,
the difference consists in this: while language also has articulate form
(its articulation being what is called syntax), the elements of which
language is composed, its words, are "independent associative symbols
with a reference fixed by convention,"[6] whereas the elements of music
(and by extension the other arts) are not conventional.

c. Meaning in the Garden: Conventional Codes

What is the case with respect to the garden? As in language, the
signifier may be fixed with respect to the community that uses it.

Speaking of Western culture, the authors of *Folklore and Symbolism of Flowers, Plants and Trees* write: "Since antiquity, mythology and religion, folklore and legend, magic and superstitious belief assigned to flowers certain emblematic symbolism. Every bouquet and garland, nosegay and posy, corsage and boutonniere, festoon and wreath was carefully composed according to the legendary meaning. Joy and grief, triumph and woe, admiration and gratitude, love and desire, every human sentiment had its floral emblem."[7]

The language of flowers is one such system of denotative meanings; it was introduced from Persia and swept Europe and America in the eighteenth and nineteenth centuries:

> Selam, the Oriental Language of Flowers, was an old Persian poetical art introduced into Europe by Charles II, king of Sweden, who, after his defeat at Poltava in 1709 by Peter the Great, czar of Russia, fled into exile to Turkey. He lived for five years at the Ottoman court, and returned in 1714 to Sweden, from where his courtiers started the mode of the Flower Language throughout the Western World. There was no more important language for the eighteenth and nineteenth century beaux and belles than the Language of Flowers. *Durch die Blume sprechen*—Speaking through Flowers became a Western proverb, meaning any flowery or poetic expression with a hidden significance or a message of love."[8]

Kate Greenaway's *Language of Flowers*,[9] for instance, is a glossary of one of these "languages," an alphabetical listing of some six hundred flowers and their meanings, from acacia (friendship—but yellow acacia is secret love) and agrimony (thankfulness, gratitude) through balm (sympathy), bay tree (glory), bay wreath (reward of merit), cardamine (paternal error), and deep red carnation (alas! for my poor heart), to yew (sorrow) and zinnia (thoughts of absent friends). Although not all garden traditions assign meanings in this way, many do have such codes, and the codes, like the lexicons of natural languages, are culture-specific. The County Demonstration Garden of the Cornwall Education Committee, for example, glosses a number of plants according to the Roman system.

The most common signifiers are plants, including fruits and flowers, but virtually any element of the garden can be used in this way—watercourses, buildings, paths, land formations like mounts and hills, and decorative motives may also refer beyond themselves. The raked sand of Japanese *kara-sansui* (flat or sand gardens) representing water is just such an arbitrary assignment.

This example shows just how constrained such "conventions" are in the case of gardens, however. What is initially an arbitrary assignment of meaning is reinforced by morphology: the design of the sand "resembles" waves. As an artistic metaphor, however, the respects in which the sand is like water remain unspecified; we are free to generate new parallels. One consequence is this: although the sand is terra firma, it is never walked on; it has come to be perceived as water, and the custom is to behave as if it were water.

These codes are largely arbitrary, although they are often seen as being based on actual similarities between the plant and the quality. But is such assignment truly unmotivated? The simplest cases are probably the emblematic uses, in which a flower or plant is used to refer to a person or country. So Lorenzo de' Medici adopts as his emblem the laurel, by reason of the assonance (strengthened no doubt by the symbolic connotations of the laurel).[10] And in virtue of the French pun on "marguerite" (daisy), the daisy has been adopted as an emblem by half a dozen Margarets: Margaret of Anjou, wife of Henry VI of England; Margaret, the sister of Francis I and her daughter Margaret; Margaret of Flanders (the wife of Philip the Bald of Burgundy); Margaret of Richmond (mother of Henry VII).[11] But while "fixed" and therefore conventional, even these uses are not arbitrary in Saussure's sense: they are not defined solely within a single system but acquire their meanings through the mediation of language (relying on puns) or by historical association.

But in most garden codes the signifier-signified relation is perceived as "natural" in some sense, for one of several reasons. 1) There may be a morphological similarity between signified and signifier, as in the Doctrine of Signatures, or, in the Persian system between the pomegranate or lemon and the breasts; the almond and the eye; and the bamboo, sugarcane, and date palms and the beloved's figure.[12] 2) Other characteristics, particularly aspects of behavior or demeanor, may be perceived as shared by signifier and signified, as happens verbally in metaphor. So in China the bamboo, which bends in the wind and the rain without breaking, comes to stand for strength in adversity, a moral and psychological resilience; the orchid, self-effacement and humility; and both, the Confucian gentleman who embodies these virtues.[13] 3) Such a relation may be further strengthened by literary or historical association. Examples would be the use of dolphins (as a decorative motif on a fountain in an Italian garden) to connote the Just based on the statement of Hermes Trismegistus that the Just become dolphins among the fish.[14]

This leaves us with an important conclusion and an important question. If codes are not arbitrary but constrained, then interpretation across traditions should be possible. And to a large extent it is. Unlike languages, gardens turn out to be universally comprehensible, at least to some degree. The question is whether these usages, however, are not closer to symbols than to signs.

d. Meaning in the Garden: Symbolic Usages

As Saussure points out, "One characteristic of the symbol is that it is never wholly arbitrary; it is not empty, for there is the rudiment of a natural bond between the signifier and the signified. The symbol of justice, a pair of scales, could not be replaced by just any other symbol, such as a chariot."[15] In all the great garden traditions, these rudimentary natural bonds between components/constituents of the garden and their meanings have been further developed in literature and in painting as well as in gardens. And the literary and artistic traditions fully inform the use and interpretation of the signifier in the garden, which is rarely understood as an isolated system, but normally—in Europe, Persia, India, Japan, China—takes its place as part of a system of arts including literature, painting, music, architecture, sculpture, and even including philosophy and history. The use of the signifier carries a vast wealth of connotation that exceeds the normal possibilities of the purely linguistic sign. (By "normal" I mean simply a use that is neither religious nor specifically artistic, either of which would become symbolic.) The "Flower Languages" of Persia and Europe overlap at many points with symbolic uses of flowers and plants, but the two usages are fundamentally distinct and ought not to be confused.

The symbolic use of plants in the garden is closer to the symbolic use of flowers in literature, as described by Barbara Sewar in *The Symbolic Rose,* than it is to the Language of Flowers. In her view, a symbol is

> the concrete embodiment of a conception too intricate, vast, or mysterious to be adequately expressed in any other way. A literary symbol contains within itself a multiplicity of meanings and can therefore be employed to suggest either a complex of concordant ideas or a fundamental harmony beneath apparent discords. Beyond this, the whole is greater than the sum of its parts. The several meanings expressed by the symbol, when these meanings are analyzed in ordinary language, cannot equal the total significance of the symbol.

For an essential aspect of symbolism is the interaction between
elements of form and content to convey a particular emotional effect
that no other combination of sounds and meanings can fully
encompass. . . . For example, the rose that culminates Dante's
Comedy embraces Mary, Paradise, grace, and Divine Love, and at the
same time reconciles these spiritual concepts with the hitherto
opposing concept of terrestrial courtly love. Moreover, in the context
of the work as a whole and in the particular language of its poetry,
these meanings gain associations and emotions impossible to
communicate in our usual words. Such a symbol can clearly be
distinguished from its cousins—the metaphor, simile, image, or
allegorical device—by its exceptional level of complexity. For though
the symbol, like the rest, is in some sense a form of imagery, the
difference in degree if not in kind is marked. A simile presents an
explicit comparison between one thing or concept and another, a
metaphor presents a like comparison implicitly, an image substitutes
identification for comparison, and an allegorical device is most
commonly employed as the vehicle of a single abstract idea. Various
as they are, all four resemble each other and differ from the symbol
in expressing little more than simple, definite correspondences
between two analogous conceptions.[16]

The complexity of the process of learning to read such symbolism
is indicated by a recent attempt by T. C. Lai to familiarize readers
of English with the plant symbolism of China.[17] Unlike the books on
the "Languages of Flowers," this does not merely list the "meanings"
and explain them. Instead, for each plant, Lai provides a selection
of poems, essays, anecdotes, quotations, and reproductions of paintings
that form part of the rich background necessary for interpretation.
Understanding on this level is a matter of living within a certain
context, sharing a culture, and of recognizing the symbolic plant as
an opening to a whole world of symbolic meaning.

I follow C. G. Jung in his contrast between semiotic (linguistic)
meaning, that is, "signs or symptoms of a fixed character," and "true
symbols, i.e., . . . expressions of a content not yet consciously recognized
or conceptually formulated . . . [although] relatively fixed symbols do
exist whose meaning must on no account be referred to anything
known and formulable as a concept."[18] Jung is notorious for his refusal
to give a succinct definition of the symbol, but two examples may
clarify the distinct type of meaning he ascribed to the symbol:

I prefer to regard the symbol as an unknown quantity, hard to
recognize and, in the last resort, never quite determinable. Take, for
instance, the so-called phallic symbols which are supposed to stand
for the *membrum virile* and nothing more. Psychologically speaking,

the *membrum* is itself. . .an emblem of something whose wider content is not at all easy to determine. But primitive people, who, like the ancients, make the freest use of phallic symbols, would never dream of confusing the phallus, as a ritualistic symbol, with the penis. The phallus always means the creative mana, the power of healing and fertility, the "extraordinarily potent,". . .whose equivalents in mythology and in dreams are the bull, the ass, the pomegranate, the yoni, the he-goat, the lightning, the horse's hoof, the dance, the magical cohabitation in the furrow, and the menstrual fluid, to mention only a few of the thousand other analogies. That which underlies all the analogies, and sexuality itself, is an archetypal image whose character is hard to define, but whose nearest psychological equivalent is perhaps the primitive mana-symbol.[19]

Similarly, regarding the symbol "mother," he says:

"Mother" is an archetype and refers to the place of origin, to nature, to that which passively creates, hence to substance and matter, to materiality, the womb, the vegetative functions. It also means the unconscious, our natural and instinctive life, the physiological realm, the body in which we dwell or are contained; for the "mother" is also the matrix, the hollow form, the vessel that carries and nourishes, and it thus stands psychologically for the foundations of consciousness. Being inside or contained in something also suggests darkness, something nocturnal and fearful, hemming one in. These allusions give the idea of the mother in many of its mythological and etymological variants; they also represent an important part of the Yin idea in Chinese philosophy. . . .The word "mother," which sounds so familiar, apparently refers to the best-known, the individual mother—to "my mother." But the mother-symbol points to a darker background which eludes conceptual formulation and can only be vaguely apprehended as the hidden, nature-bound life of the body. Yet even this is too narrow and excludes too many vital subsidiary meanings. The underlying, primary psychic reality is so inconceivably complex that it can be grasped only at the farthest reach of intuition, and then but very dimly. That is why it needs symbols.[20]

A tree or fountain in a garden can serve just such a potent role.

2. Language, Gardens, and the Type/Token Distinction

a. In Language

Another important problem for the comparison of language and gardens is that the type-token distinction pioneered by Peirce cannot be applied in the same way. One notable characteristic of language is that its components—words, letters or characters, sounds—are significant not as unique instances, but merely as tokens of a type. The "a"s on a page are interchangeable, and any given instance of a word is interchangeable with any other instance of the same word.

In semiotic systems, the signs are tokens. One general's star is interchangeable with another.

Even in language, tokens are not always enough. There are times when not just any occurrence of a word will do. But in that case, extralinguistic measures are called for. A signature must be notarized to indicate that this individual instance of the words is attested to.[21]

b. In Gardens

But is a plant in a garden serving as a token of a type? It depends completely on context. In some cases, items do function merely as tokens. In a hedge, or a massed bed, or a lawn, they *must* represent a type—must be a red tulip or a five-foot by two-foot yew or a small yellowish pebble. Should something happen to one of the plants deployed in such a way, it is a simple matter to substitute another of the same type. A deviant from the norm is disciplined or uprooted; individuality is not valued, but eliminated.

In other kinds of plantings, however, this is not the case; the item is valued for its individual qualities as well as for what it shares with others of its kind. This usage is completely opposed to (most uses of) language. In fact, it can hardly be called usage at all since to be used means to be valued for achieving a purpose. This is another kind of relation, love, appreciation, or encounter—Berleant's engagement.

Take rocks. They may be used without regard for their individuality and in such a way as not to draw attention to their individual qualities. On the other hand, in traditional Chinese and Japanese gardens and in some modern Western gardens, they are chosen with great care for their unique qualities. (The landscaping on the campus of the University of Montreal provides outstanding examples.) The same situation prevails on the Arbor Terrace at Dumbarton Oaks with regard to plants. Although a few of the potted plants seem to be mere markers in a pattern—one of four small pots of alyssum, for example—several of the others demonstrate a commanding individuality, particularly the citron and the lantanas. In Japanese gardens, trees are nearly invariably treated as individuals; they are considered irreplaceable (plate 15). Old trees in almost any setting exhibit an outstanding individuality, even where, as at Nyman's in Sussex and an outer garden at Daitokuji (plate 16), they are arranged in avenues and hence are also being used as tokens of their type. In summary, individuals may be used as either tokens of a type or as unique individuals or as both simultaneously. Different types of plantings may draw upon one of these usages at the expense of the other. But the individuality of natural objects and living beings is such that they may break out of the narrow role chosen for them and compel our attention for their unique qualities in spite of the intentions of the gardenist.

But again literature as well as photography singles out the radical individuality, the resistance to reduction to a token, the sheer otherness possible to components of a garden. As Sartre (in *Nausea*) and Nabokov (in *Pnin*) have shown us, even the most familiar and harmless natural object, such as a tree, can become a source of terror when encountered in its full otherness, as a being in its own right.[22] A number of issues are compressed here—whether trees are threatening to us as human beings, and if so, in what sense, and why, and whether they *need* be. Of course threats to human life have had a place in garden design. The gardenists in the late eighteenth century attempted to incorporate into the garden the Sublime, originally understood to inhere in natural rather than domestic landscape and to be incompatible with enclosure and domesticity. The theory of the Sublime[24] found its purest expression in the garden in the works of Sir William Chambers, who advocated the inclusion of symbolic threats and horrific sights. This touched off a vigorous debate with Sir Horace Walpole, who consistently shied away from the Sublime and its intimated threat of death, in spite of his utilization of terror and the implications of death in the arts of literature and architecture—Walpole had single-handedly invented the Gothic novel and brought to full fruition in architecture the Gothic style which until then was merely in bud. Walpole had even ridiculed his favorite gardener, Kent, for having brought dead trees into the garden. Insofar as the garden represents a consistent attempt precisely to control elements which are otherwise beyond our control, the distinction between the garden and the wild can only be one of degree. (The garden is closely related to the Japanese shrine gates (*torii*), the long flights of stone steps, ropes, and the strands of knotted white paper used in Shinto to demarcate parts of the natural environment felt to be of significance [usually numinous trees, water, or rocks.]) While the project of domesticating the Sublime could never be completely successful, given that it is self-contradictory, it is also in a sense unnecessary.

Yet the sublimity of the tree, encountered as Other, is not inevitably a threat (plates 15, 16).[23] Martin Buber outlines another approach, which he, too, contrasts with the normal approach to the tree as a simple object:

> I contemplate a tree.
>
> I can accept it as a picture: a rigid pillar in a flood of light, or splashes of green traversed by the gentleness of the blue silver ground.
>
> I can feel it as movement: the flowing veins around the sturdy, striving core, the sucking of the roots, the breathing of the leaves, the infinite commerce with earth and air—and the growing itself in its darkness.
>
> I can assign it to a species and observe it as an instance, with an eye to its construction and its way of life.
>
> I can overcome its uniqueness and form so rigorously that I recognize it only as an expression of the law—those laws according to which a constant opposition of forces is continually adjusted, or those laws according to which the elements mix and separate.
>
> I can dissolve it into a number, into a pure relation between numbers, and eternalize it.
>
> Throughout all of this the tree remains my object and has its place and its time span, its kind and condition.
>
> But it can also happen, if will and grace are joined, that as I contemplate the tree I am drawn into a relation, and the tree ceases to be an It. The power of exclusiveness has seized me.
>
> This does not require me to forego any of the modes of contemplation. There is nothing that I must not see in order to see, and there is no knowledge that I must forget. Rather is everything, picture and movement, species and instance, law and number included and inseparably fused.
>
> Whatever belongs to the tree is included: its form and its mechanics, its colors and its chemistry, its conversation with the elements and its conversation with the stars—all this in its entirety.
>
> The tree is no impression, no play of my imagination, no aspect of a mood; it confronts me bodily and has to deal with me as I must deal with it—only differently.
>
> One should not try to dilute the meaning of the relation: relation is reciprocity. Does the tree then have consciousness, similar to our

own? I have no experience of that. But thinking that you have brought this off in your own case, must you again divide the indivisible? What I encounter is neither the soul of a tree nor a dryad, but the tree itself.[23]

Different as they are, both Sartre and Buber focus on the encounter with the tree itself rather than as a token of a type which can stand for something else.

3. Language, Gardens, and Time

a. In Language

One of the critical contributions language makes to human consciousness is awareness of time. Different languages structure time in different ways, but all languages are able to differentiate states and events which have not yet happened but either might happen or are expected to happen (the future) from those which have happened in the past and those which are currently in effect or in process. By means of some device such as an adverb or verb tense, the event being discussed is related to the time of utterance. Many languages, English, for example, also articulate this same temporal sequencing with regard to the sequence of events within the utterance—"By the time she got there, he had already left"; "We will have been here an hour." Closely related to these distinctions are linguistic devices for carving out a realm of possibility—conditionals, subjunctives, counterfactuals, and so on.

b. In Other Arts

Many arts, on the other hand, have internal temporality but do not relate the internal time schema to the actual time at which the work is being experienced. In music, dance, drama, mime, the temporality of the work itself is largely unconnected to objective time or our everyday social time. The temporality of the work takes over; the attempt to correlate a dramatic or musical performance with social or objective time by looking at our watches indicates the work is not successful for us.

Visual arts have a noteworthy paucity of temporal dimensions. Without the accompaniment of physical motion, music, or language, it is rare for them to try to represent an internal sequence, though there are of course exceptions. Far Eastern calligraphy is very much a temporal art, perhaps the purest visual image of time we have. It is dependent, however, upon language—not for its content, for its significance is as a spatial image of time, rhythm, and tempi, but to establish the framework of sequence upon which this image rests. In the absence of language, painting and printmaking can convey the depiction of time through the rhythm of individual brushstrokes. Hogarth, it has been argued, depicted the temporality within the scene (the temporal aspects of the process of engraving was largely set aside):

> In contrast to literature, which is primarily a temporal art form, the visual arts have generally been considered spatial forms. Hogarth's art, however, succeeds in incorporating temporal flux and the concepts associated with it, causality and individual identity through time. Indeed the engraver's progresses and a number of his other works can accurately be described as spatial realizations of temporal categories.[25]

It is also very rare for visual arts to establish temporal continuity with the time in which they are viewed. As a material object, the work has (usually) been made before our viewing and it coexists within our present. But there is no internal clue as to whether the depiction is of something which continues to exist, or which existed but exists no longer, or which has never yet existed (and may or may not come into existence). A picture can be about something that happened in the past, but there is no way to identify it as past except through language (either a title or an iconographic identification which we know is past because of general knowledge of the world transmitted largely through language.) This poses a persistent problem for garden historians, for example, since there is no way to ascertain (without corroboratory linguistic evidence) whether a given plan of a garden was drawn of the garden as it was or as it was to be and if the latter, whether it was ever put into effect or not.

(Photographs are an interesting exception here. The time of the event or scene depicted coincides with the time of the photograph. It is therefore always in the past, and it is always of something real, not merely ideal, imaginary, or possible. Yet the photograph, in contrast to language or calligraphy, has only one level of past; it cannot differentiate the various presents of the depiction [the past to the viewer]. This poses a problem for kidnapers, who must force their photographs, which are meant to be evidence regarding the continued existence of the victim in the viewer's present, into a meta-level by means of language, incorporating within the photo a dated magazine cover or newspaper.)

c. In Gardens

Gardens like other visual arts are mute as to past and future and ambiguous as to whether what they represent is ideal or actual. So powerful is this ambiguity that the Assassins could be convinced that the garden they inhabited was Paradise.[26]

A garden may create either a present or a nontemporal (mythic) domain.

It may also speak of the past. But not of the past as past, only as present. That is, it does so only by bringing the evidence of the past into the present. Unlike verbal history which may be described without revealing any relevance to our own present, any relic of the past incorporated into the garden automatically becomes relevant, that is, part of our present. That is why gardens are cherished by cultures which want to maintain or establish connections with their history—Renaissance Italy, China, Augustan England.

A garden may acquire a past of its own, a history. This is often a deeply personal past for its visitors, created from a succession of their experiences.

As we saw in chapter 2, gardens have an internal temporality of their own. The articulation of internal time is very important to them. Where they differ from other arts is that this temporality is continuous with normal, everyday time; we do not take "time out" when we go into a garden. Everything happens at the same tempo as outside. The garden therefore reveals the temporal structure of human living.

4. Mode and Mood

a. In Language

Language is by far the most flexible of systems for expressing subtle distinctions between new and old information. Other systems present old and new information with the same force. Language consistently establishes hierarchies of significance within the information it conveys.

In addition, nearly all nonverbal systems deal with an extremely limited range of topics. The fashion "language," for all its complexity, is inadequate to the discussion of science. The biochemical "language" of genes is restricted to messages about how to put an organism together and keep it functioning. Pictures, insofar as they convey information, often seem to be able to represent anything, but they are notoriously poor at representing abstract concepts; when they do so, they nearly always must resort to allegory, which depends upon the intercession, as it were, of language (often, indeed, with a verbal label). Natural languages, on the other hand, can expand indefinitely to deal with virtually any topic. And any other system, such as symbolic logic, which is to deal with "everything" must be derived from or refer to natural language.

But more importantly, it is not merely a matter of the range of possible topics—what I will call the "capacity" of the language—that distinguishes natural languages from other systems. Language introduces certain possibilities for thinking about those topics, for presenting information, certain "capabilities," that are not otherwise available—possibilities such as time (present, past, future, continuing, or completed, etc.), number, mood, and mode (possibility, impossibility, necessity, contingency). Now, with the exception of language, virtually all communicative systems operate solely within the indicative, within the present. They give information about what is true now—or about what is false *as if* it were true now. A certain type of uniform, for example, identifies a person as a police officer within a particular government; it is the visual equivalent of a verbal statement that "I am a police officer of a certain rank, of a certain country and municipality." Occasionally the message is false, as when a person intending to commit a crime steals and wears such a uniform. But in this case, the message is still in the present tense and indicative, not "If only I were a policeman," or "I might have been a policeman," or "I should be a policeman" or "I used to be a policeman (and I feel I am still entitled to dress as one even though I am no longer on the force)." Indeed, if any of these latter were possible interpretations, there would be no point in the prospective criminal's wearing the uniform, the point of which is to make the statement and use it to facilitate the commission of a crime. The criminal wearing the uniform relies with confidence on the automatic interpretation of the message, with the full force of a present-tense indicative assertion.

The distinction between "is" and "ought" may be felt or perceived without the use of language. We may recognize, prelinguistically, without putting it into words, that, for example, "he ought not to be here." We often have a compelling feeling of this sort, for instance, in dreams unaccompanied by language, where we recognize by our feelings—of dread, of something awful about to ensue—that there is a difference between the way things are (or appear to be) and the way they ought to be.

But language provides the only conceptual tools we have to deal with such a situation. Images are of no use at all.

Yet if a nonverbal expressive-communicative system is truly a language, it ought to be able, first, to deal with the same kinds of issues and information as language deals with, and second, to present them in analogous ways, in spite of their being encoded differently. It ought, in other words, to have the same capacity and similar, if not identical, capabilities.

b. In the Garden

None of these distinctions of mode, mood, tense, etc., can be made via the garden, nor can one make any distinctions equivalent to these. All "statements" made via the garden are straightforward indicative assertions. Moreover, since there is no possibility of questioning through the garden, there is no way, within the medium of the garden, to challenge the assertions it makes. This ought not to be taken as a weakness, however; indeed, it is a strength. The peculiar facility of the garden in this regard is to fuse the actual and the possible, the real and the ideal. To be in a garden is to accept it on its own terms— terms that prove themselves viable in virtue of the fact that it exists and you are there. The garden invariably confirms its message.

This makes gardens extremely rich in ideological possibilities.

5. *Logical Form: Subject, Topic, and Disambiguation*

Artistic ideas are not logical propositions, at least not in the normal sense. The ways in which they differ are not uniform but depend upon the art; music, for instance, would seem to be resistant to being separated into subjects and predicates; in many cases, there would seem to be only happening, no independent substratum to which it is happening. To examine the logical form of each of the various arts would take us far beyond the present work, but we will consider in some detail the differences between language and gardens. Gardens differ from propositions in three ways.

First, gardens are always essentially deictic, that is, without predicative content. They show, but they do not specify. They reveal themselves, what they are like, and they show what something else (say a perceived order, or an ideal world) is like. In this they are something like deictic linguistic utterances. They depend upon context or circumstances for disambiguation.

But gardens do not specify in what respects they are like that something else. It is up to us to infer the points of similarity. They offer a model of the (real or ideal) world, not a list of criteria or points of comparison. This means that perceived criteria can change, and unlike what happens with concepts (for criteria for "justice" and "human being" can change too), this does not necessitate formal or explicit revision of the theory/proposition/concept. This means that gardens require active involvement on our part, something akin to listening but even more fundamental, since no statement is made at all until the viewer actively recognizes in what respects the analogy is being drawn. And this is all the more resistent to analysis because the recognition need not be conscious. (Empson makes a similar point about the recognition of ambiguity in literature.)[27]

Second, gardens as "statements" of ideas have two subjects, the garden itself and whatever it is symbolically referring to, an overt and a covert subject. This is much like metaphor in language, with this difference—the disinterment of the covert subject of a metaphor is usually clear from context—in fact, it is *that* that the discourse is about, not the overt subject (called the "vehicle"). The covert subject (called in metaphor studies the "tenor") can nearly always be readily identified by looking at the sentence preceding (more rarely, following) the metaphor. There is no such formal context for the determination of the covert subject in the case of the garden. The covert and overt subjects in a garden or other work of art are not interchangeable: it is not the case that everything that can be said about the one can be said about the other. Most obviously, the qualities that pertain to the artistic medium do not pertain to the referent or covert subject. "Gloomy Sunday" by Billie Holiday may convey feelings, but nothing of those feelings is slow or fast or depends upon a particular chord.

Third, gardens are inherently ambiguous, in three ways. If we think of the garden as making a statement analogous to the form "y is A," then we see that each of the three elements is independently ambiguous. First, as we have just seen, the subject is ambiguous, as the statements gardens make apply equally to two subjects, the overt and the covert; we depend upon circumstances and the garden itself to discern the covert referent. Second, the ways in which the two subjects are similar, the pertinent aspects of the metaphor, are ambiguous. (See Empson, type 2.) Finally, there is ambiguity as to whether the statement made is an "is" and/or an "ought to be," whether the relation between the subject or referent and the predicate(s) is actual or ideal. This ambiguity is inherent in visual art—which may be why the realistic portrait was such a late development. The distinction between real and ideal is not easy to make without language—language introduced this distinction to thought; visual perception took millenia to catch up—and still can't present the distinction within a work but can only present something on the basis of the distinction as offered by language. (Empson has shown for English literature that it is inherently ambiguous in various ways. This is true also of Japanese literature. Empson suspects it is significantly less true for Italian and French than for English, and he gives the example of translations from English to Latin where an author who is very adept at ambiguous adumbration of his English sentences drops them when he moves to Latin. This suggests that 1) ambiguity is not necessarily essential to all artistic ideas, at least on the syntactic and semantic levels, since it appears not to be essential to some literary art; 2) some language is purposely ambiguous, and hence nonlogical—or multilogical? It is hardly necessary to point this out to linguists and literary scholars, but it becomes a problem in writing for philosophers, who sometimes approach language as if it were logical in the philosophical sense—or can (i.e., should) be cleaned up easily and then everything will "be all right.")

C. Conclusions

We may conclude, then, that gardens are meaningful in ways that are fundamentally and importantly different from language. The comparison between gardens and language is trivial and misleading. If gardens are to give form to ideas of any sort, they must do so in ways that are quite distinct from the ways employed by language. If this much is true, then art has a unique relation to knowledge and a crucial role to play in its formulation and dissemination, parallel to, yet distinct from, language.

CHAPTER 11

❧

The Garden as Great Art:
The Presentation of Artistic Ideas

If, as I have maintained, art is Significant Form, that is, form which articulates an idea, and if the garden is to be considered art, then it must exhibit Significant Form.[1] But if, in addition, we mean by "idea" the determinate idea (as we usually do with ideas), then gardens are in trouble, on two counts. First, as we have seen, when the work of art changes as much as gardens do, it is hard, if not specious, to attribute to it a determinate form, let alone to infer from that a determinate idea. Second, when the artist is only one of two partners with equally decisive roles, when the other is not a human being but nature, it hardly seems accurate or useful to call the form the product of an idea. Does nature have ideas about what she wants when she dries up the stand of bamboo one's been nursing for three years? The human gardenist, of course, may have an idea which she strives to formulate. In a generous climate and with a well-informed idea of what can be done with given materials, she may succeed.

Is any such success more than a compromise, however, given that it must be based on a recognition of one's limitations, the limitations of the site, and of plants themselves? Is any garden fully a success? The one thing practical gardeners seem agreed on is that no garden is ever finished.

In spite of these difficulties, careful examination of gardens will suggest that they are indeed designed to articulate ideas and are understood as doing so. If the idea is broad enough to tolerate a bit of unintentional change without doing harm to the idea, or if the changes in the garden can be adequately controlled, then the idea(s) will emerge, and quite clearly.

171

A. Gardens and the Idea of Plenty

Most common is the idea of plenty, of a domain of peace and tranquility, of everlasting spring, of freedom from hunger and cold and heat and want and fear. Many gardens are based on this idea, particularly those in harsh climates like the New Orleans courtyards discussed in chapter 3. More generally, in Europe, the European-influenced Americas, and the Middle East, gardening has been suffused with the ideals encapsulated in the complementary images of the Garden of Eden and Paradise.

Referring to the court of the fifteenth- and sixteenth-century dukes of Burgundy, Roy Strong states that "the medieval *hortus conclusus,* the enclosed garden of the Virgin's chastity, was developed as a potent symbol of the reality of happiness."[2] Such a garden takes a concept, "happiness," and by its *form* adds a) the predicates (happiness consists of this and this and this, or is like this and this and this), b) the existential predicate ("there is happiness"), and c) the modal specification—not "happiness could be thus" but "happiness is possible." I have argued elsewhere that gardens are used by the illustrators of the book *The Emperor of China's Palace at Pekin...*[3] to make the claim that a certain kind of ideal *society* (just, fair, secular, etc., on the Chinese model) is possible on earth.[4] These two examples, and others such as Versailles, suggest that in at least some cases the force of the garden may lie more in the assertion that a given idea is realizable, or already pertains, than in the expression or elaboration of the idea itself.

B. Gardens and Ideas of "Home"

There is also the peculiar—and extremely labor-intensive and expensive—concern with re-creating in a new location the vegetative and topological environment associated with "home." This, of course, was the point of the Hanging Gardens of Babylon, but it is no less attention-getting in the deserts of the American Southwest, where immigrants from the Midwest and New England try to maintain lawns in the desert. One of the earliest Renaissance-style formal gardens in England was built at the request of a homesick queen from France. It is not always the political and historical past that is being re-created; often it is the personal past of an individual. Makers of gardens often talk about how they are trying to re-create in their adult gardens the gardens they remember from their childhood.

C. Gardens and Ideas of Time

Another very common class of ideas formulated by gardens is ideas of time. As we have seen, the relations between works of art and time are extremely complex. This is particularly true of the garden, whose elements live and change in both cyclical and historical dimensions of time. In addition, however, the garden may be designed and used to articulate a particular idea of time—a particular view of the relation between past and present, for example. Historical time is made available to us by gardens in two entirely different, almost unrelated ways.

In historic reconstruction and preservation, a notable garden that has been preserved intact or that has been reconstructed, like the gardens at Versailles, Het Loo, Williamsburg, and Monet's at Giverny, is being used to make accessible to modern experience something (often a good deal) of the experience of those who lived under entirely different historical circumstances. It is an attempt to re-create this past, often for its own sake, as something independent of the present that deserves cherishing, not only for the experiences it makes possible but for the knowledge it can contribute about that past. Such a garden takes for granted not only the presence of historical consciousness but the existence of a fairly sophisticated historiographic tradition as well.

Not all gardens operate within such a framework: some take upon themselves the project (shared admittedly with other arts and sciences) of the generation of historical consciousness and the delineation of patterns of relevence of the past to the present, the intertwining of past and present, or of the infusion or situation of the present within a past. This is not unique to gardens; it happens in other arts as well. It sometimes happens, for instance, that a work of art is formed to continue the present within a favored past, to expand the (present generation's) definition of the past in such a way as to make evident the "fact" that the present is included in the past. Here the work of art is put to the task of dissolving or obscuring the distinctions between past and present that might otherwise be apparent. And it can completely succeed at this—so completely that the very possibility of using the work to gain knowledge of the past as an era distinct from our own is overlooked in our dependence upon it to create a present. Such a practice can completely alter our apprehension of the present. This process is seen in the complex interweavings of Chinese painting, poetry, calligraphy, and garden design. A painting will be done "in the style of" the artist Wang Wei or Ma Yuan or Chao

Meng-fu; the full stylistic individuality of the alluded artist is not attempted, but some aspect which is commonly recognized as being part of his style is utilized to designate him, leaving the current painter a good deal of elbow room for his own individuality to come through. Yet in his visual and verbal allusions to the earlier artist, he evokes a past meant to inform the present, and to convey to that present some of the legitimation and authority of the past. Similarly, stone markers in a garden will be carved in the calligraphic style of the ancients; a garden pavilion will be named by a literary quotation or after a famous party. The styles of the pavilions themselves recall the huts well known from paintings, and so art helps to re-create a landscape of the past made familiar through painting. Entire gardens are developed to this effect in China.[5]

A similar process is at work in the English landscape gardens of the eighteenth century, although sometimes for entirely different purposes. The Englishmen on the Grand Tour in Italy saw the remains of the ancient Roman monuments; in the attempt of the Opposition Whigs to establish post-Revolutionary England politically on the model of Republican Rome, they built models of these elegant monuments on a small scale within their own estates, re-creating the landscape within which to live a similar life based on republican virtue. So the garden at Stowe re-creates in the present the landscape of the Roman Republic. (Not all Augustan landscape gardens were built to this effect. A somewhat different process took place at Stourhead, where Henry Hoare built a classical landscape, along picturesque rather than political lines, but evidently with the aim of constructing a monument to his son who died young.) And coexisting with the republican gardens of this period were gardens which sought to re-create the Gothic past. As the landscape garden evolved toward the picturesque style after midcentury, the landscape imitated was less the Roman civic landscape, based on architecture because it was a particular kind of political culture that was desirable, than a natural landscape, a countryside of a particular type, given to certain effects of light and certain kinds of crags and trees. In this later type, the art which was the basis for the derived English landscape was no longer solely architecture but poetry and painting, although architecture remained a salient feature.[6]

How much is this allusion, how much illusion? How much is it based on a sort of magical thinking: if we re-create the environment of a certain kind of life, we can ourselves live that sort of life within it? Did the designer of such a garden mean to become a certain kind of man, to acquire the virtues of a citizen of the Roman Republic by living in a similar environment? At first this hypothesis seems preposterous, and yet it gains credibility given the fact that the experiment was repeated elsewhere: in Newport, Rhode Island, whose late nineteenth-century millionaires built mansions like Rosecliffe and The Elms explicitly copying the chateaux of the pre-Revolutionary French aristocracy. In one case, the motto and insignia of Napolean ("the laurel of victory and the industrious bee") were adopted by the master of the house. A comparison was being drawn, and we may assume it was hoped that a similar life was being lived. There is an implicit assertion that "we are like they were" (though presumably stopping short of accepting a similar end) and an attempt to command similar respect which was probably fairly successful, at least within their own circle.

In such cases the creation of a totemic environment is meant to enable the inhabitants to emulate others who have lived in such an environment, much as the wearing of ceremonial lion skins or eagle feathers or bear claws effects an identification between a member of a hunting-gathering tribe and the animal and assures him its courage and strength. The difference between the so-called "primitive" and the modern sophisticate (and all of those whom we are discussing here are highly educated, wealthy, and politically powerful) is that the "primitive" relies on being in physical contact with a part of the animal with which he identifies, the sophisticate on a dual process of both acquiring special antique or commemorative objects from the persons with whom one identifies (or others like them) and on living within an environment "like" that of the human beings with whom he identifies. (The tribe-member, of course, shares with his totem figure an actual-cum-symbolic environment.)

The "cottage-garden" movement which took wing in England in the nineteenth century was also based on an effort to re-create the past. Here it was the homely, simple virtues of the English freeman and cottager which were being honored. Evidence is, however, that earlier English cottagers never did have such gardens and that certainly the plants which were being praised and planted were recent acquisitions.[7] As we've seen in other contexts, buildings are more reliable evidence of the past (and especially of their own past) than are gardens. The Gothic landscape is more accurately depicted by Gothic-style buildings than by plantings.

The reworking of one's physical relation to the land by the symbolic means of the creation of a garden raises important questions about our relation to land and about the potential of land itself to empower us. What does it mean to re-create one's environment in terms which incorporate or instantiate a particular view of one's (and one's people's) past—thereby completely redefining the present? Do the individuals who create these gardens—and thus acquire power—act solely for themselves, or as part of a family or class/clan to which they belong—or on behalf of society as a whole?

CHAPTER 12

✿

Conclusions:
Gardens and the Theory of Art

It will be evident, I am sure, that this book was written not as the definitive philosophical statement on gardens, not to solve once and for all the question of the artistic status of gardens, but as a beginning, making suggestions as to some issues which need attention, in the hope of stirring things up among philosophers and among those who care either about gardens or about the arts. I hope it raises more questions than it answers. In particular, I would like to stir up philosophical study of the significance and signifying means and processes of particular gardens and styles.

If what I have claimed about gardens in the preceeding chapters is true, then gardens have been in an important sense constitutive of social and personal reality. Their precise roles in this constitution have differed in different contexts. Different styles have addressed entirely different issues or have fostered different approaches to the same issues.

This has important, and I think overly neglected, implications for art in general. If gardens are an art, then (at least) some art is constitutive of reality, whatever else it is or does. Art constitutes not just that part of the world which it comprises but parts of the outer world as well, and it teaches us the range of possible responses open to us. Ways of knowing, ways of perceiving, ways of representing and appropriating our world, of recognizing others in our societies and our very selves, of making possible social intercourse of various kinds—these can be strongly influenced by gardens, and by other arts.[1]

Recognition of the arts as basic to the constitution of reality poses a serious challenge to the hegemony of language. For if art has these capacities, then the limits of my language are not the limits of my world.

Precisely because the arts signify in ways that are so radically different from language, art occupies a unique place in relation to knowledge and to consciousness—and gardens occupy a unique place among the arts.

Gardens present their illusions with a strength of conviction that is unique among the arts. This peculiar conviction is derived most importantly from the fact that they are demonstrably successful in a special way: they are—like us—alive. This fact, along with several other features—their vulnerability to their environment, their inability to express negation, the commensurability of their temporal and spatial scales with those of normal everyday life—make the illusions presented by gardens more compelling than those of many other arts, and less easily distinguished from reality itself.

Garden styles may differ considerably from one another, so much so that their motivation may be unintelligible (remember Pope and the formal garden). But underlying the stylistic and cultural variation and the conventional codes of assigned meanings, there is a solid foundation of shared ("universal") comprehensibility and preferences, based on the nature of our relation as biological organisms to our environment and subsequently on the structure of human cognition, especially environmental cognitive processing. We understand unfamiliar garden styles far better than we understand unfamiliar languages; if we don't like them, as we often don't, it is usually because we don't accept the ideas or illusions (again in Langer's sense) they present.[2] Such a "universalist" claim, I realize, runs against the current of contemporary thought, but it is important nonetheless.

If gardens are works of art, as it now seems they are, and if they are sometimes great works of art, they are so in spite of the fact that they do not fit our definitions of art. Theories of art have tended to be prescriptive rather than descriptive, embodying modernist biases and preferences and helping to inculcate disinterest and distance as customary ways of seeing, knowing, and relating to the world. Gardens point up the absurdity of a number of distinctions which continue to lie close to the heart of aesthetic theory, long after they have been abandoned by much of the practicing art world. In particular, the garden, by providing an environment for experience rather than an object of experience, collapses the very foundation of modern aesthetic theory, aesthetic disinterest/distance, or the subject-object dichotomy. With it go concomitant notions of sharp distinctions between art and craft, fine and applied arts, and the utilitarian and the aesthetic.

A tendency toward naive realism has prevailed in philosophical aesthetics, a tendency which accepts, and even helps to guarantee, a fallacious but convincing and comfortable taken-for-grantedness of the world, an apparent naturalness, without recognition of the facts that our realities are constructed, are not the same for everyone, and are not even the same for us at different times. Not only "common-sense" attitudes but the modern philosophical enterprise itself help to cover up this process at least as often as they disclose it.

Buttressing this has been an oversimplification of the purposes and functioning of art, which originates in philosophical bias. When Kant strove to account for the apparent universality of the aesthetic, and located it in distance/disinterest or the absence of instrumentality, he gave to instrumentality too concrete a focus. The aesthetic attitude is distinguished from our normal attitude, in which the object is perceived in its capacity to accomplish some purpose of ours; subsequently art has even come to be defined as that activity for which no end is known in advance. But the ends in terms of which instrumentality and the aesthetic are to be distinguished are tangible and specific—tools, objects of lust and hunger, and other forms of immediate desire; on the less tangible side, persuasive or commanding language, and so on. This omits from our examination a whole spectrum of ways in which things serve some function which is vague or less well understood or unsuspected or unacknowledged. Not only the end but the means by which it is to be achieved may be vague. When we take as our end a better life in some sense not yet well understood, or the articulation of a greater or more subtle sense of personal agency or responsibility, or a more self-reliant or consistent self, or a more firmly defined society, our sense of instrumentality may be extremely attenuated. Art is very well suited to the elucidation and adumbration of such emerging experiences, insights, and concepts. Precisely where ends and the means to them are well understood and well established, art fades away, technology and craft in the most instrumental sense take over. Kant has deflected our attention to the two extremes of instrumentality and disinterest, at the expense of the vast middle range that forms the bulk of our experience, and particularly our experience with art.

To be sure, there are good artistic reasons for separating art from even this sort of instrumentality: moralizing literature, propagandist drama or painting, tend to be boring and obvious. They are rarely successful in artistic terms. But this is not because ("good" or "true" or "pure") art serves no purpose but because its very purpose is discovery and exploration and elucidation—the clarification and adumbration and elaboration of the as-yet-but-vaguely intuited.

A philosophy of art which covers up or ignores such purposes cannot be useful except as a form of ideology, an obfuscation, a means to the perpetuation of alienation. When theory insists upon distance and disinterest as a precondition for art and the aesthetic, then art and the aesthetic become means of alienation and objectification. It is time to bring gardens back into the company of the arts and to accept the challenge that their inclusion poses for our understanding of the other arts as well.

Notes

Chapter 1.

1. A number of excellent studies of this kind have been made, especially in the past two decades, and I have made extensive use of them, but their questions are not those of this book.

2. An exception to this general *modus operandi* is provided by two recent books on aesthetics, Arnold Berleant's *Art and Engagement* (Philadelphia: Temple University Press, 1991) and Richard Wollheim's *Painting as an Art* (Bollingen Series 35. 33, Princeton, N.J.: Princeton University Press, 1987).

3. See Frederick P. Bargebuhr, *The Alhambra: A Cycle of Studies on the Eleventh Century in Moorish Spain* (Berlin: Walter de Gruyter & Co., 1968), esp. chap. 2.D., "The Court of Lions."

4. The words "yard" and "garden" have the same root.

5. Dorothy Kent Hill, "Roman Domestic Architecture," in Dumbarton Oaks *Colloquium on the History of Landscape Architecture* (7th: 1979), *Ancient Roman Gardens*, Elisabeth B. MacDougall and Wilhelmina F. Jashemski, eds. Washington, D.C.: Dumbarton Oaks and the Trustees of Harvard University, 1981, p. 85.

6. Bertolt Brecht, *The Good Person of Setzuan*, trans. Ralph Manheim, Washington, D.C.: Arena Stage Production, 1985.

7. Edith Wharton, *Italian Villas and their Gardens* (New York: Century Co., 1904), p. 46.

8. The astute reader will detect the occasional note of bitterness creeping into the text, the result of the author's experiments, so to speak.

9. David A. Slawson, *Secret Teachings in the Art of Japanese Gardens: Design Principles, Aesthetic Values* (New York and Tokyo: Kodansha International, 1987).

Chapter 2.

1. It may well be that the development of gardens from the practical and ritual space of agriculture and religion to more elaborated space as art is dependent upon the preexistence of a body of lyric nature poetry.

2. *The Gulistan or Rose Garden of Sa'di,* trans. Edward Rehatsek (New York: G. P. Putnam's Sons, 1964); *The Secret Garden: An Anthology in the Kabbalah,* David Meltzer, ed. (New York: Seabury Press, 1976).

3. Interestingly, we do not seem to have appropriated the concept of dropping one's leaves—whether because periodic death is not part of our life cycle (pace Eliade and *From Ritual to Romance*) or because our more characteristic preparation for lean and bitter times lies more with squirrels and grasshoppers and ants, I cannot say.

4. T. C. Lai, *Noble Fragrance: Chinese Flowers and Trees,* (Kowloon and Hong Kong: Swindon Book Co., 1977), p. 150.

5. Lai, p. 100.

6. Lu Kuei-meng: "Preface to a Eulogy on a Grotesque Pine," qtd. in T. C. Lai, p. 7, 8–9.

7. Liu Yen-fu: "Planting Bamboos," in T. C. Lai, p. 48, 50.

8. *Richard II:* act 3, sc. 4, 11–25ff.

9. *Othello,* act 1, sc. 3.

10. From *Captain Hume's Musical Humours: The First Part of Ayres, French, Pollish, and others together, some in tabliture, and some in Prickesong. . .* (London: 1604). I am indebted to Brent Wissick for bringing this to my attention through an enchanting performance of this song at the Aston Magna Academy, 1987.

11. Cao Xueqin. *The Story of the Stone* (China: 1792; trans. David Hawkes, Harmondsworth, Middlesex, England: Penguin, 1975).

12. (1809; trans. Elizabeth Mayer and Louise Bogan [Chicago: Henry Regnery Co., 1963]).

13. Murasaki Shikibu, *The Tale of Genji,* trans. Edward G. Seidensticker (New York: Alfred A. Knopf, 1977), pp. 215–16.

14. Ibid., p. 217.

15. Ibid., p. 100.

16. Quoted in John Harvey, *Mediaeval Gardens* (London: B. T. Batsford, 1981), p. 6.

17. Potted cactus is a conceptual art. The enjoyment some find in cactus is not in being warned or threatened, which would be dire, but in the fact that it encourages us to feel it imaginatively without experiencing the pain.

18. Derek Plint Clifford, *A History of Garden Design* (New York: Praeger, 1963; rev. ed., 1966); Wilhelmina Mary Feemster Jashemski, *The Gardens of Pompeii, Herculaneum, and the Villas destroyed by Vesuvius* (New Rochelle, N.Y.: Caratzas Bros., 1979). Eugene C. Hargrove argues for the importance of purely aesthetic considerations to the general environment and sees environmental beauty, which he views as an intrinsic value, as foundational to environmental ethics; see *Foundations of Environmental Ethics* (Englewood Cliffs, New Jersey: Prentice Hall, 1989).

19. Harvey, p. xi.

20. Again as with the grand/humble distinction, size has an impact: the cherry orchard has greater self-sufficiency than the pot of chives; in other words, its effects are less easily ignored, and the viewer need not make as great an effort to take delight in it.

21. People do, of course, sometimes plant gardens (as opposed to farms) to *save* money, but a) this doesn't mean they in fact do save money, and b) this very gesture may in the right circumstances reveal economic status or some complex social/economic attitude.

22. Anne Scott-James, *The Cottage Garden* (Harmondsworth, Middlesex, England: Penguin, 1982), p. 27.

23. See, for example, Mavis Batey, "The Way to View Rousham by Kent's Gardener," *Garden History*, 2, no. 2 (Autumn 1983).

24. Gerald van der Kemp, "Claude Monet and his Garden," in *The Gardens at Giverny*, Stephen Shore, ed., (Millerton, N.Y.: Aperture, 1983).

25. Paige Rense, ed., "Hilo Estate on the Island of Hawaii," in *Gardens: Architectural Digest* (Los Angeles: Knapp Press, 1983), pp. 132–37.

26. Rense, pp. 138–43.

27. David Marshall, "Figures in the Landscape." Paper read at a symposium on "Land and Landscape in the Eighteenth Century," April 1982, Yale Center for British Art.

28. Examples may be found in the British Museum and the Metropolitan Museum of Art in New York.

29. Florence Lee Powell, *In the Chinese Garden* (New York: John Day Company, 1943).

30. Interestingly such handscrolls rarely focus on the experience of a garden alone—perhaps because the experience of a garden is essentially

three-dimensional space from the East Asian point of view. Landscape handscrolls are always of natural landscape or a garden as a single scene within a natural landscape.

31. Susanne K. Langer, *Feeling and Form: A Theory of Art* (New York: Charles Scribner's Sons, 1953), pp. 88–9.

32. This was the response evoked from a Washington, D.C. businessman under whom I was employed as an office "temp" in an attempt to fight "cabin fever" while finishing my dissertation. My immediate supervisor introduced me to him as someone who was writing on the philosophy of gardens. He paused a moment and asked, "Philosophy of gardens? You want to know my philosophy of gardens? You plant 'em and they die."

33. Richard A. Etlin, *The Architecture of Death* (Cambridge: Massachusetts Institute of Technology Press, 1984).

34. This is not quite true: there are two such gardens, or parts of gardens: the Italian Bomarzo, north of Rome, and the Temple of Modern Virtue at Stowe. And they can become ludicrous, as Pope showed in the "Epistle to Lord Burlington" (in *The Poems of Alexander Pope: a one-volume edition of the Twickenham text with selected annotations*, John Butt, ed. (London: Methuen & Co., 1963; corrected 1968)—but only unintentionally. Yet these possibilities which I have just excluded may have to be reconsidered in the light of Jane Owen's recent *Eccentric Gardens* (New York: Villarel Books, 1990), which suggests that the postmodern period may usher in not only new kinds of garden design but new stances, modes, or attitudes.

35. Well illustrated and discussed by Peter S. Beagle, *The Garden of Earthly Delights* (New York: Viking Press, 1982).

Chapter 3.

1. See Stephen Kaplan and Rachel Kaplan, eds., *Humanscape: Environments for People* (North Scituate, Mass.: Duxbury Press, 1978) selections in sections 4 ("Caring"), 8 ("Coping Strategies: Choice and Control"), and 9 ("Coping Strategies: Interpretation"), and "Coping and Cognition" and "Problem Solving and Planning" in *Cognition and Environment: Functioning in an Uncertain World* (New York: Praeger, 1982).

2. Robert Sommer, *Personal Space: The Behavioral Basis of Design* (Englewood Cliffs, N.J.: Prentice-Hall, 1969).

3. For a discussion of the relation between houses and gardens and of the establishment of social territory in England, see Mark Girouard, *Life in the English Country House* (New Haven: Yale University Press, 1978; New York: Penguin Books, 1980).

4. Humphrey Repton, in *The Art of Landscape Gardening, by Humphrey Repton, esq.*, including his "Sketches and Hints on Landscape Gardening" and "The Theory and Practice of Landscape Gardening," ed. John Nolan (Boston, New York: Houghton Mifflin & Co., 1907), p. 7.

5. Repton, p. 14.

6. By "world" I mean here that part of the universe which is known or imaginable to a given human being or society.

7. Of course, this is not invariably the case. There are island societies in the Pacific, for example, in which the whole world has been transformed, according to human vision and to accommodate human needs, in such a way that the very concept of garden, as a term of contrast to the rest of the world (either the wilderness or the city) is rendered meaningless.

8. This is not to argue of course that virtuality is a sufficient condition for art or that it is restricted to art.

9. Susan Sontag, *On Photography* (New York: Farrar, Straus and Giroux; paperback ed., Dell Publishing Co., 1978), pp. 105–6.

10. Other arts utilize human beings as performers. But in these cases, what the performers require of their environment is little more than what they would require in any case, even if they were not creating art. The situation is therefore neither as complex nor as compelling as with gardens.

11. The problem of course is one that Aristotle addressed regarding tragedy in his *Poetics*, namely how can the artist ensure that his message carries conviction, that the audience will extrapolate beyond the work itself? His solution there, to use historical characters, is based upon the same principle: in essence "if it is/was alive (and happened this way), it is a true model."

12. But not all biological features work against differentiation and toward universalization in gardens. One feature which accentuates diversity is climate. It is true that climate may be ignored during stylistic obsessions. The English built grottoes; the French hammered out lawns. But there can be no question but that climate provides the overarching values defining the unity of the various garden styles. There are few gardens without fountains in the hot or dry climates—Spain, Italy, Persia, New Orleans.

13. Classic studies in psychology have shown that processes such as perception and memory differ in important ways depending on whether they are in controlled laboratory situations or in "naturalistic" or "real-life" environments. See for example E. J. Gibson, *Principles of Perceptual Learning and Development* (1969); J. J. Gibson, *An Ecological Approach to Visual Perception* (Ithaca, N.Y.: Cornell University Press, 1976); Ulric Neisser, *Cognition and Reality: Principles and Implications of Cognitive Psychology* (San Francisco: W. H. Freeman & Co., 1976) and *Memory Observed:*

Remembering in Natural Contexts (San Francisco: W. H. Freeman & Co., 1982); and *Perceiving, Acting and Knowing: Toward an Ecological Psychology*, ed. Robert Shaw and John Bransford (Hillsdale, N.J.: Lawrence Erlbaum Assocs., 1977).

14. There is a certain irony to our claim that the same kinds of processing that placed a premium on knowledge without contemplation should have led to the development of the garden, whose connection with contemplation is ancient, universal, and well explored. (See Terry Comito, *The Idea of the Garden in the Renaissance* (New Brunswick, N.J.: Rutgers University Press, 1978); Eliot Deutsch, "An Invitation to Contemplation: The Rock Gardens of Ryoanji and the Concept of *Yugen*" in *Studies in Comparative Aesthetics*, Monograph no. 2 of the Society for Asian and Comparative Philosophy (Honolulu: University Press of Hawaii, 1975); A. Bartlett Giamatti, *The Earthly Paradise and the Renaissance Epic* (Princeton, N.J.: Princeton University Press, 1966); Maggie Keswick, *The Chinese Garden: History, Art and Architecture*, especially chap. 4, "The Gardens of the Literati," (London: Academy Editions and New York: St. Martin's Press, 1978, 1986); Maynard Mack's study of the dialectics of retirement and involvement in the life of Alexander Pope, *The Garden and the City: Retirement and Politics in the Later Poetry of Pope*, (Toronto, 1969); Edwin T. Morris, *The Gardens of China: History, Art, and Meanings* (New York: Charles Scribner's Sons, 1983); and Michael O'Loughlin, *The Garlands of Repose: The Literary Celebration of Civic and Retired Leisure: The Traditions of Homer and Vergil, Horace and Montaigne* (Chicago, 1978).) It may be that as environments grow increasingly complex, allowing less and less time for contemplation before action, the garden is invented as a necessary complement.

15. Stephen Kaplan and Rachel Kaplan, eds., *Humanscape*, pp. 5–6.

16. Kaplan and Kaplan, *Humanscape*, p. 147; see also S. Kaplan, "Cognitive maps, human needs, and the designed environment," in *Environmental Design Research*, ed. W. F. E. Preiser (Stroudsberg, Pa.: Dowden, Hutchinson and Ross, 1973).

17. Ibid.

18. Naomi Miller's study *Heavenly Caves: Reflections on the Garden Grotto*, (New York: George Braziller, 1982) treats caves and water. Similarities in the English tradition between natural landscape, garden design, and landscape preference as evidenced in painting have been the focus of a number of scholarly studies. See I. W. U Chase, *Horace Walpole: Gardenist. An Edition of Walpole's 'The History of the Modern Taste in Gardening', with an Estimate of Walpole's Contribution to Landscape Architecture* (Princeton, N.J.: Princeton University Press, 1943); Louis Hawes, *Presences of Nature* (New Haven: Yale Center for British Art, 1982); Elizabeth Wheeler Manwaring, *Italian Landscape in Eighteenth Century England: A Study Chiefly of the Influence*

of Claude Lorrain and Salvator Rosa on English Taste, 1700–1800 (New York: Oxford University Press, 1925); David Watkin, *The English Vision: The Picturesque in Architecture, Landscape and Garden Design* (New York: Harper & Row, 1982).

19. Kaplan and Kaplan, *Humanscape*, pp. 148–49. For a more detailed discussion of mystery, see also R. Kaplan, "Predictors of Environmental Preference: Designers and 'Clients,'" in *Environmental Design Research*, and "Down by the Riverside: Informational factors in waterscape preference," in *Proceedings of river recreation management and research symposium* (North Central Forest Experiment Station, Forest Service, USDA, 1977), and S. Kaplan, "An Informal Model for the Prediction of Preference" in *Landscape Assessment* ed. E. H. Zube, R. O. Brush, and J. G. Fabos (Stroudsberg, Pa., 1975).

20. J. D. Balling and J. H. Falk, *Environment and Behavior,* 14, no. 5 (1982).

21. See L. Partridge, *Animal Behavior,* 24, 534 (1976); L. Partridge, in *Behavioral Ecology: An Evolutionary Approach* ed. J. R. Krebs and N. B. Davies (Sunderland, Mass.: Sinauer, 1978); and S. C. Wecker, *Ecological Monographs* 33, 307 (1963).

22. Falk and Balling, "Evolutionary Influence on Human Visual Preference." Unpublished paper.

23. See D. Stroud, *Capability Brown* (London: Faber & Faber, 1975); Roger Turner, *Capability Brown and the Eighteenth-century English Landscape* (New York: Rizzoli International, 1985); E. Hyams, *Capability Brown and Humphrey Repton* (London: J. M. Dent & Sons, 1971); Humphrey Repton, *The Art of Landscape Gardening.*

24. For the impact of English landscape gardening on the design of modern cemeteries, see Richard A. Etlin, *The Architecture of Death* (Cambridge: Massachusetts Institute of Technology Press, 1984).

25. G. Orians, *The Evolution of Human Social Behavior* J. S. Lockard, ed. (Amsterdam: Elsevier, 1980), p. 49.

Chapter 4.

1. Part of this chapter was published as "Gardens as Works of Art: The Problem of Uniqueness," in *British Journal of Aesthetics*, 26, no. 3, (Summer 1986) pp. 252–56.

2. Stephanie Ross, "Ut Hortus Poesis—Gardening and her Sister Arts in Eighteenth-Century England," *The British Journal of Aesthetics*, 25, no. 1, (Winter 1985), pp. 17–32.

3. George Dickie, *Art and the Aesthetic* (Ithaca, N.Y.: Cornell University Press, 1974), p. 34; or, as poet E. Ethelbert Miller puts it, "A poem is anything you want it to be, anything you can get away with." Quoted by Patrice Gaines-Carter, *The Washington Post Magazine*, February 3, 1985, p. 10.

4. There are other, more generally relevant problems with the institutional theory, such as its circularity, but these, having been analyzed elsewhere, need not concern us here.

5. There are exceptions, to be sure. For example, I gather from the signage that at least some people go to botanical gardens in order to get information about plants.

6. Monroe Beardsley, "Redefining Art," in *The Aesthetic Point of View: Selected Essays* (Ithaca, N.Y.: Cornell University Press, 1982), p. 306.

7. Beardsley, p. 304.

8. Nelson Goodman, *Languages of Art: An Approach to a Theory of Symbols* (Indianapolis and Cambridge: Hacket Publishing Co., 1976).

9. That these practices which are so problematic in the Western context may legitimately coexist with the highest quality of fine art is shown by any number of non-Western cases such as Chinese painting.

10. Alexander Pope, "Epistle to Burlington", 11.57–64, in *The Poems of Alexander Pope: a one-volume edition of the Twickenham text with selected annotations*, ed. John Butt (London: Methuen & Co., 1963; corrected 1968).

11. See Peter L. Hornbeck, "The Garden as Fine Art; Its Maintenance and Preservation," in Dumbarton Oaks Colloquium on the History of Landscape Architecture, *Beatrix Jones Farrand (1872–1959): Fifty Years of American Landscape Architecture* (Washington, D.C.: Dumbarton Oaks, Trustees for Harvard University, 1982).

12. Walter Ong, *Orality and Literacy*, (London: Methuen & Co., 1982); see also Albert B. Lord, *The Singer of Tales*, in Harvard Studies in Comparative Literature, 24 (Cambridge: Harvard University Press, 1960).

13. Of course, literal identity only becomes a matter of concern 1) if notation is available and 2) if your values have been heavily shaped by literacy.

14. From a lecture on Bridgeman by Clarke before the Garden History Society on September 16, 1981; reported in R. J. Bisgrove, *Newsletter*, no. 4, of the Garden History Society, September 1982, p. 13.

15. From conversation with gardeners.

16. James Cahill, "Confucian Elements in the Theory of Painting," in *The Confucian Persuasion*, ed. Arthur F. Wright (Stanford: Stanford University Press, 1960).

17. The tension engendered by such relationships, although largely ignored, is attested by novelists like Agatha Christie, presenting the constant friction between the employers of gardeners and the gardeners themselves who so frequently refuse to carry out orders, and by the ironic, even hostile, carvings of the Yale Law School building, where craftsmen subvert the self-serious "college gothic" architecture with images of students sleeping during lectures, professors sleeping during student discussions, and Justice blind not to position and power, but to the demands of justice.

18. Based on observations of the Emerson String Quartet (in rehearsal at the Renwick Gallery); The Classical Quartet, Philomel, and other groups in rehearsal with The Aston Magna Academy; and other quartets in practice at the Library of Congress.

19. Lillian Elliott and Pat Hickman, "Lillian Elliott and Pat Hickman: The Pleasures and Problems of Collaboration," *Fiberarts: The Magazine of Textiles*, September/October 1985, special issue on collaboration, pp. 22–25.

20. Ibid., p. 25.

21. Sally Rudich, "New Works: David Johnson and Geary Jones," *Fiberarts: The Magazine of Textiles*, September/October 1985, special issue on collaboration, p. 18.

22. On the respect of a potter for her materials, see Seonaid Mairi Robertson, *Craft and Contemporary Culture* (London: George G. Harrap & Co. and United Nations Educational, Scientific, and Cultural Organization, 1961), esp. chap. 1, "On Being a Potter." We must not equate sensitivity to materials with the self-conscious analysis and articulation of this sensitivity; not all craftspeople are as self-reflective about their work as Albers and Robertson, but that doesn't reflect on their sensitivity and effectiveness in working with their materials.

23. Susan Fillin-Yeh, *Charles Sheeler: American Interiors* (New Haven, Conn.: Yale University Art Gallery, 1987).

24. The capabilities of an art are also a function of the materials available, so that technical advances often change the most fundamental aspects of what an artist can strive for. The change from fresco to oil painting, from accoustic to electric guitar, from manual harness to jacquard loom, from harpsichord to piano, from single-block wood carving to jointed carvings, from post-and-lintel to arch construction, etc., all significantly affected the range and type of formal effects that were possible.

25. See Nicholas Fox Weber, *The Woven and Graphic Art of Anni Albers: Published in conjunction with a retrospective exhibition of the artist's weavings and prints*, held at the Renwick Gallery, Washington, D.C., June 12, 1985–Jan. 5, 1986. (Washington, D.C.: Smithsonian Institution, 1985), p. 71.

26. Anni Albers, *Anni Albers: On Designing* (New Haven, Conn.: Pellango Press, 1959; reprint, Middletown, Conn.: Wesleyan University Press, 1961), p. 8; italics in the original.

27. Weber, p. 69. For Robertson's work, see note 22, this chapter.

28. For a discussion and reproduction of the works of these gardenists, see Dumbarton Oaks Colloquium on the History of Landscape Architecture, *Beatrix Jones Farrand (1872–1959): Fifty Years of American Landscape Architecture* (Washington, D.C.: Dumbarton Oaks, Trustees for Harvard University, 1982); P. M. Bardi, *The Tropical Gardens of Burle Marx* (New York: Reinhold Publishing Corp., 1964); Russell Page *The Education of a Gardener* (London: Collins Publishers; New York: Vintage Books, 1985).

29. In an age of mechanical reproduction, when technical perfection is more easily attainable than ever, this deliberate incorporation of mistakes has spread to other craft traditions. I was taught during my weaving apprenticeship to Bessie Caffery Lowrie to leave in an occasional mistake, which would reveal the handcrafted origin of the work.

30. The custom in crafts of deliberately including "mistakes" or deviations draws attention to a peculiar feature of the garden. It would be absurd to orchestrate deliberate mistakes in a garden; such orchestration would be redundant because deviations are always occurring on their own—weeds proliferate, plants wither. The garden is never fully under human control. However one may strive after a finished perfect "product," it must always be illusory—or at the best, ephemeral. The garden resists reification, insists upon process. It is always unfinished. A fixed result may be desirable, but it is always elusive.

31. I am indebted for these examples to Professor Peter Williams and Professor Rulon S. Wells, respectively.

32. Herbert Read, *Icon and Idea: The Function of Art in the Development of Human Consciousness.* (New York: Schocken Books, 1965), p. 18.

33. See the discussion of the complex interrelations of form and the possibilities of significance in this and other palettes in H. A. Groenewegen-Frankfort, *Arrest and Movement: An Essay on Space and Time in the Representational Art of the Ancient Near East* (New York: Hacker Art Books, 1951, 1972), pp. 20–23.

34. Margaret Jourdain, *The Work of William Kent, Artist, Painter, Desinger and Landscape Gardener* (London: Country Life; New York: Charles Scribner's Sons, 1948); Kotosuke (?Naruo?) Kumakura, *Sen no Rikyu: Wabi-sa no bi to kokoro (Sen no Rikyu: The Beauty and Spirit of Tea)* (Tokyo: Heibonsha: 1978).

Chapter 5.

1. Immanuel Kant, *Critique of Judgment* (Berlin, 1790); Eng. ed. trans. J. H. Bernard, (New York: Hafner Press, 1951). I am also indebted to Ted Cohen and Paul Guyer, eds., *Essays in Kant's Aesthetics* (Chicago and London: University of Chicago Press, 1982).

2. Edward Bullough, " 'Psychical Distance' as a Factor in Art and an Aesthetic Principle," reprinted in *Critical Theory since Plato*, ed. Hazard Adams (New York: Harcourt Brace Jovanovich, 1971) and *A Modern Book of Esthetics*, ed. Melvin Rader (New York: Holt, Rinehart and Winston, 1936; 1962), pp. 394 and 397 respectively.

3. Ibid., p. 396.

4. Ibid., p. 397.

5. Stefan Morawski, *Inquiries into the Fundamentals of Aesthetics* (Cambridge: Massachusetts Institute of Technology Press, 1974; 1978), p. 106.

6. This is not the place to explore the need for the concept of art as a distinct and distinctive enterprise. Briefly, I believe it comes down to the following: art must be preserved with a special status because 1) only if artists are relatively free from constraint by the laws and mores of their society will they be able to develop the new insights and visions which it is the purpose of art to discover and develop; 2) life is difficult enough; if we add to our actions the burden of bearing aesthetic value, on top of the normal burdens of legality, morality, practicality, etc., we may find ourselves overwhelmed. This is not to say that it cannot be done—it has been done, and continues to be done, by individuals, by subcultures, and by societies. But it does exact an enormous price in terms of human effort and attention. Of course, these are both arguments based upon expediency, not upon an ontological distinction.

7. Morawski, p. 67.

8. P. O. Kristeller, "The Modern System of the Arts: A Study in the History of Aesthetics," *Journal of the History of Ideas*, 12 (October 1951), pp. 496–527, and 13 (January 1952), pp. 17–46; also W. Tatarkiewicz, "The Classification of the Arts in Antiquity," *Journal of the History of Ideas*," 24 (April 1963), pp. 231–40; also Meyer Schapiro, "On the Aesthetic Attitude in Romanesque Art," in *Art and Thought: Issued in Honour of Dr. Ananda K. Coomeraswamy*, ed. K. Bharatha Iyer (London, 1947).

9. Nature is another, as Kant, of course, recognized; in fact, the notion of the aesthetic was first developed in regard to nature, not art. Nonetheless both in the popular mind and in much, if not most, of contemporary philosophy of art, nature has become secondary to art as far as the legitimacy of its claims to the aesthetic.

10. Roger S. Ulrich, "View Through a Window May Influence Recovery from Surgery," *Science*, 224 (April 27, 1984) pp. 420–21.

11. Jacques Maritain, *Creative Intuition in Art and Poetry* (New York: Pantheon, 1953). Compare Buber's point regarding unlimited freedom in the realm of ethics. Martin Buber, *Good and Evil* (New York: Scribner's, 1953).

12. Edith Wharton, *Italian Villas and their Gardens* (New York: Century Co., 1904), pp. 7–8.

13. Jane Merrill, "Tea Alfresco," in *Garden*, January/February 1986, p. 24. "By the 1720s, London had a score of tea gardens in the most pleasant spots of the city and its outskirts. Mazzinghi's *History of London*, published in 1792, gives a list of the twenty-two most-frequented pleasure gardens of the period," she writes on the same page.

14. Susan Littlefield, "Waking up the Beds," in *House and Garden*, November 1986.

15. This affliction, depression induced by insufficient exposure to light, was recently entered in *The Diagnostic and Statistical Manual of Mental Disorders* (*DSMIII*) under the term "Seasonal Affective Disorder."

16. Morawski, p. 105.

Chapter 6.

1. A preliminary version of the first part of this chapter was read by invitation at the Eastern Division meeting of the American Philosophical Association in December 1985 as commentary on the paper by Arnold Berleant (see note 2 below).

2. Arnold Berleant, "Art without Object," paper read at the Eastern Division Meeting of the American Philosophical Association, December 1985. Unfortunately I discovered Yrjö Sepänmaa's *The Beauty of Environment* (Helsinki: Suomolainen Tiedeakatemia, 1986), which is also of great relevance, too late to consider it for this work; readers interested in the topic, however, will find it rewarding.

3. Such as is found in Richard Wollheim's *Art and its Objects: An Introduction to Aesthetics* (New York: Harper and Row, Harper Torchbooks, 1968, 1971).

4. Berleant's position here is in fundamental agreement with Suzanne Langer's.

5. Ibid., p. 11.

6. Ibid.

7. Ibid., p. 9.

8. See, for example, my "Art and the Construction of Self and Subject in Japan," in *Self and Symbolic Expression*, ed. Wimal Dissanayake (Albany, N.Y.: State University of New York Press, 1992).

9. Christopher Hussey, *The Picturesque: Studies in a Point of View* (London, 1967; first edition, 1927).

10. Peter 1:24–25.

11. See Sir Thomas Browne, "The Garden of Cyrus, or the Quincunx," *Sir Thomas Browne: Selected Writings*, ed. Sir Geoffrey Keynes (Chicago: University of Chicago Press, 1968).

12. See Maynard Mack, *The Garden and the City* and Peter Martin, *Pursuing Innocent Pleasures: The Gardening World of Alexander Pope* (Hamden, Conn.: Archon Books, 1984). Lorenzo de' Medici's garden might also fall into this category.

13. Edmund Husserl, *The Phenomenology of Internal Time Consciousness* (Bloomington: Indiana University Press, 1964).

14. See William Empson, *Seven Kinds of Ambiguity*, rev. ed. (New York: New Directions, 1947; paperback ed., 1966).

15. Alison Lurie, *The Language of Clothes* (New York: Vintage Books, 1983), p. 14.

Chapter 7.

1. An earlier version of part of this chapter appeared as "The Garden as Significant Form" in *The Journal of Speculative Philosophy*, 2, no. 4 (1988). pp. 267–87.

2. Suzanne K. Langer, *Feeling and Form* and *Philosophy in a New Key* (Cambridge: Harvard University Press, 1942; New York: New American Library, Mentor, 1951). The discussion of the principles of generalizability is on p. 8 of the former.

3. Langer, *Feeling and Form*, p. 45.

4. Illusion thus seems to correspond to what Berger and Luckman call the "social construction of reality," (taking "construction" here to be the achievement, or result, rather than the process itself) in *The Social Construction of Reality: A Treatise in the Sociology of Knowledge* (New York: Doubleday Anchor, 1966; 1967), and art as Langer understands it would be one of the means to that construction (although she would never use the term "reality" to describe the result).

5. Langer, *Feeling and Form,* p. 101.

6. Ibid., p. 84–85.

7. Ibid., chap. 7.

8. Ibid., p. 71.

9. Ibid., p. 74.

10. Ibid., p. 75.

11. "This purely visual space is an illusion, for our sensory experiences do not agree on it in their report." Ibid., p. 72.

12. Ibid., p. 72.

13. This example is taken from William Howard Adams, *The French Garden, 1500–1800* (New York: George Braziller, 1979), p. 25.

14. Katherine Whiteside, "Wing Haven," in *House and Garden,* 159, no. 6 (June 1987).

15. Langer, *Feeling and Form,* p. 188.

16. An apparent exception, *The Garden of Malice,* a mystery novel by Susan Kenney (New York: Ballantine Books, 1983), turned out to be not a malicious garden but a normal garden destroyed by the malice of a human being.

17. This ambiguity with regard to the "is/ought" distinction is discussed briefly in chapters 10 and 11.

18. Maurice Natanson, ed., "Common-Sense and Scientific Interpretation of Human Action," in *Alfred Schutz: Collected Papers,* vol. I of *The Problem of Social Reality,* (The Hague: Martinus Nijhoff, 1973), p. 25 and passim.

Chapter 8.

1. The terms are Alexander's. See Bertram Jessup, "What is Great Art?" *British Journal of Aesthetics* 2 (January 1962). Bertram mentions S. Alexander, Katherine Gilbert, Theodore Greene, S. C. Pepper, I. A. Richards as all holding this view, which would seem to be consonant with that of Suzanne Langer, Paul Weiss, and Ernst Cassirer as well.

2. It is by no means the case that all philosophers of art agree that content is important in art; see, for example, Susan Sontag, *Against Interpretation and Other Essays* (New York: Farrar Straus Giroux, 1966) for a recent and influential exposition of the opposing point of view.

3. Richard Wollheim's recent and highly innovative *Painting as an Art* (Princeton: Princeton University Press, 1987) analyzes the first two types of meaning and develops possibilities of their interrelations as well. Arnold Berleant explores the implications of the environmental level in his recent *Art and Engagement.*

4. Jessup, p. 29.

5. Ibid., p. 30.

6. Ibid., p. 31.

7. Ibid., p. 23.

8. Readers will find a suggestive preliminary study in my "Knot Gardens and the Genesis of the Scientific Attitude," *Comparative Civilizations Review,* no. 18 (Spring 1988), 58–90.

9. Roy Strong, *The Renaissance Garden in England* (London: Thames and Hudson, 1979); Michel Baridon, see chapter 11, note 6, p. 199.

10. Walpole, *The History of the British Taste in Gardening,* reprinted in I. W. U. Chase, *Horace Walpole: Gardenist* (Princeton: Princeton University Press, 1943).

11. Hussey, *The Picturesque;* John Dixon Hunt, *The Figure in the Landscape* (Baltimore: Johns Hopkins University Press, 1976); David Marshall, "Figures in the Landscape," paper read at a symposium on "Land and Landscape in the Eighteenth Century," April 1982, Yale Center for British Art.

12. See Elizabeth Eisenstein on print, for example. *The Printing Press as an Agent of Change: Communications and Cultural Transformation in Early Modern Europe.* (Cambridge: Cambridge University Press, 1979).

13. Mara Miller, "Knot Gardens. . . ."

14. I would like to thank Dr. Scott Robertson for bringing this point to my attention.

Chapter 9.

1. Langer's position is similar to that of Paul Weiss in *Nine Basic Arts* (Carbondale and Edwardsville: Southern Illinois University Press, 1961). Weiss finds the idea inherent in the work to be one of three valid approaches to art, the others being the process of creation and the final result, the work created (p. 7). As he puts it, "Ideas are made determinate in the process of creation and are fully expressed only in the resulting work" (ibid.). Although

for Weiss, the idea is ultimately less important than the process or the result, "All three—idea, creativity, and work—must therefore be understood if one is to do justice to what is in fact essential to art" (ibid.).

2. *Feeling and Form*, p. 24.

3. Ibid., p. 40.

4. Ibid., p. 31.

5. See also Empson's discussion of Wentworth and Hyde in Johnson's *The Vanity of Human Wishes,* in Empson, p. 68.

6. Aristotle recognized the importance of this issue; see his discussion in *The Poetics* of the use of actual historical individuals in tragedy. *The Basic Works of Aristotle,* ed. Richard McKeon (New York: Random House, 1941).

7. *Philosophy in a New Key.*

8. This also means that Dewey's argument that the audience must re-create the work, and so has a task analogous to that of the artist, is only partly valid. The audience has been provided with an end point, a solution, to the problem, which the artist had to struggle for—and may not have reached to his satisfaction, despite the satisfaction of the audience.

9. All three are reproduced in John Berger, *Ways of Seeing* (London: Penguin Books, 1972), pp. 45, 63.

Chapter 10.

1. Roland Barthes, *The Fashion System,* (Paris: Editions du Seuil, 1967); Eng. trans. by Matthey Ward and Richard Howard (New York: Hill & Wang div. of Farrar, Straus & Giroux, 1983), Petr Bogatyrev, "Costume as a Sign," reprinted in *Semiotics of Art,* eds. Ladislav Matejkia and Irwin R. Titunik (Cambridge: Massachusetts Institute of Technology Press, 1976) and Lurie, op. cit.

Niels K. Jerne, "The Generative Grammar of the Immune System," in *Science,* 229, (Sept. 13, 1985).

3. Ferdinand de Saussure, *Course in General Linguistics,* (New York: McGraw-Hill Book Company, 1966), pp. 67–68.

4. Ibid., p. 69.

5. Ibid., p. 71.

6. *Feeling and Form*, p. 31.

7. Ernst and Johanna Lehner, *Folklore and Symbolism of Flowers, Plants and Trees* (New York: Tudor Publishing Co., 1960), p. 109.

8. Ibid.

9. Reprinted New York: Avenel Books, 1974.

10. Eugenio Battisti, "Natura Artificiosa to Natura Artificialis" in *The Italian Garden* (Washington, D.C.: Dumbarton Oaks and the Trustees for Harvard University, 1972).

11. Beals, pp. 84–85.

12. William L. Hanaway, Jr., "The Vegetation of the Earthly Garden," in *Fourth Dumbarton Oaks Colloquium, The Islamic Garden,* (Washington, D.C.: Dumbarton Oaks, 1976) and reprinted in Elizabeth Moynihan, *Paradise as a Garden in Persia and Mughal India* (New York: George Braziller, 1979), p. 153.

13. Richard Barnhart, *Peach Blossom Spring* (New York: The Metropolitan Museum of Art, 1983).

14. This reading is suggested by Eugenio Battisti, p. 19.

15. Saussure, p. 68.

16. Barbara Seward, *The Symbolic Rose* (New York: Columbia University Press, 1960), p. 3.

17. T. C. Lai. Quoted in chapter 2.

18. C. G. Jung, "The Practical Use of Dream Analysis," in *The Practice of Psychotherapy: Essays on the Psychology of the Transference and Other Subjects,* vol. 16 of *The Collected Works of C. G. Jung,* trans. R. F. C. Hull, Bollingen Series 20 (New York: Pantheon Books, 1954), pp. 156–57.

19. Ibid.

20. Ibid., p. 158–59.

21. Such extrasemiotic procedures indicate a special category of linguistic usage; notarization, for instance, indicates a performative utterance.

22. Jean-Paul Sartre, *Nausea* (Paris: Gallimard, 1938; Cambridge, Mass: R. Bentley, 1964, 1979); Vladimir Nabokov, *Pnin* (Garden City, N.Y.: Doubleday, 1957).

23. Martin Buber, *I and Thou,* 2d ed.; trans. Ronald Gregor Smith (New York: Charles Scribner's Sons, 1958), pp. 57–59. This description of the experience of a tree points up a factor crucial to the experience of art, namely that the effects and effectiveness of a work of art are due as much to the response of the viewer as to the work of art itself.

24. Edmund Burke, *The Sublime and The Beautiful* (1756; revised 1757; New York: P. F. Collier & Son, 1909, 1937).

25. Sean Shesgreen, ed., "Time," in *Engravings by Hogarth,* (New York: Dover Publications, 1973), p. xix.

26. F. A. Ridley, *Assassins: A Study of the Cult of the Assassins in Persia and Islam* (New York: Gordon Press, 1980).

27. Epson, passim.

Chapter 11.

1. Compare too Weiss's comment that "art cannot, I think, be properly understood without taking into account ideas, the process of creation, and the work created. Ideas are made determinate in the process of creation and are fully expressed only in the resulting work. The creative act is no mere unending process; it is fractionated by the ideas and brought to a proper close by the work. An art object gives a sensuous, material locus for ideas and epitomizes the process by which it was achieved" (p. 7).

2. Roy Strong, *The Renaissance Garden in England* (London: Thames and Hudson, 1979), p. 32.

3. Anonymous (London: Robert Sayer, et al., 1753).

4. "Political Dimensions of the English Reception of Chinese Garden Design, 1712–1770: Modes of Representation and Strategies of Interpretation," read before the East-West Conference on Eighteenth-Century Aesthetics sponsored by the International Society for Eighteenth Century Studies in Paris, August 1990.

5. Robert E. Harrist, Jr. described this process in a paper read before the College Art Assoc. (New York: February 1986), entitled "Topography, Poetry, and the Past in *Mountain Villa* by Li Kung-lin."

6. On the development of the English landscape garden during this time see Chase, *Horace Walpole: Gardenist*; Miles Hadfield, *The English Landscape Garden* (Princes Risborough, Aylesbury, Bucks.: Shire Publications, 1977); Jourdain, *The Work of William Kent*; Mack, *The Garden and the City*; and Martin, *Pursuing Innocent Pleasures.* For additional material on the relation of this gardening style to politics and political debate, see Judith Colton, "Merlin's Cave and Queen Caroline: Garden Art as Political Propaganda," *Eighteenth Century Studies,* 10 (1976), 1–20; Mara Miller, "Political Significance of the Garden in the Age of Walpole" and "Political Gardens II: Gothicism and Exoticism in the Late 18th Century," *Proceedings* of the Folger Institute for the History of British Political Thought (Washington, D.C.: The Folger Shakespeare Library, 1993); and Richard E. Quaintance, "Walpole's Whig Interpretation of Landscaping History," *Studies in Eighteenth-Century Culture,* 9 (1979). I hope to elaborate the political implications of eighteenth-

century English gardens, especially their relations to Ideas of political legitimacy, in a separate work. Michel Baridon has explored the epistemological and political issues of both English and French gardens in a series of papers: "Arcadia and Utopia: The Gardens of Enlightenment," read at Dumbarton Oaks, (1986(?)); *"Jardins et Paysage: Existe-il un style anglais?" Dix-huitieme Siecle,* no. 18 (1987); *"Le Pouvoir et son image. Politique et Jardin Paysager en Angleterre,"* VRBI, x, (1987).

7. Anne Scott-James, *The Cottage Garden,* (London: Allen Lane, 1981; Harmondsworth, Middlesex, and New York: Penguin Books, 1982, 1984).

Chapter 12.

1. It may seem inadvisable to recognize for art such a fundamental role, and the more so if we remain determined to preserve artistic freedom of expression. On the other hand, it is equally dangerous to proceed in ignorance as to the real nature of any force as universal and powerful as art. Nor, after all, is artistic freedom an insuperable problem; in spite of the political difficulties involved, a number of cultures have worked out ways to preserve freedom in language in spite of the very real tensions and difficulties. In fact, for both art and language, it is the potential importance of the messages, reinforced by the importance of speaking out (as an act which creates and preserves liberty and which makes selves and societies of certain kinds possible), that makes freedom of expression vitally important. Art in current theory has been designated as without responsibility, rendering it impotent and trivial, for it has nothing to be free about.

2. This is something of an oversimplification, because it ignores those failures to understand which are based on inadequate knowledge. Such knowledge, however, is usually based on physical experience—one cannot understand a garden meant to be seen from above if one does not have access to the privileged viewpoint; similarly, appreciation of most gardens depends upon experience of them in the weather for which they were designed. The determined garden visitor may make up for such experiential deprivation by active imaginative re-creation.

Bibliography

Adams, William Howard. *The French Garden, 1500–1800.* New York: George Braziller, 1979.

Albers, Anni. *Anni Albers: On Designing.* New Haven: Pellango Press, 1959; reprint, Middletown, Conn.: Wesleyan University Press, 1961.

Aristotle. *The Poetics. The Basic Works of Aristotle,* ed. Richard McKeon. New York: Random House, 1941.

Aurenhammer, Hans. *J. B. Fischer von Erlach.* Cambridge: Harvard University Press, 1973.

Balling, J. D. and J. H. Falk. *Environment and Behavior 14,* 5 (1982).

Bardi, P. M. *The Tropical Gardens of Burle Marx.* New York: Reinhold Publishing Corp., 1964.

Bargebuhr, Frederick P. *The Alhambra: A Cycle of Studies on the Eleventh Century in Moorish Spain.* Berlin: Walter de Gruyter & Co., 1968.

Baridon, Michel. "Arcadia and Utopia: The Gardens of the Enlightenment," read at Dumbarton Oaks (Spring 1988).

———. "History, Myth and the English Garden." In *The Fashioning and Functioning of the British Country House,* ed. Gervase Jackson-Stops, et al. Washington, D.C.: National Gallery of Art, 1989.

———. *"Jardins et Paysage: Existe-il un style anglais?" Dix-huitième Siècle,* no. 18, 1987.

———. "Le Pouvoir et son Image. Politique et Jardin Paysager en Angleterre." *VRBI,* x, 1987.

Barnhart, Richard. *Peach Blossom Spring.* New York: Metropolitan Museum of Art, 1983.

Barthes, Roland. *The Fashion System.* Paris: Editions du Seuil, 1967; Eng. trans. Matthey Ward and Richard Howard. New York: Hill & Wang Div. of Farrar, Straus & Giroux, 1983.

Batey, Mavis. "The Way to View Rousham by Kent's Gardener." *Garden History,* 2, no. 2 (Autumn 1983).

Battisti, Eugenio. "Natura Artificiosa to Natura Artificialis." In *The Italian Garden.* Washington, D.C.: Dumbarton Oaks and the Trustees for Harvard University, 1972.

Beagle, Peter S. *The Garden of Earthly Delights.* New York: Viking Press, 1982.

Beardsley, Monroe. "Redefining Art." In *The Aesthetic Point of View: Selected Essays.* Ithaca: Cornell University Press, 1982.

Berger, John. *Ways of Seeing.* London: Penguin Books, 1972.

Berger, Peter L., and Thomas Luckman. *The Social Construction of Reality: A Treatise in the Sociology of Knowledge.* New York: Doubleday Anchor, 1966, 1967.

Berleant, Arnold. *Art and Engagement.* Philadelphia: Temple University Press, 1991.

Bogatyrev, Petr. "Costume as a Sign," reprinted in *Semiotics of Art,* ed. Ladislav Matejkia and Irwin R. Titunik. Cambridge: Massachusetts Institute of Technology Press, 1976.

Bord, Janet. *Mazes and Labyrinths of the World.* London: Latimer New Directions, 1976.

Brecht, Bertolt. *The Good Person of Setzuan.* Trans. Ralph Manheim. Washington, D.C.: Arena Stage Production, 1985.

Browne, Sir Thomas. "The Garden of Cyrus, or the Quincunx." In *Sir Thomas Browne: Selected Writings,* Sir Geoffrey Keynes, ed. Chicago: University of Chicago Press, 1968.

Buber, Martin. *Good and Evil.* New York: Charles Scribner's Sons, 1953.

———. *I and Thou.* 2d ed., Trans. Ronald Gregor Smith. New York: Charles Scribner's Sons, 1958.

Bullough, Edward. " 'Psychical Distance' as a Factor in Art and an Aesthetic Principle." In *Critical Theory since Plato,* ed. Hazard Adams. New York: Harcourt Brace Jovanovich, 1971, and *A Modern Book of Esthetics.* Ed. Melvin Rader. New York: Holt, Rinehart and Winston, 1935, 1962.

Burke, Edmund. *The Sublime and Beautiful.* 1756; revised 1757; New York: P. F. Collier & Son, 1909, 1937.

Cahill, James. "Confucian Elements in the Theory of Painting." In *The Confucian Persuasion,* ed. Arthur F. Wright. Stanford, Calif.: Stanford University Press, 1960.

Campbell, Joseph. "The Symbol without Meaning." In *The Flight of the Wild Gander.* Zurich: RheinVerlag, 1958, and South Bend, Ind.: Regnery/Gateway, 1951, 1969, 1979.

Cao Xueqin. *The Story of Stone.* Trans. David Hawkes. China, 1792; Harmondsworth, Middlesex, England: Penguin Books Ltd., 1973.

Cassirer, Ernst. *The Philosophy of Symbolic Forms,* 3 vol. Trans. Ralph Manheim. New Haven: Yale University Press, 1955.

Castile, Rand. *The Way of Tea.* New York: Weatherhill, 1971.

Chase, I. W. U. *Horace Walpole: Gardenist. An Edition of Walpole's 'The History of the Modern Taste in Gardening', with an Estimate of Walpole's Contribution to Landscape Architecture.* Princeton, N.J.: Princeton University Press, 1943.

Clarke, George. Speech before the Garden History Society on September 16, 1981; reported in R. J. Bisgrove. *Newsletter,* no. 4 of the Garden History Society, September 1982.

Clifford, Derek Plint. *A History of Garden Design.* New York: Praeger, 1963; rev. ed., 1966.

Cohen, Ted and Paul Guyer, eds. *Essays in Kant's Aesthetics.* Chicago and London: University of Chicago Press, 1982.

Colton, Judith. "Kent's Hermitage for Queen Caroline at Richmond." *Architectura* 2 (1974).

———. "Merlin's Cave and Queen Caroline: Garden Art as Political Propaganda." *Eighteenth Century Studies,* 10 (1976).

Comito, Terry. *The Idea of the Garden in the Renaissance.* New Brunswick, N.J.: Rutgers University Press, 1978.

Deutsch, Eliot. "An Invitation to Contemplation: The Rock Gardens of Ryoanji and the Concept of *Yugen.*" *Studies in Comparative Aesthetics,* Monograph no. 2 of the Society for Asian and Comparative Philosophy. Honolulu: University Press of Hawaii, 1975.

Dickie, George. *Art and the Aesthetic* Ithaca: Cornell University Press, 1974.

Dumbarton Oaks Colloquium on the History of Landscape Architecture. *Beatrix Jones Farrand (1872–1959): Fifty Years of American Landscape Architecture.* Washington, D.C.: Dumbarton Oaks, Trustees for Harvard University, 1982.

Eisenstein, Elizabeth L. *The Printing Press as an Agent of Change: Communications and Cultural Transformations in Early Modern Europe.* Cambridge: Cambridge University Press, 1979.

Eliade, Mircea. *Images and Symbols.* London: Havrill Press, 1961.

Elliott, Lillian, and Pat Hickman. "Lillian Elliott and Pat Hickman: The Pleasures and Problems of Collaboration." *Fiberarts: The Magazine of Textiles,* September/October 1985, special issue on collaboration.

Empson, William. *Seven Types of Ambiguity.* Rev. ed. New York: New Directions, 1947; paperback ed., 1966.

Etlin, Richard A. *The Architecture of Death.* Cambridge: Massachusetts Institute of Technology Press, 1984.

Falk, John J. and John D. Balling. "Evolutionary Influence on Human Visual Preference." Unpublished paper.

Ferrari, Giovanni Battisti. *De Florum Cultura Libri IV.* 1633.

Fillin-Yeh, Susan. *Charles Sheeler: American Interiors.* New Haven, Conn.: Yale University Art Gallery, 1987.

Fischer von Erlach, Johann Bernhard. *Entwurff einer historischen Architectur.* . . Leipzig: 1742; Reprint. Ridgewood, N.J.: Gregg Press, 1964.

Giamatti, A. Bartlett. *The Earthly Paradise and the Renaissance Epic.* Princeton, N.J.: Princeton University Press, 1966.

Gibson, E. *Principles of Perceptual Learning and Development.* Englewood Cliffs, N.J.: Prentice Hall, 1969.

Gibson, J. J. *An Ecological Aproach to Visual Perception.* Ithaca, N.Y.: Cornell University Press, 1976.

Girouard, Mark. *Life in the English Country House.* New Haven: Yale University Press, 1978; New York: Penguin Books, 1980.

Goethe Johann Wolfgang von. *Elective Affinities.* Trans. Elizabeth Mayer and Louise Bogan. Chicago: Henry Regnery Company.

Goodman, Nelson. *Languages of Art: An Approach to a Theory of Symbols.* Indianapolis and Cambridge: Hackett Publishing Co., 1976.

Greenaway, Kate. *Language of Flowers.* Reprint. New York: Avenel Books, 1974.

Groenewegen-Frankfort, H. A. *Arrest and Movement: An Essay on Space and Time in the Representational Art of the Ancient Near East.* New York: Hacker Art Books, 1951, 1972.

Hadfield, Miles. *The English Landscape Garden.* Princes Risborough, Aylesbury, Bucks.: Shire Publications, 1977.

Hanaway, William L., Jr. "The Vegetation of the Earthly Garden," In *Fourth Dumbarton Oaks Colloquium, The Islamic Garden.* Washington, D.C.: Dumbarton Oaks, 1976; reprinted in Elizabeth Moynihan. *Paradise as a Garden in Persia and Mughal India.* New York: George Braziller, 1979.

Hargrove, Eugene C. *Foundations of Environmental Ethics.* Englewood Cliffs, N.J.: Prentice Hall, 1989.

Harries, Karsten. *The Meaning of Modern Art: A Philosophical Interpretation.* Evanston, Ill.: Northwestern University Press, Northwestern University Studies in Phenomenology and Existential Philosophy. 1968.

Harrist, Robert E., Jr. "Topography, Poetry, and the Past in *Mountain Villa by Li Kung-lin*," paper read before the College Art Association. New York: Feb. 1986.

Harvey, John. *Medieval Gardens.* London: B. T. Batsford, 1981.

Hawes, Louis. *Presences of Nature.* New Haven: Yale Center for British Art, 1982.

Hibbert, Christopher, et al. *Versailles.* New York: Newsweek Book Division, 1972.

Hill, Dorothy Kent. "Roman Domestic Architecture." In *Ancient Roman Gardens.* Washington, D.C.: Dumbarton Oaks and the Trustees of Harvard University.

Hornbeck, Peter L. "The Garden as Fine Art; Its Maintenance and Preservation." In Dumbarton Oaks Colloquium on the History of Landscape Architecture: *Beatrix Jones Farrand (1872–1959): Fifty Years of American Landscape Architecture.* Washington, D.C.: Dumbarton Oaks, Trustees for Harvard University, 1982.

Hunt, John Dixon. *The Figure in the Landscape.* Baltimore: Johns Hopkins University Press, 1976.

Husserl, Edmund. *The Phenomenology of Internal Time Consciousness.* Bloomington: Indiana University Press, 1964.

Hussey, Christopher. *The Picturesque. Studies in a Point of View.* London, 1967; 1st ed., 1927.

Hyams E. *Capability Brown and Humphrey Repton.* London: J. M. Dent & Sons, 1971.

Jakobson, Roman. "Aphasia as a Linguistic Topic." *Selected Writings II: Word and Language.* The Hague and Paris: Mouton, 1971.

Jashemski, Wilhelmina Mary Feemster. *The Gardens of Pompeii, Herculaneum, and the Villas destroyed by Vesuvius.* New Rochelle, N.Y.: Caratzas Bros., 1979.

Jerne, Niels K. "The Generative Grammar of the Immune System." In *Science,* 229 (Sept. 13, 1985).

Jessup, Bertram. "What is Great Art?" *British Journal of Aesthetics* 2 (January 1962).

Jourdain, Margaret. *The Works of William Kent*. London, 1948.

Jung, C. G. "The Practical Use of Dream Analysis." *The Practice of Psychotherapy: Essays on the Psychology of the Transference and Other Subjects*. Vol. 16 of *The Collected Works of C. G. Jung*, trans. R. F. C. Hull. Bollingen Series 20. New York: Pantheon Books, 1954.

———. *Mandala Symbolism*. Princeton: Princeton University Press, Bollingen Series, 1959, 1972.

Kant, Immanuel. *Critique of Judgment*. Berlin, 1790; Eng. ed. trans. J. H. Bernard. New York: Hafner Press, 1951.

Kaplan, R. "Predictors of Environmental Preference: Designers and 'Clients.'" In *Environmental Design Research*, ed. W. F. E. Preiser. 1973.

———. "Down by the Riverside: Informational factors in waterscape preference." In *Proceedings of river recreation management and research symposium*. North Central Forest Experiment Station, Forest Service, USDA, 1977.

Kaplan, S. "Cognitive maps, human needs, and the designed environment." In *Environmental Design Research*, ed. W. F. E. Preiser. Stroudsberg, Pa.: Dowden, Hutchinson and Ross. 1973.

———. "An Informal Model for the Prediction of Preference." In *Landscape Assessment*, ed. E. H. Zube, R. O. Brush, and J. G. Fabos. Stroudsberg, Pa., 1975.

Kaplan, R., and Kaplan, S. *Cognition and Environment: Functioning in an Uncertain World*. New York: Praeger, 1982.

Kaplan, Stephen, and Rachel Kaplan, eds. *Humanscape: Environments for People*. North Scituate, Mass.: Duxbury Press, 1978.

Kenney, Susan. *The Garden of Malice*. New York: Ballantine Books, 1983.

Kemp, Gerald van der. "Claude Monet and his Garden." Stephen Shore, ed. *The Gardens at Giverny*. Millerton, New York: Aperture, 1983.

Kern, Hermann. "Image of the World and Sacred Realm. Labyrinth-Cities— City-Labyrinths." *Daedalus*, no. 3 (March 15, 1982).

Keswick, Maggie. *The Chinese Garden: History, Art and Architecture*. London: Academy Editions; New York: St. Martin's Press, 1978, 1986.

Knight, W. F. Jackson. *Cumaean Gates: A Reference of the Sixth Aeneid to the Initiation Pattern*. Oxford: Basil Blackwell, 1936.

Kravitz, David. *Who's Who in Greek and Roman Mythology*. New York: Clarkson N. Potter, 1975.

Kristeller, P. O. "The Modern System of the Arts: A Study in the History of Aesthetics." *Journal of the History of Ideas*. 12 (Oct. 1951) and 13 (Jan. 1952).

Kumakura, Kotosuke (?Naruo?). *Sen no Rikyu: Wabi-sa no bi to kokoro* (Sen no Rikyu: The Beauty and Spirit of Tea). Tokyo: Heibonsha, 1978.

Lai, T. C. *Noble Fragrance: Chinese Flowers and Trees.* Kowloon and Hong Kong: Swindon Book Co., 1977.

Langer, Suzanne. *Feeling and Form: A Theory of Art.* New York: Charles Scribner's Sons, 1953.

———. *Philosophy in a New Key.* Cambridge: Harvard University Press, 1942; New York: New American Library, Mentor, 1951.

Langley, Batty. *New Principles of Gardening.* London, 1728.

Layard, John. "Labyrinth Ritual in South India—Threshold and Tattoo Designs." *Folklore,* 48 (1937).

Lehner, Ernst, and Johanna Lehner. *Folklore and Symbolism of Flowers, Plants and Trees.* New York: Tudor Publishing Co., 1960.

Littlefield, Susan. "Waking up the Beds." *House and Garden,* November 1986.

Lord, Albert B. *The Singer of Tales.* In vol. 24 of *Harvard Studies in Comparative Literature.* Cambridge: Harvard University Press, 1960.

Lurie, Alison. *The Language of Clothes.* New York: Vintage Books, 1983.

Mack, Maynard. *The Garden and the City: Retirement and Politics in the Later Poetry of Pope.* Toronto: University of Toronto Press, 1969.

Manwaring, Elizabeth Wheeler. *Italian Landscape in Eighteenth Century England: A Study Chiefly of the Influence of Claude Lorrain and Salvator Rosa on English Taste, 1700–1800.* New York: Oxford University Press, 1925.

Markham, Gervase. *Excellent and New Invented Knots and Mazes.* London, 1623.

Maritain, Jacques. *Creative Intuition in Art and Poetry.* New York: Pantheon, 1953.

Marshall, David. "Figures in the Landscape." Paper read at the symposium on "Land and Landscape in the Eighteenth Century," Yale Center for British Art. New Haven: April 1982.

Martin, Peter. *Pursuing Innocent Pleasures: The Gardening World of Alexander Pope.* Hamden, Conn.: Archon Books, 1984.

Matthews, William Henry. *Mazes and Labyrinths: A General Account of their History and Development.* London, New York: Longmans, Green, 1922; Detroit, Singing Tree Press, 1969.

Meltzer, David, ed. *The Secret Garden: An Anthology in the Kabbalah.* New York: Seabury Press, 1976.

Merrill, Jane. "Tea Alfresco." *Garden,* January/February 1986.

Miller, E. Ethelbert. Qtd. by Patricia Gaines-Carter. *The Washington Post Magazine,* Feb. 3, 1985.

Miller, Mara. "Art and the Construction of Self and Subject in Japan." In Wimal Dissanayake, ed. *Self and Symbolic Expression.* Albany, New York: State University of New York Press, 1994.

––––. *"The Emperor of China's Palace at Pekin:* A New Source of English Garden Design." *Apollo,* 119, no. 265 (April 1984).

––––. "The Garden as Significant Form." *The Journal of Speculative Philosophy,* 2, no. 4 (1988).

––––. "Gardens as Works of Art: The Problem of Uniqueness." *British Journal of Aesthetics* (Summer 1986).

––––. "Knot Gardens and the Genesis of the Scientific Attitude." *Comparative Civilizations Review,* no. 18 (Spring 1988).

––––. "Political Dimensions of the English Reception of Chinese Garden Design, 1712–1770: Modes of Representation and Strategies of Interpretation." Paper read at the East-West Conference on Eighteenth-Century Studies, Paris, August 1990, sponsored by the International Society for Eighteenth-Century Studies.

––––. "Political Gardens II: Gothicism and Exoticism in the Late Eighteenth Century." In *Proceedings* of the Folger Center for the History of British Political Thought. Washington, D.C.: Folger Institute, 1993.

––––. "Political Significance of the Garden in the Age of Walpole." In *Proceedings* of the Folger Center for the History of British Political Thought. Washington, D.C.: Folger Institute, 1993.

Miller, Naomi. *Heavenly Caves: Reflections on the Garden Grotto.* New York: George Braziller, 1982.

Morawski, Stefan. *Inquiries into the Fundamentals of Aesthetics.* Cambridge: Massachusetts Institute of Technology Press, 1974; 1978.

Morris, Edwin T. *The Gardens of China: History, Art and Meanings.* New York: Charles Scribner's Sons, 1983.

Murasaki, Shikibu. *The Tale of Genji.* Trans. Edwin O. Seidensticker. New York: Alfred A. Knopf, 1977.

Murck, Alfreda and Wen Fong. *A Chinese Garden Court. The Astor Court at the Metropolitan Museum of Art.* New York: The Metropolitan Museum of Art, 1980.

Nabokov, Vladimir. *Pnin.* Garden City, N.Y.: Doubleday, 1957.

Neisser, Ulric. *Cognition and Reality: Principles and Implications of Cognitive Psychology.* San Francisco: W. H. Freeman & Co., 1976.

————. *Memory Observed: Remembering in Natural Contexts.* San Francisco: W. H. Freeman & Co., 1982.

O'Loughlin, Michael. *The Garlands of Repose: The Literary Celebration of Civic and Retired Leisure: The Traditions of Homer and Vergil, Horace and Montaigne.* Chicago, 1978.

Ong, Walter. *Orality and Literacy.* London: Methuen & Co., 1982.

Orians, G. *The Evolution of Human Social Behavior.* Ed. J. S. Lockard. Amsterdam: Elsevier, 1980.

Owen, Jane. *Eccentric Gardens.* New York: Villard Books, 1990.

Page, Russell. *The Education of a Gardener.* London: Collins Publishers; New York: Vintage Books, 1985.

Panofsky, Erwin. "History of Art as a Humanistic Discipline." In *Meaning in the Visual Arts.* Garden City, New Jersey: Doubleday, 1957.

Partridge, Linda B. "Field and Laboratory Observations on the Foraging and Feeding Techniques of bluetits cearulus and coldtits teausater in relation to their Habitats," *Animal Behavior 24,* no. 534 (1976).

————. "Habitat Selection," *Behavioral Ecology: An Evolutionary Approach.* Ed. J. R. Krebs and N. B. Davies. Sunderland, Mass.: Sinauer, 1978.

Pepper, S. C. "Is Non-Objective Art Superficial?" *The Journal of Aesthetics and Art Criticism,* 11, no. 3, (March 1953): 255–61.

Pope, Alexander. *Epistle to Lord Burlington* in *The Poems of Alexander Pope: a one-volume edition of the Twickenham text with selected annotations.* Ed. John Butt. London: Methuen & Co., 1963; corrected 1968.

Powell, Florence Lee. *In the Chinese Garden.* New York: John Day Company, 1943.

Prest, John. *The Garden of Eden: The Botanic Garden and the Recreation of Paradise.* New Haven and London: Yale University Press, 1981.

Quaintance, Richard E. "Walpole's Whig Interpretation of Landscaping History." *Studies in Eighteenth-Century Culture,* 9 (1979).

Read, Herbert. *Icon and Idea: The Function of Art in the Development of Human Consciousness.* New York: Schocken Books, 1965.

Rehatsek, Edward, trans. *The Gulistan or Rose Garden of Sa'di.* New York: G. P. Putnam's Sons, 1964.

Rense, Paige, ed. *Gardens: Architectural Digest*. Los Angeles: Knapp Press, 1983.

Repton, Humphrey. *The Art of Landscape Gardening, by Humphry Repton, esq.*, including his "Sketches and Hints on Landscape Gardening" and "The Theory and Practice of Landscape Gardening." Ed. John Nolan. Boston, New York: Houghton Mifflin & Co., 1907.

Ridley, F. A. *Assassins: A Study of the Cult of the Assassins in Persia and Islam*. New York: Gordon Press, 1980.

Robertson, Seonaid Mairi. *Craft and Contemporary Culture*. London: George G. Harrap & Co. and United Nations Educational, Scientific, and Cultural Organization, 1961.

Ross, Stephanie. "Ut Hortus Poesis—Gardening and her Sister Arts in Eighteenth-Century England." *The British Journal of Aesthetics*, 25, no. 1 (Winter 1985).

Rudich, Sally. "New Works: David Johnson and Geary Jones." *Fiberarts: The Magazine of Textiles*, September/October 1985, special issue on collaboration.

Sartre, Jean-Paul. *Nausea*. Paris: Gallimard, 1938; Cambridge: R. Bentley, 1964, 1979.

Saussure, Ferdinand de. *Course in General Linguistics*. New York: McGraw-Hill Book Company, 1966.

Schapiro, Meyer. "On the Aesthetic Attitude in Romanesque Art." *Art and Thought: Issued in Honor of Ananda K. Coomeraswamy*, K. Bharatha Iyer, ed. London: 1947.

Scott-James, Anne. *The Cottage Garden*. Harmondsworth, Middlesex, England: Penguin, 1982.

Schutz, Alfred. "Common-Sense and Scientific Interpretation of Human Action." In *Alfred Schutz: Collected Papers, vol. I: The Problem of Social Reality*, ed. Maurice Natanson. The Hague: Martinus Nijhoff, 1973.

Sepänmaa, Yrjö. *The Beauty of Environment: A general model for environmental aesthetics*. Helsinki: Suomalainen Tiedeakatemia, 1986.

Seward, Barbara. *The Symbolic Rose*. New York: Columbia University Press, 1960.

Shaw, Robert, and John Bransford, eds. *Perceiving, Acting and Knowing: Toward an Ecological Psychology*. Hillsdale, N.J.: Lawrence Erlbaum Assocs., 1977.

Shesgreen, Sean, ed. *Engravings by Hogarth*. New York: Dover Publications, 1973.

Shore, Stephen. *The Gardens at Giverney.* Millerton, New York: Aperture, 1983.

Slawson, David A. *Secret Teachings in the Art of Japanese Gardens: Design Principles, Aesthetic Values.* Tokyo and New York: Kodansha International, 1987.

Sommer, Robert. *Personal Space: The Behavioral Basis of Design.* Englewood Cliffs, N.J.: Prentice-Hall, 1969.

Sontag, Susan. *Against Interpretation and Other Essays.* New York: Farrar Straus Giroux, 1966.

———. *On Photography.* New York: Farrar, Straus and Giroux; paperback ed., Dell Publishing Co., 1978.

Steinberg, Leo. "The Eye is Part of the Mind." *Partisan Review,* 20, no. 2 (March 1953); Reprint. In *Reflections on Art.* Ed. Susanne K. Langer. 1958.

———. "The Line of Fate in Michelangelo's Painting." *Critical Inquiry* 6, no. 3 (Spring 1980).

Stokstad, Marilyn and Jerry Stannard. *Gardens of the Middle Ages.* Lawrence, Kans.: Spencer Museum of Art, 1983.

Strong, Roy. *The Renaissance Garden in England.* London: Thames and Hudson, 1979.

Stroud, Dorothy. *Capability Brown.* London: Faber & Faber, 1975.

Scully, Vincent. *The Earth, The Temple and the Gods: Greek Sacred Architecture.* New Haven: Yale University Press, 1962; rev. ed., 1979.

Tatarkiewicz, W. "The Classification of the Arts in Antiquity." *Journal of the History of Ideas,* 24 (April 1963).

Treib, Marc, and Ron Herman. *A Guide to the Gardens of Kyoto.* Tokyo: Shufunotomo Company, 1980.

Turner, Roger. *Capability Brown and the eighteenth-century English landscape.* New York: Rizzoli International, 1985.

Ulrich, Roger S. "View Through a Window May Influence Recovery from Surgery." *Science,* 224, (April 27, 1984).

Watkin, David. *The English Vision: The Picturesque in Architecture, Landscape and Garden Design.* New York: Harper & Row, 1982.

Weber, Nicholas Fox. *The Woven and Graphic Art of Anni Albers: Published in conjunction with a retrospective exhibition of the artist's weavings and prints, held at the Renwick Gallery, Washington, D.C., June 12, 1985–Jan. 5, 1986.* Washington, D.C.: Smithsonian Insitution, 1985.

Wecker, Stanley C. "Role of early experience in habitat selection by the prairie deermouse Berumyeus Manialatus Bairdi," *Ecological Monographs* 33, (1963), pp. 306–325.

Weiss, Paul. *Nine Basic Arts.* Carbondale and Edwardsville: Southern Illinois University Press, 1961.

Wells, Rulon. "Immediate Constituents." *Language* 23 (1947) 81–117.

Wharton, Edith. *Italian Villas and their Gardens.* New York: Century Co., 1904.

Whiteside, Katherine. "Wing Haven." *House and Garden,* (June 1987).

Wilkinson, Charles K. *Egyptian Wall Paintings.* New York: Metropolitan Museum of Art, 1983.

Wollheim, Richard. *Art and Its Objects: An Introduction to Aesthetics.* New York: Harper and Row, Harper Torchbooks, 1968.

———. *Painting as an Art.* Bollingen Series 35.33. Princeton, N.J.: Princeton University Press, 1987.

Index to Gardens

A

Alhambra, Lion Court, 10
Arbor Terrace (Dumbarton Oaks), 161
Astor Court (Metropolitan Museum of
  Art, New York City), 10, 74

B

Babylon, Hanging Gardens of. *See*
  Hanging Gardens of Babylon
Beinecke Plaza, 15
Blenheim, 16, 39, 135
Bomarzo, ch. 2, n. 34, 184

C

Chantilly, 12, 16, pl. 8
Clarkson, Edwin and Elizabeth, garden
  of, 128
Clivedon, 39, 144
Copacabana (Beach), 39
Cotswolds style, 56

D

Daisen-in. *See* Daitoku-ji
Daitoku-ji, 22, 36–7, 104, 142, pl. 2, 16
Dumbarton Oaks, 16, 79, 161–2

E

Eden, Garden of, 25, 52, 172
Elms, The, 175
Elysian Fields. *See* Stowe

G

Gamberaia, Villa, 21, 39
Garden of the Fisherman's Nets, 74
Giverny, 38, 173

H

Hanging Gardens of Babylon, 10, 172
Haupt Garden, Enid A. (Smithsonian
  Institution), 10
Het Loo, 173

I

Ichworth, pl. 7

J

Jehol, Imperial Garden at, 15, pl. 4

K

Katsura, 16, 22, 38, 135, 177
Kokiden, 39

L

Library of Congress (Madison
  Building), 126
Lion Court (Alhambra), 10
Longwood Gardens, 16

M

Madison Building (Library of
  Congress), 126
de' Medici, Marie, aviary of, 128
Meiji Shrine, garden at, 22

213

Name Index

215

Subject Index

Japanese literature. *See* Literature,
    Japanese
Japanese painting. *See* Painting,
    Japanese
Japanese tea ceremony, 150
Jardin anglo-chinois, 24
Judgment, 148–9
Judiciary, 16

K
Karasansui, 156
"Keeping away," 129
Kitchen gardens, 100
Knot gardens, 84, 143
Knowing, 62. *See also* Cognition
Knowledge, 151, 173

L
Labor intensity, 21, pl. 10
Landscape, 4, 12, 22, 24, 39, 53, 54, 57,
    64, 70, 100, 110, 143, 162, 175
    adaptation to, 100
    in handscroll painting, ch. 2, n. 30,
        183–4
    integration of garden into, 21
    natural, 22, 174
    preference, 61–5; ch. 3, n. 18, 186–7
Landscape gardens, 22, 125, 174
    English, 46. *See also* English gardens
    Japanese, 22, 39, 125. *See also*
        Japanese gardens
Language(s), 3–4, 127, 147–152, 166.
    See also Implicit; Ineffable; Pre-
    linguistic; Sign; Tacit; Translation
    analogy to art, 153–170
    arbitrariness of, 152
    as opposed to art, 6
    of clothes, etc. (semiotic systems) 120,
        153–4
    limits of, 166
    hegemony of, 4, 177
    lexicons, compared to gardens, 156
    limits of, 166–7
    and limits of my world, 3, 177
    mood and mode, 166–168
    mutual unintellibility, 153
    in photographs, 165
    power of, 3
Language of Flowers, 156–7

Lanterns (in gardens), 117
Lawns, 90; ch. 3, n. 12, 185
Lebensweld, art and, 122
Legal aspects of gardens, 154–5
Legibility (feature of landscape), 64
Leisure, 36
Light, 38, 102
Literary traditions and gardens,
    158–60
Literati, 35, 69, pl. 4
Literature, 97–104, 110, 119
    ambiguity in, 169–70
    Chinese, 30
    compared with gardens, 40
    English, 170
    gardeners in. *See* Gardeners, in
        literature
    and gardens, 10, 30, 36, 52; ch. 7, n.
        16, 194
    Gothic, 162
    Japanese, 30, 170
    Persian, 25
    view of trees in, 162
Logic, 152
Logic of gardens, 168–70
Love, 87, 89
    as mode of relation to art, 119, 131,
        150–1
    association of gardens with, 131

M
Macrocosm. *See also* Microcosm
Maintenance of gardens, 126
"Making sense," 64
Mammals, 53
Mass art, 120
Mastery, 108–9
Materials, 82, 85, 100, 123
Maze, 52
Meaning, 108, 124, 136, 141–4, 156–7
    environmental, 136, 143–4
    in art, 107, 155
    in gardens, 10, 15, 124, 155–64
    in language, 153–5
Mediation of polarities by gardens, 25
Medicine, 101, 109
Medieval gardens, 32, 144, 172, pl. 5.
    See also Cloister
Medieval illustrations of gardens, 84